CONCERTINA

CONCERTINA

The Life and Loves of A Dominatrix

SUSAN WINEMAKER

London · New York · Sydney · Toronto

A CBS COMPANY

First published in Great Britain by Simon & Schuster UK Ltd, 2007
A CBS COMPANY

1 3 5 7 9 10 8 6 4 2

Simon & Schuster UK Ltd
Africa House
64-78 Kingsway
London WC2B 6AH

www.simonsays.co.uk

Simon & Schuster Australia
Sydney

A CIP catalogue record for this book is available
from the British Library

ISBN 13: 978-0-7432-9557-4
ISBN 10: 0-7432-9557-9

Typeset in Granjon by M Rules
Printed and bound in Great Britain by
CPI Bath

Art breathes from containment and suffocates from freedom.

Leonardo

Contents

Acknowledgements

For inspiring, for your support and encouragements, for your open minds and appetites, I'm so grateful to: Peter Clasen, Tamara Berger, Sita Schutt, Louise Kattenhorn, Sophie Caston, Mark Winemaker, my parents, Joanna Freedman, agent Charlie Viney, editor Kerri Sharp, the Mistresses, Adam, and all the clients.

Concertina *noun*, *adjective*, & *verb*.

A *noun*. 1. A portable free-reed musical instrument consisting of a pair of bellows usu. Polygonal in form, with a set of finger-studs at each end controlling valves which admit wind to the reeds.
2. In full *concertina wire*. Wire used for entanglements.
B *attrib*. Or as *adjective*. (Able to be) compressed or closed like a concertina; involving such action.
C *verb trans. & intrans.* Shut up like a concertina; compress; collapse; wrinkle.

PART ONE

CHAPTER 1

Work Ethics

It's 11:25 a.m. and I'm sitting on and suffocating Bernie. I'm wearing a black rubber skirt that looks like a ballerina's tutu and in my hands are ten-pence coins with which I'm rapidly flicking his nipples. In thirty-six seconds, by a matter of inches, I will suddenly lift from my sitting position which releases the seal from my rubber-clad crotch, and listen to his fitful gasps for air. Together with Mozart's piano concerto in E flat, these are the sounds that fill the tiny room. And today I can add the maniacal whine of a remote-controlled toy car and the shouting of boys in an otherwise sleepy suburban street. I can see my reflection in a wall of mirrors. There's a pair of scissors by my left and a clock with a seconds hand to my right.

The unknown is an instrument of control full of endless possibilities – which is half the reason I blindfold Bernie. Of course he knows what's coming, but he never knows exactly when it's coming. There's no time for him to prepare, to fill his lungs, when suddenly I shift from a squat position to place my full weight on his mouth and nose. Bernie has never dictated my style, nor has he ever acknowledged its effectiveness. It's me that imagines the unknown makes suffocation more frightening and exciting.

You can't see me, Bernie, but I see you: lying naked on the floor, tightly bound and blindfolded. I know your feet and matching hands, how delicate and elfin they are. I've memorised the patterns of dark hair on your body, the barrel of your chest, and the small, compact frame that is you. I have always admired the curve and definition of your yoga calves. Over the seasons I've watched your tan lines come and go, watched your hair grow, always noticed when it was cut.

Bernie is single, Jewish, and well preserved for his late forties. He has a small, pointed head, beady, scrutinising eyes, and a very stressed brow. He teaches physics, referees football, and practises his yoga. He has a playful, puckish streak, and is extremely keen on winning. From stories he has told me while doing up his trousers, I've gathered that he has never been comfortable in the company of women. And not just women; he seems to resent his colleagues, all but his brightest students, and certain figures of authority. Bernie thinks he's clever, brilliant even. I think he sees himself as a trenchant martyr who's been suffocating his whole life under the weight of fools and mediocres. He always lingers before taking his departure; he never wants to leave. He dresses very slowly and talks with the rapid giddiness of a post-traumatic, post-orgasmic, lonely man.

I'm suffocating Bernie but I'm not a sadist. When it comes to pleasure, I think giving it is the greatest source of power.

*

Bernie's body is bound with seven ropes. The object is complete immobilisation and reasonable comfort. Rope burn is unpleasant and potentially embarrassing. Although we're about to play a deadly game, tingling toes, numb limbs and alarming shades of purple are dangers that can, and should be, avoided. The foreplay of tying him up is more free form and fun than what's about to follow and, because I know this, I take my time and draw it out. I devote myself to the weaving of a secure and elaborate web. Although I improvise, I use symmetry as my guide. As I proceed, I cast aside my glacial role to ask him if a thigh or a wrist feels too tight. 'Is the rope chafing your ankles? Are you sure that wrist's not too tight? Do tell me if that arm begins to tingle.' After about thirteen minutes, when I feel he's getting impatient, I finish what I'm doing, stand back, and assess my creation. 'Let's see what you can move,' I say. So what does he do? He rocks his torso from side to side, shakes his pointy head and bows one finger, facetiously.

In the case of Bernie, bondage is a preliminary, a physical and psychological set-up for the main event. I know what Bernie wants: he wants me to be effective but as quick as possible. Still, I'm hoping he appreciates the act of attention and the ever-tightening embrace as an end in itself. After all, this is for you, Bernie; it's all about you. And isn't that half the pleasure?

I'm suffocating Bernie, but that's not the only thing I'm thinking about.

I'm thinking of feta cheese broken like shale and stacked like an ivory tower on a dark wooden plate. I'm thinking of a bone-white, porous sculpture glistening with olive oil and speckled green with ripped mint leaves. Pomegranate seeds, crushed and scattered about like jewels stain the white and the wood with their ruby juice. It just came to me and I see it now like I saw it then in a food magazine, years ago. Amazingly, I get the same thrill from imagining as I got when I was looking – and in neither case have I tasted what I've eaten with my eyes. To see is one pleasure, to taste is yet another.

Bondage alters both the body and the mind. First he can't see and then by degrees he can't move. I wonder where his mind is while his ankles are rubbing, while his thighs are squeezed together and his back is pressed against a cold tiled floor. When his veins are crushed and the flow of blood is hindered, does he focus on his breathing? Is he fantasising? How does he prepare? He's vulnerable, exposed, and in danger – is that what he thinks about? Does he think of me? And how does it happen that bondage, nudity, helplessness, anticipation, the music, the setting, and my presence collide and conspire into a sexual experience? I haven't even begun to suffocate Bernie, and he has an erection.

My mind drifts on to the dramatics of food: the shocking effect of orange carrot on a bed of bloody purple beetroot. I'm thinking of unlikely couples, daring threesomes, orgies of texture, taste and tone. I'm thinking of a theatre of food that pushes boundaries and explores the possibilities of contrast. I'm thinking sweet with savoury, watermelon in chilled tomato soup, chocolate and chilli pasta, shellfish and vanilla beans, tea-steamed fish, dates marinated in coffee. Why's there not more lemon and chocolate, chocolate and red wine, red wine and lentils? I once came across a recipe for a sauce that called for tobacco, of all things. At a Paris food show I had the singular experience of tasting dried goat's cheese: it was like a sharp infection in the throat that lingered for an hour. What would it be like to host a dinner party where all the guests were blindfolded? I want to make a meal that mocks size and proportions: infant vegetables, one communal fried ostrich egg with buttered croutons on spikes or forks for dipping into a giant soft yolk, or miniature sandwiches, jumbo shrimp, a sequence of soups, just a spoonful of each.

Today I felt like playing. So, in addition to the ropes, I've used whatever I could find: cling film twisted into twine, stockings, shoestring and dental floss. I've tied individual fingers and toes to various parts of the body and the big toes I've tied to each other. The middle toes of each foot are tied to a rope around the upper thighs, and his index fingers are attached to his upper arms in such a way that his wrists are stretched backwards, bending his elbows in a forty-five degree angle. It looks like he's trying to hold up a wall; it looks comical. I've hooked the rope around his ankles to a pulley hanging from the ceiling so that when I turn the crank, his feet and lower legs are lifted an inch off the ground.

The result is impressive; it's a comedy of excess, an art installation that nobody but me will ever see. No one sees my handiwork. Nobody sees him as I do in these unique yet temporary configurations. Nothing in this red room lasts, and yet it all seems destined to be repeated. What's the lesson? I pick up two ten-pence coins with their milled rims, squat above his head facing his feet, and begin flicking his nipples in time to the music.

I fantasised that cooking school was an arcane and cloistered institute that exposed the secrets of flavours and their harmony, and explored the laws and principles governing taste. I imagined a community of keen students standing around a table sampling different herbs and spices, and avidly discussing the workings of the palate, the tongue, the role of the nose, and the function of the eyes with regards to the taste buds. The reality of cooking school was far less romantic and much more pragmatic: poultry modules, seafood modules, sanitation & safety modules. Thirteen of us learned the mother sauces and the daughter sauces of classic French cuisine. We were taught to identify four dry and three moist-heat cooking methods. We memorised the correct temperature for storing mayonnaise and meat, learned the five signs of a fresh fish, how to rescue a broken sauce, and where to carve the carcass. We baked rolls, we baked potatoes, we baked Alaska. We competed for the clearest consommé, the fluffiest meringues and the tallest, lightest soufflé. Thirteen of us stirred our bouillabaisse in tandem and reproduced five hundred standard recipes over the course of eighteen months.

When we begin, Bernie's nipples are like calluses; they look as if they've been painted in now dried and translucent glue. But after flicking them a couple of hundred times the skin begins to crack and flake and then shed onto the tiled floor. Every now and again for an instant and then gone, I cringe and recoil at the sight of peeling skin and the thought of dead cells blowing around the room. After two hours his nipples are red and raw, and the silver coins look like a blood-stained saw.

Over the years I've spent many hours conducting the manic concerto of these flickflickflickflickflicks and observing their effects – yet I still don't know what's going on. Inevitably I empathise with the cruel shock of the first few flicks. I'm conscious of his pain, and of being the cause of it. It's in those first seconds that I feel I'm committing an act of violence, and crossing a line. But it's humanly impossible to empathise for any length of time. As the music builds momentum, so do I. My focus breaks, my mind drifts, and it's as if pain itself has receded into the background.

But what's it like for Bernie? As his nipples become increasingly raw and tender, does the sensation intensify, or does the repetition dull the pain? Or, has he learned a way to manage the pain? All I know is that sheer repetition and his sanctioning of this game, including the pain, alters my perception and renders me somewhat detached. From a privileged, distant perch, I can afford to appreciate the humour and absurdity of playing a bound man's nipples as if he were a musical instrument.

My first day in London was sweltering and cloudless, nothing like I'd expected. I'd arranged to stay with an acquaintance of mine, a woman I hadn't seen in over a decade, just until I secured a job and found a flat to rent. As it turned out, she and her husband and their two-year-old son would be away the week of my arrival, so it was arranged that her friend, Sabrina, who'd be house-sitting and watering the flowers, would be at the flat to welcome me when I arrived. A black cab took me from Victoria Station to an address off Holland Park Road, a crescent of purpose-built flats in a cul-de-sac behind the Hilton Hotel.

I paid the fare – the equivalent of my weekly grocery bill back in Montreal – and thought: I've got to get a job immediately. I rang the buzzer at number nine. No answer. I knocked. I knocked on the window, rang again, knocked again, and then I sat down on my luggage and looked over my shoulder. Waving from along the crescent at number three was a middle-aged man listening to the radio and sunning himself on a plastic lawn chair outside his paved entrance. After ten or twelve minutes of polite smiles and peripheral stares, he went inside and soon reappeared, approaching me with an offering of digestive biscuits and a cup of tea, which was very kind indeed, and then raved about the splendid weather. At last, pleasantries aside, he saw an opportunity to indulge in a neighbourly gripe.

'Not surprised they aren't here to greet you. Bloody awful, excuse my language. Loud, hippy types with their stinking compost bin and that child. Top it all off, bloke's trying to shame everyone in the street with his roses and prize-winning sunflowers. You came all the way from . . . Canada? Blimey. And they're not even here to greet you. Disgrace! Least you caught the brilliant weather, that's something. It's been a lousy summer until now. Cheers.'

I didn't bother explaining that it was not the feckless neighbours but their friend who was annoyingly absent. When Frank went back to number three with my emptied cup, I sat down on a full bladder and stared at the tubular chimneys and blackened brick buildings. I remember admiring the contrast between dirty urban and the green lace of leaves of a tall acacia tree. When I closed my eyes I could smell pavement, island mist and pollution in the air. I heard the hum of traffic, the chatter of birds, and felt the London sun reaching my face through a warm haze.

Nearly an hour passed before I began reviewing my options. There was the Hilton Hotel staring me in the face if I could afford it, but that would be a waste. I'd read of a hostel in

Holland Park if it came to that. But first I thought to leave my bags with the neighbour, use his toilet, and write a note to Sabrina. I was looking for my pen when a black cab pulled up and out stepped a beautiful blonde waif with opalescent streaks in her hair. Whatever she wore she wore it well, as she skipped my way, unapologetically. By her whimsical jaunt, her nasal and high-pitched squeal and flighty eyes, I could tell that aside from being English, she was capricious, and slightly off her axis.

When she opened the door, we entered the skinniest house I'd ever seen. 'These are council flats,' she explained, 'affordable housing in what happens to be one of London's richest neighbourhoods', and she giggled for no apparent reason. The kitchen was 'barely large enough to swing a cat' – that was the expression she used. The living room/dining room, the only other room on the first of three storeys, was only slightly larger. Then, incessantly and without reserve, Sabrina began to 'educate' me. She talked about London, the mayor, the tube and the buses, the zones and the fares, the best markets, how to shop economically in the neighbourhood, her favourite parks and department stores, the useful *A–Z*, *Loot*, *Time Out*, and did I want some tea?

While I sat drinking a second cup on my first English day, Sabrina lay supine on an old, frayed, red and cream striped sofa, eating half an avocado with soy sauce and a spoon. And then, after having known her for all of an hour I learned that she was my age, twenty-six, and married, but she didn't live with her husband. He was a workaholic who slept in his recording studio and dined on a dream, which she never doubted would be realised. She fluttered about, unemployed, staying with Steve's parents and sometimes friends.

She'd been a pop singer, recorded a single that hit the charts for one brief, effervescent moment, and then shrunk into anonymity in order to nurse the wounds she'd received on her journey to and from fame. 'My father pushed me, wanted fame for me, and I did it to please him.' She was anorexic throughout her teens and early twenties and spent nine years in therapy.

Sabrina and her parents – American, ex-model mother and failed artist/inventor father – had lived as inseparable 'best friends' throughout her childhood and adolescence in London and New York. 'I dropped my first acid with them, and we smoked marijuana together all the time. They were bohemians. Sometimes there was money, lots of money, and granny's wealthy, but I remember times when we were broke. And my father never had real work.'

When she was twenty-one she fell in love with Steve. When she was twenty-three her parents hatched a financial scheme that involved moving to Bali. It had simply been assumed that Sabrina would join them. When she refused to leave London they pretended not to hear. Arrangements were made, months of organising; the boxes began to stack up, and then one day a plane ticket appeared on her bedroom dresser. Again she told them that she wasn't prepared to leave Steve and her life in London. Still they wouldn't listen. She described departure day in tragic detail: the taxi waiting outside to take them to Heathrow, her stoic refusal, the words and tears that ensued, and finally the bitter sight of her parents, her 'best friends' driving away. 'That was three years ago and, until five months ago, I didn't answer their calls, not that there were all that many, or reply to their picture postcards of white sandy beaches, sapphire water, brilliant sunsets and piña coladas.'

Abandoned by her parents, neglected by her workaholic husband, having tasted and rejected fame, she was, she admitted, a woman with issues.

It was too beautiful a day to spend inside tiny, dark interiors, and so I accompanied her on her quest for a 'decent' umbrella. We strolled through the rich, creamy Borough of Kensington and Chelsea, down the wide Holland Park Road lined with pruned trees and stately white embassies, pillars, flags, and iron fences. We walked down cobblestone mews, and lingered in Holland Park itself, where peacocks wandered freely and the stinky rose garden was in full bloom. She said peacocks were cruel birds. She knew the names of native trees and the trendy dogs on leads, and she pointed out where Paul McCartney and Richard Branson lived.

We walked by the playground where she has fond childhood memories, and were almost at Kensington High Street when suddenly she turned her focus on me.

Since meeting Sabrina, I'd been very quiet. My mind's blank page had been busy recording her incessant monologue, and absorbing an onslaught of new impressions. But she was curious to know why a Canadian woman would choose to live and work in London, in an extremely stressful, competitive, testosterone-driven industry that was hierarchical, exploitative, underpaid and all-consuming. Good question. As she saw it, professional cooking was a form of madness, an imbalance like all singular obsessions. Either you thrived in the environment due to some compulsive force of nature, or you were a slave in an oppressive, abusive industry. And she knew, she knew all about it. So why, she pressed, would someone *choose* that life? Was it my vocation? Was I compelled to become a great chef?

Well, what could I say? I didn't aspire to mediocrity and I was passionate about food, but I couldn't in all honestly admit that becoming a 'great' chef, whatever it means, was my singular aim in life. Where did that leave me, who was pursuing a career, gaining experience, and using my culinary skills as a passport to travel and a way of engaging with the world? London was on the brink of a culinary revival, so I was told, and the gastro pubs were thriving. And London was English speaking (my French wasn't strong enough to keep up in a kitchen in France), and England was so close to so many places. But suddenly a dark cloud of doubt and foreboding began to shadow my mood and muddle my motives. Meanwhile a pale-grey umbrella had caught Sabrina's eye.

Sometimes I surprise Bernie with an extremely sharp flick of the coin, which incites a curdling groan that seems to cling to the walls of the room. I always tense at that instant of contact, but then it's done and I can only watch and wait for his recovery – which is surprisingly quick. He's very resilient and free of resentment. He's not angry with me; on the contrary, he pays and encourages me to establish his helplessness in preparation for his pleasure.

My trial day began in the so-called 'dungeon', the downstairs preparation kitchen of a renowned restaurant. I was paired with a panicky, pimply boy of twenty and invited to watch and assist him for half the day. When the clock struck eleven he was whisking mustard mayonnaise in a frenzy while I picked coriander leaves and squeezed lemons. He was too flustered to talk to me and explain, and he kept muttering, 'There's too much to do, it's impossible, impossible' under his breath. The instant he finished spooning some mayonnaise into a ramekin, he grabbed the tray balancing twelve ramekins and a glass of water, and rushed off in search of the head chef. I put down my knife and followed swiftly behind.

It was 11:07 when we caught up with the chef, who automatically referred to the clock on the wall.

'What time is it, Michael?' he asked with mock curiosity, a threat ringing in his throat.

'11:06, Chef. I'm sorry, Chef, I was trying to – I had to –'

'You're late! You're late. Stop excusing yourself, Michael. So boring. It's always something with you. Or done to you, but it's never you, is it? You're useless and slow. Everyone else meets the tasting time. Today there were two of you and you still couldn't manage yourself. I don't want to hear any excuses. Tomorrow I want to see you ready at ten-thirty on the dot. Understood?'

'Yes, Chef.'

The chef was in his mid-thirties, boyishly handsome, long-lashed and tall. He had brown, clever eyes and a gigantic nose, but I couldn't yet tell if he was an artist, a perfectionist, or just a bully.

He took his time making quite a performance out of sampling the contents of each ramekin. He brought the first spoon under his nose, sniffed it, examined it, glanced at Michael, glanced at me, and then finally put the spoon in his mouth. He smacked his tongue against his palate and masticated slowly. His face was inscrutable until he'd sipped some water and rinsed his mouth, at which point his features contorted into an expression of total disgust as he spat, 'This isn't guacamole. This is revolting! Too much garlic. Fix it. Add another avocado or two . . . What do you mean there are no more avocados? Idiot! Figure it out.'

And so it went until all twelve ramekins had been sampled and critiqued and we had nineteen minutes left to make a new plum sauce, bribe a porter to go to the shop for avocados, add lemon and zest to the vinaigrette and more cinnamon to the soup, pit olives, rip lettuce, chop parsley, pull the meat off a dozen cooked duck legs for the salad, make a beer batter and set up station in the kitchen upstairs before the lunch hour service. Impossible, impossible, I thought.

At 12:39, upstairs in the service kitchen, there was a thunderous crash, a slap on the tiled wall, and a terrifying roar – the service in full swing and the chef yelling, 'Dunce. Useless girl. Pick up the pace, keep moving, get it out there, eight seconds, *Scotty*, watch the bloody soup, where's the potato gratin? I need three risotto fucking Neros. Not tomorrow, not next week, I want it now. Now.' Stomp, clap, slap, pound. 'Now, God damn it!'

I was shocked by the belligerence, the bellicosity, and the sheer violence of the scene before me, but the target of this chef's wicked rant was especially confounding. From where I stood, the sinewy Scottish boy behind the hot entrée section was a pantomime of grace and control. He flipped crêpes with the left hand, sautéed broad beans and pine nuts in brown butter with the right, and manned the deep fryer, stirred the soup, checked the oven below and the salamander above with a dancer's coordination. Food orders and insults were flying, the room was hot and heated, speed and concentration were everything, and only a zigzagging blue vein bulging across his temple betrayed his tension.

'Hurry up. Sauce on the side. Fucking moron. Sauce on the side! You've got the memory of a bloody goldfish.'

For two hours, taunting and terrorising, the head chef marshalled the service forward. He pursed his face, beat his brow and howled as if in pain, but when the service was over, as if a curtain had closed, he dropped the act. 'Good work, lads.' He winked, and then made a point of shaking everyone's hand. He poked a waiter in the ribs – a waiter still in the whirl of service – and how we laughed at his strained and frazzled face now that *our* panic was over. Stations were then cleared, food was wrapped, surfaces wiped, and the porters were ascending from the dungeon to collect the pots and pans, clean the stoves, sweep and wash the floor.

Meanwhile, my gaze and sympathy lingered on the Scot, whistling cheerfully as he wiped his station clean. I wanted to say something to him, give him some of the praise I felt he deserved or console him for the abuse he'd received. I waited until he glided past me on his way downstairs and tapped him on the shoulder. He swung around and faced me, and I asked him if he was all right. He looked confused, then suspicious.

'The way the chef screamed at you. You really don't deserve that sort of treatment.'

They were poorly chosen words, I'll admit, and I can see how they might have been construed as condescending or just odd.

First he looked incredulous but that seemed to amend into a sarcastic sneer, finding me naïve, stupid or both, before finally setting me straight.

'You kidding? I deserved every bit of it and more. We all did! I couldn't respect a chef that didn't whip my ass. He's one of the best around, and don't you forget it.'

With that he flung around and disappeared downstairs, while I just stood there, reeling with molten embarrassment. I'd misunderstood the psychology of the game. The fear, the intensity, the strict discipline and verbal abuse actually stimulated the Scot. He was wholly in his element, but I was not. I didn't see why a kitchen had to be run so brutally. What about the delicate rapture of food? And I thought: can I submit to this infernal kitchen and its tyranny? But if the Scot was right, if he was a great chef and there was something to learn, then it would be worth the pain and the thickening of my skin.

When I went back to Holland Park, Sabrina was on the sofa reading a book called *Spiritual IQ*. She was wearing a winter coat, a wool hat and a scarf, even though it was summertime. 'Sweating out a cold,' she explained without taking her eyes off the page. I was feeling slightly nauseous so I sat down on the chair across from her and recounted the trial of my day. It's possible I exaggerated the sadism of the chef and the submission of his staff in search of sympathy. Perhaps I hoped she'd convince me that I'd made a mistake in taking the job. So when she put down her book and spoke, what she said took me by surprise.

'The thing you've got to do is observe this mad chef and his brute methods so you can learn how not to lead. Treat the kitchen as a psychological study in power and discipline.'

Easy for you to say, I thought. But inspirational all the same. Entering that kitchen battlefield, I planned to wear her words like a plate in my armour.

Bernie invites me to punch him and kick him in the stomach as hard as I can and as often as I want. It's an extreme request on several counts, and yet he behaves as if he's offering me a sweetie, or an occasion for me to act out my violent nature and find my release. I'm sure he wants me to enjoy myself, but the truth is, I never punch him or kick him as hard as I can, thus I never experience that sweet release. This is my profession and Bernie's under my protection. Besides, without serious provocation and a surge of adrenaline, violence is a controlled, concerted effort, a sort of inverted athleticism. But for the sake of fantasy, or authenticity, I'm not sure which, I indulge him by pretending I'm delighted by the workout, while he takes pleasure in his fitness and mental resilience.

Because he's blindfolded, he never knows exactly when the next blow's coming. He hears me stand up, senses me hovering, and knows it's coming. I tease his belly with my stockinged foot as if I'm testing the waters. He can't help but brace himself by clenching his stomach muscles. So I wait for that moment when he inevitably relaxes his hold, and then I stomp on his belly with the heel of my foot. I can only judge my force after impact, and then adjust myself and aim . . . for what? Balance? That elusive, superlative blow that safely but effectively knocks the wind out of him?

No matter how physically powerless, in attitude Bernie will never submit. The nature of the game is triumph-by-trial, again and again. On the surface, it's harmless bravado, but underneath, I sense desperation and fear. The grin that rushes across Bernie's face just as soon as he recovers from a gasping fit is almost perverse. It seems to say, 'Never mind how I look, drooling, gagging, choking, bleeding. Never mind how contrived, how dangerous, destructive, solitary and expensive; play along with this deception, and share in my bona fide high.'

Which is exactly what I do, and Bernie's penis stays erect for two solid hours.

For nine months the restaurant was my masochism. I was a machine, an assembly-line worker, and a captive. I worked sixteen-hour shifts – we all did in order to get the time-and-a-half that plumped our paltry pay. The anxiety and build-up, the adrenaline rush of the service, the sheer stamina, speed and strength required to survive the day became an exhausting end in itself. There's no time to celebrate the myriad wonders and pleasures of food when fourteen tomato and mozzarella salads need assembling in three minutes, two duck salads, four Caesar salads – not too much dressing, eight croutons each, one with no dressing, six mixed salads, and one beef tartare. So, caper berries chopped, Dijon mustard out of the fridge, ketchup, Worcester sauce, salt, pepper, need to get Tabasco sauce, where's the Tabasco sauce? Can't find the fucking Tabasco sauce! When consistency and volume are the name of the game, there's no room to improvise and be taken by one's mood. We spec-sheeted, weighed, priced and portioned the artichoke salad in Styrofoam cups, thirty, forty at a time, and then tore off the cling film and dropped them on the plate at the very last second.

I found it humiliating to be yelled at in front of, and teased by, my boyish colleagues. It brought me back to my girlhood and the relentless teasing I endured growing up with three brothers. I resented the time I spent picking the flesh off ten lamb shanks at ten at night with heavy eyelids and an empty belly. I wanted time and money to explore the maze of London. I wanted to feed my interests, to visit the food markets and halls, hunt out the best fish and chips, find good sushi, fresh roasted coffee, and helpful health food shops. I wanted to eat curry on Brick Lane, swallow oysters at Selfridges, and drink high tea at Fortnum & Mason's. I wanted to go treasure hunting in Spitalfields Market and meander along the rainbow rows of narrow homes down the Portobello Road. I wanted to walk through the parks, get lost in the city's serpentine streets, visit art galleries and museums, attend ballet classes, host elaborate dinner parties, cook my own breakfast every morning, take photographs, do arts and crafts, write letters and emails, spend afternoons in the Reading Room at the British Museum, and ride the tube to the end of each line.

The restaurant provided staff meals three times daily for the waiters, porters and chefs. If meal duty fell upon you that day it meant preparing breakfast for twelve chefs and three porters, lunch for around thirty staff, and dinner for as many as forty. All but me frowned upon meal duty for it was considered an interruption and additional chore to the day's impossible list. The consequence was baked beans from a can, cheap white bread held under the salamander for fifteen seconds, sausages, bacon, and scrambled eggs for breakfast every day of every week for months, even years. Occasionally the eggs were poached or there were sautéed mushrooms, black pudding or grilled tomatoes thrown in for a treat. My colleagues didn't mind. On the contrary, it was the kind of fuel they fancied in the morning. And there I stood alone. I couldn't understand why chefs who cooked beautiful, quality food for strangers all day wouldn't want to take the same care over their own meals.

When it was my turn to cook breakfast I prepared a buffet of roasted vegetables with maple syrup and fresh herbs; porridge with wild berries, raisins, walnuts, and pumpkin seeds; melted cheese, tomatoes, lemon and grainy mustard on toast; pancakes with yoghurt, pinto beans, salsa, or stir-fry. And there was an outcry. The masochistic Scot was most vociferous. 'Roasted vegetables? *Berries?* Where's the fucking meat! What the hell's happening around here? Cooking's about pain and stamina. What next? No more double shifts? Soymilk options with our coffee?'

I thought he was being ridiculous with his no-pain-no-gain philosophy, and turned to making my own breakfast every morning – breakfast being my favourite meal. I was not one of the guys, but that didn't make me feel any more of a woman. I found it virtually impossible to feel attractive and feminine, or intelligent and confident, while being scolded for burning the butter, while running around in a tizzy with an unflattering cap on my head, a dirty apron tied around my check polyester men's trousers and thick chef's jacket, bits of lettuce and a cherry tomato stuck in between the grids of my shoe – sunless, sweaty-faced, greasy and exhausted.

At half past midnight I'd return home from a double shift and lonely Sabrina would be waiting up to mother me and smother me. We'd rented a two-bedroom flat in North London together as soon as I took the job, but what a dreary, dank place it was, and in such a bland neighbourhood: row after row, street upon deserted street of white stucco flats before any sign of a high street and its fluorescent-lit cafés, kebab shops and curry houses. There was a carpet shop, an off-licence, a sports pub, an internet café, and it all depressed me more than I realised at the time.

Sabrina had found the flat one afternoon while I was at work, and deluded herself into thinking it could be converted into a Zen temple or an artist's loft with some imagination and a couple of hundred quid. I didn't even have that to spare and she didn't have any money, but nonetheless she spent her days ripping out the mouldy carpet, tearing off the wallpaper and linoleum, choosing paint colours, reading self-help books and absorbing home décor magazines. On my time off I was too physically and emotionally pulverised to show much enthusiasm for Nordic grey, bamboo and cappuccino paint chips, Ikea catalogues, feng shui experiments, and make-up sessions (because, said Sabrina, 'everyone looks better in make-up'). It was only a matter of time before my exhaustion was mistaken for rejection and she splashed back at me.

'Look at you. You look terrible. You're a *slave*. Why are you driving yourself into the ground? You never get out. You never smile. You're afraid to admit it isn't for you. Afraid to quit because you think it makes you a failure . . . and 'cause you don't know what to do if you weren't cooking. God, think bigger. Start your own business. I could help you. We could sell *biscotti* to the local cafés or you could cater to parties at Steve's music studio. Steve has connections. Stop limiting yourself. Stop beating yourself up!'

Our final altercation was over a pen. We were at Heal's and she wanted to borrow my fountain pen so she could write a wish list as she came across the objects of her desire. We parted aisles to wander separately, but when we convened at the prohibitively pricey plates, saucers, and mugs, I noticed that she wasn't holding my pen. She sort of giggled and shrugged, and said a bit too casually that it dropped along the way but she didn't know where. 'That's fine, just get me a new one.' That's what I said, and I would say it again.

'It was an accident, you bitch. You don't have to scold me, punish me, and treat me like a child. It's not enough that I'm sorry, you want to slap my hand and make me feel ashamed of myself.'

It had been six months and not a day too soon when I broke free from that North London psychodrama to stay with my friends in Holland Park before moving into a flat-share in Brixton, advertised in *Time Out.* And after nine months of restaurant labour, I delivered myself from that as well.

11:42 a.m.: *Bernie's toes are grey and bloodless and I've been following the chromatic progression of one presently plum-coloured thumb. It's a disturbing sight, but when I ask him about it he assures me it's fine, is even a bit annoyed that I ask. Mozart's 'Serenade for Winds' is in gentle submission and the toy car has finally stopped screeching outside.*

I suffocate him and I strike him, yet I never stroke him. I never touch him tenderly or genitally. I never speak to him seductively. I never draw attention to the fact that my pubis is either pressed against, or hovering just above his face. We never speak about his erection, his masturbation, or the inevitable orgasm – not during the session, and not afterwards. The topic of sex is plainly not up for discussion. He's not here to analyse his sexual penchants but to satisfy them. He wants it to be playful and cheeky. He wants our time together to be spiced with wit and infused with good sportsmanship. I'm not the sexual object. And yet, curiously, when I have tried blocking his nose and mouth with my palms, smothering him with a pillow, and strangling him with my bare hands, he's lost his erection. Thus I have to conclude that his arousal is contingent upon my sitting on his face.

I was searching for alternatives to the restaurant scene when I came across an advertisement for an assistant private chef. Together with the indefatigably cheerful chef Jerome, we prepared dinner five nights a week and brunch on Saturdays for a wiry twenty-eight-year-old millionaire and his thin, anaemic wife. We spent our days creating a single, impeccable, French-inspired masterpiece for *him*, Mr M, the young epicurean, and a low-salt, low-carbohydrate, sugar-free, organic, wheat-free, dairy-free, red-meatless meal for *her*. 'If possible,' she implored in a tone of meek defeat, 'something tasty.'

Jerome was an Alsatian who'd been working in French kitchens since he was fifteen, and at twenty-five he was a stalwart of classic French cuisine, thus her dietary restrictions proved an insurmountable barrier for him. That was the real reason I was hired, because, after all, you don't need two trained chefs to do what we did. It was Jerome's impression from looking at my CV, and our subsequent interview, that I was a culinary misfit: I was a woman for starters, and then he could see that I'd never stayed in one kitchen for longer than nine months, and that I hadn't worked in a single Michelin-starred restaurant, whereas he had been poached from a three-star Michelin restaurant, Mr M's favourite, in order to come and work for him at the mansion. I'd hopped from Malaysian to fusion, from Cajun to French, to Japanese, to vegan to Mediterranean, to running my own catering business and bakery for a year. I told him I was interested in international, vegetarian and nutritional cuisine. I remember harping on for too long about pickling watermelon rind and caramelising tomatoes for dessert.

'*C'est fou, Suzanne*. There's nothing new in cooking. *Rien*. Nothing that hasn't been done before. What works is what's always worked. There's no *innovation* in flavour combination. These things, they're what you call gimmicks.'

His outlook and life experience were somewhat limited but he was young, handsome, full of energy, and extremely kind hearted. He hired me because he thought I had nowhere else to go, and he thought the job would suit me, and I think he warmed to me, found me oddly amusing, and felt I'd be good company.

In addition to preparing dinner for the couple, we made lunch for a staff of nine, which included a gardener, a maid, an elderly housekeeper, two bodyguards, a chauffeur, a butler and ourselves. The staff, the house and the business had been recently bequeathed to Mr M. Mr M Senior had died the previous winter, and it would be the young couple's year to grieve, inherit, adapt and fine-dine at home.

There was not a single adrenaline rush in the mansion. I was no longer conducting services on a full bladder just to keep me on my toes. I was never punished, never yelled at, and never reduced to frustrated or humiliated tears. We worked nine, ten-hour days, got paid above the restaurant standard, and considered ourselves fortunate. There was time to dry the tomatoes in the oven at ninety degrees Celsius for ten hours overnight. We cooked game stocks on the back burner for two days, reduced our sauces for hours until what precious little remained from the initial litres was intensely flavoured and poured like honey into a couple of ice-trays that were then frozen.

We baked a brioche and a cake twice a week, browsed through cookbooks that we bought on an unlimited and chauffeured shopping spree, and practised various cooking techniques. Since Mrs M was my exclusive concern, I tested vegetable juices, played with potions, elixirs, ancient grains and algae, while Jerome obsessed over foie gras pâté. He poached a new log every third day until he got the texture, the bain-marie temperature, the colour and saltpetre exactly right. Never mind that most of the buttery, diabetic livers of force-fed geese were then thrown away or force-fed to the staff, their families and the freezer. Jerome soon ordered a second freezer to accommodate the accumulation of experiments. He concentrated on cassoulets, home-made pasta and pastry, sugar design, and ice creams. He treated his year at the mansion as a dress rehearsal for the running of his own bed and breakfast in France, intended for the following year.

We had no budget to my knowledge, which meant we could stock the larder and the cupboards with an excess of the finest ingredients: first-press olive oil from a small Spanish grove that tasted like lemons and meadows; French Valhrona chocolate, £10 a bar, just for baking; balsamic vinegar aged thirty years that poured like molasses. When it was white truffle season the expensive tubers were flown over in a wooden crate and we stored the dozen of them in containers of dry Arborio rice. For ten days, the shelf life of those unearthed treasures, the kitchen smelled like a petrol station, and it was truffles with scrambled eggs, truffle mashed and baked and sautéed potatoes, truffle ice cream, truffle risotto, truffle dumplings, foie gras and truffle paté. Even so, six of the pricey gems (maybe a thousand pounds worth) went mouldy before they could be consumed.

One day a bottle of wine was delivered, which Jerome signed for, and he told me it was a hundred years old (probably undrinkable) and cost £18,000. We plucked the feathers off the birds that Mr M had shot, figs were flown in from Turkey, the fish was rare and endangered, the Spanish pig had been fed exclusively on acorns, the cheese came from a friend's dairy farm in France. Even the French sea salt was sublime.

It certainly was a privilege to be surrounded by the best that money could buy, as well as a bit comical and fantastical at first. But after a month I felt restless and trapped by my limited role, the removed surroundings, and too much time on my hands. The rest of the mansion was tacitly off limits. But once, only once on that rare occasion when the fey Mrs M left her nest, the ailing Portuguese housekeeper who had known Mr M since he was a boy and had been very fond of the late, great Mr M, gave me a whirlwind tour. How I would have loved to explore for hours. I wanted to look at their books, their photograph albums, see what sheets they slept in, what their shower-head looked like, what pictures hung on the walls. What toys did they hide in their drawers, what soap did she use, how did he organise his suits and shoes? Unfortunately, the house was under video surveillance but I surveyed a gold and burgundy lounge, embossed wallpaper, Turkish carpets, and a descent into a lavishly decorated salon with a white baby grand piano. I remember the wainscoting, a black lacquered vase on a marble podium, and a gilded portrait of the late Mr M: stern eyes, a sharp nose and sagging jowls. There was a pink crystal chandelier, an indoor swimming pool and sauna, skylights, and stretches of shimmering turquoise tiles.

Weekday evenings, after her yoga instructor and his personal trainer had gone, the couple showered and dressed and seated themselves in the lower dining room next to the kitchen. Then the hirsute butler sprang into action for the first time that day. The young couple always sat side by side, dwarfed at one far end of a long mahogany table, a telephone beside his plate. After our day's creations had been served, it was only a matter of minutes before the telephone rang through to the kitchen and Jerome jumped up eagerly to receive the critique.

Six days a week I walked for twenty minutes from the tube at Hampstead through a North London village: exclusive, leafy, evocative and charming. I passed tantalising shops, narrow mews, and then hills and winding roads flanked with only half exposed, grand, picture-book homes. And I inhaled the noticeably lighter, fresher more fragrant air. I dreamt of grandeur, of things rich and exquisite – and felt simultaneously taunted. A certain quality of life was resonating with me, and yet eluding me. I wanted time and money to prepare beautiful food, host elaborate dinner parties, collect books, eat off nice dishes, learn more about wine, and decorate my home with wood and velvet, rich colours, found treasure, plants and fresh flowers. Instead I was a servant in a millionaire's home. I made some depressing calculations, counting the sacrifices I'd made and would continue to make for a career that wasn't nourishing all of me. By the time I reached the gate and waved to the man in the tiny box, whose job it was to guard the private street for nine-hour shifts, my heart had hit the fancy pavement.

To this day I hear Jerome yelling after me, 'So what you doing now, eh, Suzanne? *Qu'est ce que tu fait maintenant?*' He's asking out of concern. He cares for me. He wants the best for me, but he just can't see what that might be. He'd always known what his life would be. I felt guilty because he'd tried to help me, tried to get me enthusiastic about bone-marrow sandwiches and sweetly buttered organs, and I'd let him down. But the insinuation that I was lost was something I resented; there were so many things to do. Anything could happen. Something *must* happen. Life is both long and short. It expands and contracts. It breathes. It's an implosion of possibility. I remember turning away from Jerome. I remember consciously tuning him out. I remember waving behind me, as if I were wiping away my profession. And then, without any warning, a sort of convulsion, and tears sprang to my eyes and flooded my mind. It was foolish, reckless, impulsive and unwise: I leapt without knowing my ground. And the sensation wouldn't last – I'd have to land – but for that suspended moment, I was bathing in bright light, a gentle breeze in my hair, and I felt gushingly, buoyantly free.

I began today like I've always begun with Bernie – with good intentions. I'm intent on achieving a state of mind that will transcend boredom and make good use of the time. It's the challenge of Bernie: avoid dwelling on the time, relax, reflect, enjoy the weirdness and appreciate the music. I try, but I've never wholly succeeded. The activity's too repetitious to be fully engaging, and yet too dangerous for me to indulge in a leisurely daydream. And then this up and down, these flickflickflicks: the truth is, sometimes I feel like a punching, flicking, suffocating machine.

CHAPTER 2

Why

It begins with a lie. The plan was to call Angel from the train station at noon and she'd come to greet me and escort me back to a place that was so discreet it didn't have a numerical address. I'd given myself plenty of time to get to a North London tube station that I may never have ventured to otherwise, and so arrived fourteen minutes early. It was the end of winter but I remember the day felt more like springtime. The air was balmy and invigorating. A pale yellow light was breaking through a matt of charcoal cloud, casting constellations on the leaves, and angular beams on the platform. It was, I decided, a very London light. A child was throwing peanut shells onto the tracks, a pregnant teenager was smoking, and there were pigeons at my feet, but I sat down on a bench on the outdoor platform and ignored them all. I focused on a lacquered blue ceramic rooftop half hidden by foliage about a hundred yards beyond the tracks. With concerted, telescopic effort I could hold the exotic rooftop, a patch of blue sky and some foliage in my frame long enough to believe it was a peasant's house in Malaysia, or a modest temple in rural Japan. Long enough to convince myself it was springtime and that I was elsewhere. And to be honest, when I got it right, I couldn't tell the difference between being there and pretending I was there. So there I sat, daydreaming and stalling. When I finally called Angel at a quarter past noon she was alarmingly sharp on the phone.

After quitting the mansion, and professional cooking, my immediate concern was money. I applied for a job at a major bookshop chain but they never got back to me. Eric, the husband of my friend in that skinny council flat in Holland Park where I first stayed with Sabrina, and to where I returned after Sabrina, was a builder, and he always needed an extra pair of hands.

So I worked part-time on various building sites, and part-time at a Brixton juice bar/book shop/café. The proprietor hired me to help redesign the menu and standardise the kitchen. He paid me five pounds an hour, took none of my suggestions and, as it transpired, really only wanted someone to serve juice during the busy peaks on weekends. Mid-shift one weekend, some of my flatmates came to visit me. I went over to talk to them and was publicly scolded by the boss for doing so. I felt humiliated; it was all wrong: I'd come all the way from Canada craving challenge and expansion, hungering for adventure, and there I was getting yelled at by a sexually frustrated man while holding a banana watermelon smoothie.

On the construction site I found myself in a familiar plight: the odd female in the company of men. I tried to be one of the guys while painting the baseboards of a dusty flat and listening to the radio and banter of blokes; but I was really just a tourist in their world. We went to the pub for lunch every day, and I ate fish and chips and swallowed two pints of Guinness along with them, and returned to work sluggish and quietly drunk.

Eric had another mate working for him: petite and Peter Pan-like with a plummy accent. He was an actor, a manic-depressive, a fantasist, a fabulist, one-time jockey, now sometime carpenter. Over lunch, or while plastering a wall, he would expand on the most elaborate stories: how he smuggled carpets from Saudi Arabia; the family plot to drug him and section him; the mendacity of doctors; his ingenious escape from the psyche ward; a business plan involving the exploit of his great-great-grandmother's herbal recipe. While I was painting the floorboards and he was on a ladder, fiddling with wires, he boasted of a toga party he'd orchestrated that became a legendary orgy. Instead of invitations, he'd used a password; hundreds turned up. He rented a warehouse in Ladbroke Grove, charged a fee at the door, more for alcohol, and made a clean fortune.

'I could do that. I've done it.' I shrugged. 'I've organised an orgy in Montreal.' There was white glossy paint in my tangled hair and my turpentined, sawdusted overalls were scratching my thighs and that was the moment I chose to assert my sexual prowess and startle him. 'I've had a lot of lovers, you'd be surprised. I've been to peep shows, have a friend who does internet pornography; and I used to live with someone who became a dominatrix.' He looked at me and squinted his bespectacled grey eyes like a prophet. 'Hmm. I see. Tell me more. Tell me about the dominatrix.'

Eve was, more accurately, a friend of a friend. We'd attended the same university, and the summer after her graduation she needed a room to rent. She was American and planned to go back to New York in the autumn. Indifferent to the blazing splendour outdoors, she spent her days locked in her bedroom, reading. She chain-smoked Marlboros, spoke with husky irreverence and maniacal speed, and had no patience for what she referred to as 'lazy minds'. But in the presence of the truly vulnerable her cool wrath seemed to change. She became exceedingly affectionate, maternal and protective. She was only twenty-one but her long black hair was already streaked with grey. Her bespectacled eyes were small and precocious, and her wispy hair was always falling in her face. I feel I never really saw her, that she was either masquerading as plain, or always shifting to greet the situation. She seemed so duplicitous. Despite a mousy, somewhat careless exterior – baggy jumpers, dark colours and cloistered clothing – her presence was bewitchingly powerful, and feminine. I never knew her, and I knew I never would . . . and, actually, I wanted it that way. I wanted to keep the mystique of Eve intact.

That autumn, Eve returned to New York and I enrolled in culinary school. Six months later I heard through our mutual friend that she was working at a literary agency in the day and as a dominatrix by night. I had only the vaguest idea of what either job involved, but, it being of Eve, her choices had become of interest to me. The impression that really resonated with me was the one of Eve living a double life. Double lives, and multiple lives, fascinated me.

Just once when visiting New York, I made a special trip to

upper Manhattan to visit Eve on her lunch break. We sat on the steps outside her brownstone office drinking cappuccinos and eating these sensational chocolate and black cherry croissants. We were revelling in food: baby cauliflowers baked with truffles, roasted beetroots and grilled grapefruit, mountains of squash mash with sage, brown butter and maple syrup. I was working in a 'fusion' restaurant owned by the Mafia, and she was business-lunching with writers and publishers in New York's finest restaurants. The conversation segued into insecure writers, commercial-minded publishers, fiery egos, and the brute 'winter' of book buying, but domination was a subject that was never broached.

Near the end of the visit a gang of loud teenage girls with menacing intent came marching our way. From where we sat at the top of the steps we couldn't help but watch them as they approached and watch as they came to a deliberate halt. The leader of the gang, a girl of maybe thirteen, wearing a track suit and flashy trainers put her arms akimbo, lifted her pugnacious chin, and called up, 'And what do *you* think you're staring at?'

I sort of snorted. Their numbers, their youth, and their flagrant arrogance were making me twitch with two angry impulses that amounted to the same thing: defend our pride, and undermine theirs. I was about to tell her not to flatter herself, that we weren't looking at them, or something, and it would have escalated, no doubt, but it was Eve who came forth with the diplomatic masterstroke. Beamingly friendly while retaining her dignity, she called down, 'We were admiring your shoes.'

I saw the child's face freeze for an instant before blossoming into a proud smile. She called up, 'Why thank you, they're new.'

And with that the gang marched on to rule their turf, but I lingered longer, silently edified and inspired by Eve's social grace, her sharp and effective deflective.

A few days after mentioning Eve and domination, Peter Pan presented me with a mint-green advert the size of a postcard. He'd plucked it off the interior of a phone box in central London. I stared at the illustration: a voluptuous vixen wearing stilettos, spectacles and a schoolmistress cap, dangling a whip over a man bent over a desk, his trousers at his ankles. For severe discipline, expertly administered, one could call the mobile number. 'Was that Eve? Could that be you?' asked Peter. And that's when I considered doing it.

I brought up the word domination with a stranger at a party who was bragging to me about the porno film he'd just shot. He gave me the name of a fetish contact magazine. I bought it and studied the adverts of about fifty mistresses. I chose seven that intrigued me, and prepared myself to call them and offer myself as their apprentice. I made the seven calls, left seven messages, and left it at that.

Five days later, coming home to the flat-share in Brixton, I saw a note on the big blue fridge addressed to me. In bold red marker it read: call Angel about domination. I remember the large, pointy A. I remember the word domination as a shape like Manhattan or Chinatown, before the meaning of the word and then the message registered. At first I felt the downward slope of disappointment because it seemed a secret door had opened far too easily. Then the motion shifted and I began to swell with fear and exhilaration as I felt myself encroaching upon a seductive unknown.

Angel's advert was elegant and intriguing. I was attracted to its sparse simplicity and my own associations with the words *mind*, *body*, *bizarre* and *control* written in a tasteful font. The advert had no photograph and I had no idea what Angel looked like, or how she'd dress to greet me at the station. But then, just a few minutes later, there she was, and there was no doubt it was her.

She looked like the witch of a fairytale, but also a crow with her aquiline nose, her pale, wan face and long jet-black hair streaked with cobalt blue. Beneath a forest-green skirt that started just below her breast and flared all of a sudden at her ankles, you could tell she was thin like a twig. The nails on the ends of her small, wrinkled fingers were painted black, and she had a frightening, dark, jagged mouth. The overall effect was Gothic and unapproachable and yet there she was, approaching me. When she stood three feet in front of me, I saw what I hadn't seen from the distance: two beautifully shaped, shy eyes like paisleys, and long, long, little girl lashes. I had a sort of double vision, a present/future collision. I saw her immediate ephemeral exoticism, and I saw her in the future, where and when I knew her.

She seemed so genuinely offended by my lateness that my childish impulse was to lie. I launched on a lengthy description of a diabetic friend having gone into seizure that morning at a breakfast café in Brixton. I told her about the orange juice that had saved the situation and how shaken I was when I boarded a train on the wrong branch and had to switch at Camden. For a moment I took a moment's delight in my finesse for fibbing before realising it was having no effect on her. She was intent on punishing me with silence as she led me through one hundred yards of orthodox Jewish suburbia, and then through a tall, wooden gate set in a grey stone wall. The lacquered wooden plaque on the door read 'The Cottage' and on the outside it looked the part.

Inside, the place was impossibly small: a reception area sandwiched between two tiny rooms, the dungeon and the medical room, plus a toilet. Yet the ceiling was very high and when the padded door of the dungeon was shut the smallness worked and gave a sense of subterranean, subversive enclosure. At eye-level along the length of one red wall hung an impressive display of whips, chains, and other instruments of the trade: blindfolds, ball gags, inflatable gags, bite gags, leather belts, wooden paddles, rubber whips, horsehair whips, wrist cuffs, ankle cuffs, a single-lashed whip, tawses, canes, neck collars, dog leads, suede floggers, crops and birches. One by one Angel named them all.

There was a black leather bench, purpose-built for corporal punishment, a cast-iron chamber that looked like a standing coffin, and a bondage chair that doubled as a throne. There was a trolley for nipple clamps, cock rings, penis bondage contraptions, weights for the genitals, and thumb traps. On a long shelf sat hoods and wigs on Styrofoam heads, and on the floor a wooden treasure chest full of ropes. In a single glance I saw a blowtorch and baby oil, a metal head cage resembling a birdcage, a tattered slipper, a quill, a wooden kitchen spoon and a rolling pin. There were boxes filled with clothes pegs, leather strings, elastic bands, thumbtacks, condoms, latex gloves, wet wipes and tissues.

The medical room looked just like any doctor's office: white, sterile, and sparkling with chrome. A white leather gynaecological chair stood as the centrepiece, and a narrow, fold-up examination bed was pushed against one wall. There was an IV stand from which hung a saline bag, medical masks, an enema funnel and a gas mask.

Upon closer examination I saw jars of medicines and ointments, boxes of needles, syringes, medical swabs, suturing thread, catheters and bandages. There was a shelf displaying surgical tools: scalpels, medical scissors, a speculum, a stethoscope, and dental picks. There was a shelf for electrical devices: wires and attachments for the penis, the balls, the rectum, the nipples and urethra. There was an electric speculum, an electric pinwheel and a wire brush. Another shelf supported dildos, vibrators and anal plugs in every shape, length, circumference and colour, lined up like toy soldiers. One of the walls was all mirror, the others were adorned with medical posters; drawings of the inner ear, the female reproductive organs, the endocrine system.

Back in the dungeon Angel explained stocks and pillars, the pulley and suspension harness, male chastity belts, and a vice for crushing penises and testicles – or fingers and toes. Holding blonde and brunette horsehair whips in each hand, she encouraged me to stroke them and compare. And then with such suaveness she said, 'Bend over and I'll show you the difference.' After taking an instant to consider it correct that I should know how all these instruments felt, I began to bend, but she stopped me with her laugh and said she was only kidding. And then she apologised for overwhelming me with information.

We settled in the reception area, she on a tall chair and me on an embarrassingly squat stool, and she talked sisterly and soberly about work as a dominatrix. She appeared to be in a precarious position of needing to sell me the job while feeling obliged to present some of its less attractive sides. She tempted me with inflated financial prospects – a couple of thousand pounds a week if I was willing to work for it – but then she insisted that money could never be my only motive. 'You need to enjoy what you're doing; it makes all the difference. Despite how it appears, you need to like men if you want to do the job and do it well. You'll be seeing them at their most needy and vulnerable. And you need to care for them. You're there to facilitate their fantasy, and they will pay you a lot of money for energetic and attentive service. Some of them will worship you for it. But don't forget that they came to you predisposed to worship. They don't know you. You're playing a role. Don't let it go to your head. Don't take it too seriously. It's a game. It's a job. Make sure to have fun with it and you'll be fine. Keep a life outside the dungeon, save your money, pursue other interests, and remember you don't have to do anything that makes you feel uncomfortable.'

She reckoned that imagination, sensitivity, intelligence, and eloquence were the attributes of a successful mistress. She stressed that 'sex' and any other 'personal services' were strictly not on offer. 'They need never touch you, but usually the more you're willing to touch them the more grateful they'll be. At the end of the session, 95 per cent of the time, a client expects to come. Give them hand relief if you feel like it, but let them do it themselves if that suits you better. You can guess what they usually prefer but the point is it's your choice. Use your intuition, follow your instinct, observe, and improvise. It's a difficult thing to teach.'

But I was grateful for her guidance and her balance. We discussed the differences between humiliation, embarrassment and degradation. What is a fetish? What's domination? Who really holds the power in the session? What's the difference between crossing-dressing, transvestism and enforced feminisation? She introduced professional terms and abbreviations such as 'hard sports', CBT, T&T and 'golden showers'. She warned me that I'd be in regular contact with pungent, sweaty bodies, semen, blood, faeces, urine, halitosis, skin conditions and dandruff among other things, and she cautioned me that it was draining, exhausting and surprisingly hard work.

Answering the telephones that rang between twenty and sixty times a day would be my introduction, she said, a way of getting a taste for who was out there and what they wanted to explore. We went over the prices, the directions for getting to the dungeon if the client was coming by car, the appointment booking system, and the services on offer: fantasy, fetish, role play, humiliation, domination, bondage, torture, suspension, medical and school room scenarios, feminisation, and electrics. I'd have to learn how to lure in a client and distinguish a time-waster from a genuine caller. As for familiarising myself with all the equipment, I could practise on Denise, the housemaid, as well as stand in on a few of Angel's sessions. She lent me a couple of novels, a stack of fetish magazines, a rope-tying manual, some essays on sadomasochism, and a documentary about a New York dungeon which she had on video.

When all was said and done, I was sold on a psychosexual challenge. But then she stared at me, was trying to surmise me, seemed to penetrate me, before deciding it necessary to ask, 'Why do you want to be a dominatrix?' The answer wasn't obvious, not to her and not to me. Why *do* I want to be a dominatrix? I wasn't a sadist, as she claimed to be. I couldn't confess to any sexual fantasies that involved the abuse and torture of men, and couldn't even say with complete conviction that I was a dominant woman. Still, I was intrigued by what I'd seen and heard so far, and neither repelled nor intimidated. But she was asking, and I had to say something . . . except no answer jumped out at me. I hadn't even asked myself the question. Instead I thought, 'why' is such an open, such a silly, snoopy, sloppy question. 'Why' requires so much guesswork and retrospect. How and where do I begin to sieve through the facts and fictions, the accidents, influences and circumstance, the whims and serendipity that brought me to her door?

And for that matter, why does anyone do what they do? Why do I like gummy textures, tart things, and extremely spicy food? Why do I cringe at the thought of salt in my coffee or on my apple, and almost gag at the sight of undercooked egg white? Yet I really don't mind the tang of slightly rancid butter, the sight of blood, or putting my finger up somebody's bottom. I don't know why the smells of frying onions, spearmint and fresh thyme make me nostalgic for some imaginary, happy time.

She wants to know: was it the people you've known, your family, the way you were raised, have you always felt this way? And I thought, must be. Possibly. I have a brother who's a twin, does that factor in? I thought of my dominant mother. She smoked voraciously, was brazen, brash and loud. She liked to joke, to cackle, to shout. There were seven of us, all for whom my mother begrudgingly cooked. She preferred to sit on the back porch, sipping instant coffee with saccharine, reading a book.

I have three brothers and a much older sister, and they teased me relentlessly. They laughed and taunted, hung me by my ankles over the upstairs banister, and wrestled me to the ground. It was chaotic and unruly, intellectual and angry; a family of screamers, know-it-alls, raucous laughers, game players and fun-pokers. If it weren't for all the noise and activity, I might not have spent my childhood and adolescence hidden in a quiet space, absorbed in a book. It's where I met so many strangers, had countless adventures, did all my travelling. Do I tell her how much I like to read? That I'm fascinated by people, by characters, by that sense of the absurd that's lurking in everyone. Do I tell her about moving to Montreal and studying philosophy? How, after reading Plato and the Theory of Ideals, the toll of truth rang within me, like an epiphany. Aristotle and aesthetics, concepts of Beauty, possessed me.

I followed the games of Logic, while Nietzsche's existentialism and moral philosophy entangled me. I remember sleepless nights spent at my desk, my head in my palms, thinking, thinking, wrestling, trying to solve the mind/body problem. How can a thought move my arm? Or the vision of figs coated in honey on the right colour plate make me salivate? One of my professors actually warned me that I was getting too passionate about philosophy, while my classmates mostly saw it as a prerequisite for a law degree.

Maybe I should tell her about Montreal, about the sexually liberal crowd, a subculture of artists, anarchists, musicians, bohemians – lots of piercings and tattoos and very few taboos. Then I thought of Harvey Ealing Bennett III, the blue-eyed baker who ran away from his billionaire family. He was a cross-dresser, a master storyteller, and a self-harmer. Actually he used to set up these sessions with a friend. They would slash their shoulders with razor blades, slowly and deeply, and then pour salt into the fresh cut to make it part and swell.

I have a friend whom I've known since I was six or seven. She wrote stories for pornographic magazines when we were at university, and now she writes erotic literature. I dated a guy who drew a cartoon he called *Pervert*. He was into sexual role-play and videos, owned fifty-two pairs of trainers and liked his women, when in the bedroom, to wear white socks up to their knees. And then of course there was Eve, whom I admired for her grace, her power, her secret sexual life, her double life, her multiple faces. And there was the film course where we studied Lacan, fetishism, alternative pornography and the male gaze – that interested me.

Working in the kitchen . . . that must be part of the answer. I should tell her about sadistic chefs, constantly working with men, the bully, banter and humiliation during a busy dinner service. How pain, violence, discipline and a good grasp of the trade's tools could produce something succulent and beautiful.

Working at the mansion turned me to domination. Living in London drove me to the dungeon. London: so attractive, so enticing, so grandiose and exciting, and yet everything seems to happen behind a mask, behind a door, according to social codes and class.

I'm Canadian, single, anonymous. I want to make some money and taste it all. I have this burning desire to break through and infiltrate. I thought of all the ways that sex and food relate: the visuals and textures, desire, tastes and appetites. Aren't these two of the great human levellers, and the best way to know one another?

After a very long pause, while Angel sat patiently staring at me, I finally spoke, more of a choke, and said I didn't know why, wasn't exactly sure, but I was curious, I wanted to learn, I thought I'd be good at it. And then I told her that I wanted to save some money, enough to some day open a porridge bar, maybe in the City, because porridge is underrated and nobody, amazingly, has done it before.

For nine minutes I haven't said a word. I've been watching the hands on the clock and flicking his nipples over and over and over again. I've been crouching above his face, sitting on it, and leaping up at the very last second. Maybe he's not bothered by the silence but I feel it's my job to say something, engage with him, entertain.

'Bernie, I know someone that can hold their breath for six minutes, I'm being serious, I wouldn't lie. And I can hold mine for at least a minute, but I've noticed you can't hold yours for more than forty seconds. I've timed you. It's obvious I've been too easy on you. So I'm setting the target at fifty seconds and I'm not getting up, not a second before that.'

'Nothing I can do about it,' he says to goad me on. And if he could, he would shrug.

'No, Bernie, that's absolutely right, there's nothing you can do about it.'

And then I collapse on his face with the aplomb of someone that's done this sort of thing before. I adjust my weight and placement in order to achieve an effective seal, and then I note the exact position of the seconds hand on the clock, and calculate its position in fifty seconds before turning away. I flick his nipples in time to the music, stare at myself and at the smears on the mirror, the dust and a condom wrapper in the corner, and drips of candle wax on the floor that will have to be scraped off with a tool from the medical room. I think of my tuna sandwich sweating in my bag; I have leftover brown rice in the fridge at home, I'll steam mustard greens and stir-fry with oyster sauce . . .

Graphically, I imagine Bernie's pleasure as a series of climbing peaks and mounting desperation. I think I can even imagine his womb-like, obliterating euphoria, and the compressed, terrified excitement of his suffocation. But who can say whether it's worth the price he's willing to pay: progressive brain damage, risk of stroke or death, and a guesstimated third of his salary.

I can't help but fantasise about his death. In the aftermath, I'm reaching into his pockets, opening up his wallet and discovering the missing piece to Bernie's puzzle, the punch line to a long and twisted joke; a folded piece of paper, a photograph, a talisman, a dried flower. Sometimes I fantasise that I'm of a mind that knows no guilt, and I'm taking my time over his body, calmly watching death, meticulously dealing with the consequences. I've rehearsed several defences for the court of law and others for my conscience. Involve Angel? Drag him across the garden into her house and change the scenario? Bury him in the garden? Get an excellent lawyer? Lie or tell the truth?

His chest contracts and I become alert. It's only 32 seconds, 33, 34, 35, but I feel him getting desperate. I flick his nipples, flick his nipples, and wait for a second sign, a twitch or quiver to inform me he's reaching his limit. 38, 39, 40 seconds, and my heart, these rapidly flicking coins, and a fevered Mozart are all mimicking the crisis. Forty-one seconds and I'm genuinely swept up in the dilemma of safely holding back or pushing on. I'm imagining that these final seconds, 42, are what he craves, 43, and that each second is more potent and pleasurable than the last. Forty-four seconds, 45, and then a morbid premonition . . . and instantly I leap, sparked by fear. The grandiosity of his first gasp for air is the mark of our success. It's like watching a man waking from the dream that he's drowning, over and over and over again.

And then I lie. I pretend we've reached the 50-second mark since anything less would call my bluff. 'Well that was easy, wasn't it? This time, let's go for 51, 52, no, 53 sec–' Before I finish the word I take him by surprise and drop back down on his face.

CHAPTER 3

Truth

Three days after our first meeting, Angel was guiding me through her garden between the cottage and her mock Tudor corner house. We entered the house through the kitchen, which reeked of cat litter, cat food, rancid dairy and rotten rubbish. The sink was stacked with dirty dishes that might have been there a week, and dried food was splashed here, there, and everywhere. I suppressed my shock and revulsion but I was disturbed, all the more so because she showed no signs of embarrassment and made no excuses. I followed her through the darkened house, up a dusty staircase and into a fuchsia-painted bedroom where the housemaid, Denise, was hunched over a dressing table, applying glue to a false eyelash balanced on thumb and fingertip. Startled and over-eager, he tripped as he swivelled to stand, and lost the long lash in the process. When he recovered his composure, I got my first full-frontal impression of the transvestite housemaid.

He was wearing a curly blonde wig that sat slightly cockeyed, a pink hair band, which was lost in the nest of locks, an excess of glittery blue eye shadow, and the one long-lashed eye. He had on a black vinyl maid's outfit, white fishnet stockings, and black, high-heeled sandals. The overall effect was egregious, save for the glassy melancholy in his grey and earnest eyes, and the humility with which he curtsied and then whispered, 'Hello, Mistress.' It was the first time anyone had addressed me so submissively, meanwhile my borrowed skirt was hanging unflatteringly off my hips, my boots were all wrong, and I was in the grip of stage fright. In a flash I saw dozens of possible inflections, projections and all manners of responding to his greeting, but what came out was a flat and feeble 'Hello.'

What a relief then that Angel ordered Denise back to the dressing table while she showed me her 'transformation wardrobe'. I remember that her back was facing him and only I could see his furtive glances as he did something, I couldn't tell what, with his hands.

Angel showed me bras, silicon breast pads, silk slips, a man-size pink satin baby doll dress, a silver-sequinned evening gown, a ballerina's tutu, a tarty red dress with spaghetti straps, and equestrian gear. Meanwhile Denise kept stealing glances and, and . . . painting his fingernails. So that's what he'd been doing. Angel showed me feather boas, a leather glove collection and suspender belts. She was stretching a leopard-patterned dress to prove the point that it was *the* dress that flattered most men's figures, when all of a sudden she whipped around and stormed, 'What do you think you're doing with my nail polish? What did I tell you about painting your nails!'

Indeed, what was the story with the nail polish, and how had she known what he was doing when her back had been turned to him? He dropped his head in a pose of feigned remorse, his wig slipping over his eyes, and whispered an apology.

'You don't look sorry. Does he look sorry to you, Mistress?' she asked to my immediate distress. I shook my head. 'See, we don't think you're sorry. *We* think you did it on purpose because you know how I feel about you and nail polish. Give me the nail polish remover. Now!' and she slapped her hands like she meant business.

'Oh, but, Mistress, please. Please let me leave it on.'

She snatched the bottle from his stubborn grip and hid it behind her back. 'I'm off to fetch your cleaning bucket. Mistress will help you finish your make-up. This bottle stays with me. If after two hours the downstairs is not sparkling clean, then you can ride the tube home with bright red nails for all the world to see. That'll be one of your punishments. You do take public transport, don't you? Yes, I thought so. Good, then I'm off.'

And I was left alone with him.

Here was my chance to play a role and be whoever I wanted to be – but who *was* that? What did I want him to see? And who did *he* expect me to be? I felt overwhelmed by too much choice and freedom. So I leaned against the wall with my hands behind my back, and played it safe with silence and a cool stare. But I nearly slid into a smile while watching his obvious confusion. He was torn between relief because Angel had gone and apprehension – because I was still a mystery. Timorous *and* brave, testing the boundaries, he took a single step towards me, and then stopped to gauge my reaction. Getting no response, he braved a second step, and stopped again. Still I said nothing, did nothing, not knowing what to do or say. On the third step he broke the silence by bombarding me with questions.

'Where are you from, if I may ask, because your accent, it sounds American . . . are you Canadian? I'm sorry. Did I offend you? How long have you lived in London? Do you like it here? What's it like in Canada? How long have you known Mistress Angel? Isn't she so kind?'

I couldn't decide whether he should be asking me those questions, or if he was stepping out of line. Was this a test? And did he really find her kind? Was it all a game? But something, I had to say something. I could have lied, or told him to mind his own business, but it was easier to speak the truth and play myself.

'I'm Canadian and I'm not offended. I've been in London eighteen months. I love it and I hate it. I don't know Angel, I've just met her, and we better finish your make-up before she comes back.'

I applied hot-pink lipstick to his thin forty-three-year-old lips, and rouge to pale and gristly cheeks. I struggled with the eyeliner and his twitching, false lashes while he told me about his frail mother with whom he'd always lived, and his hobby of painting animals, especially squirrels, in watercolours. He'd been working for Mistress Angel for eight months, whenever he could get away from Mother, which was not nearly as often as he'd like, maybe once a month. He couldn't afford to pay her from his disability allowance, so he tried to make himself useful to Mistress in exchange for her company, the clothes and the environment. While he chattered away, I had the embarrassing realisation that my inexperience was all over his face. I'd never worn make-up, let alone applied it to the flaccid skin of a twitching man, and it was far more difficult than I'd imagined.

When Angel burst on the scene, she punctured our precarious peace and I caught her wincing at my make-up job. However, the first thing she asked was, 'Has Denise been annoying you while I've been gone?'

I recall opening my mouth to say 'no', which was the truth, when Denise so rudely interjected. 'Oh no, no, no, Mistress, I wasn't annoying, not at all, I promise.' And then he shot me a conspiratorial smile – which, in my opinion, was going too far. I turned to him and asked with laced curiosity, 'And how would you know if you were annoying me or not?' I meant it too, only I wouldn't have said so had I not been playing Mistress to a passive-aggressive, cross-dressing maid.

Suddenly I saw how protective Angel was of Denise, whose face blushed beyond the rouge, whose eyes were filling with incipient tears, and whose lower lip was quivering. He thought I'd deliberately tricked him, or betrayed him, or set him up only to turn on him later, which was not the truth, but he was now whimpering and dolorous, and Angel was gently warning him to get started on the cleaning because in exactly two hours we'd *both* be inspecting his work. With that Denise wobbled off, a feather duster in one red-nailed hand, and a bucket of cleaning products in the other.

11:55: *Blind and immobilised, his ears are especially keen. I know he hears me unwrap my sandwich and eat it while sitting on his face, even though I do this as quietly as possible. He has never explicitly said so, but I know it's not part of the game or the service he's paying for if I abandon him for a cigarette outside – which I do anyway to break up the two hours – or just get up and stretch my legs. It's extremely difficult to coordinate these squats and leaps and flicks for two mindless hours. I've placed cushions under my knees and I'm constantly shifting my weight and adjusting my position, but the ache from the sudden descents, the sitting, and the last-second leap is inescapable. The truth is, I'm suffering with him, and I don't want him to know. If he did, I'm concerned that it would distract him or subtract from the fantasy. In the fantasy I'm invulnerable and having a wonderfully wicked time beating, tormenting and suffocating Bernie.*

When I administered my first enema I noticed how much fatter the client looked without his clothes. In fact, I was very conscious of his nudity, imagining that if it were I in his place I'd be riddled with self-consciousness, whereas he seemed aware of nothing but me. I had never been so intimate with a body like his before. His belly hung in one large fold over his groin, his toenails were yellow and cracked, his shoulders freckled. He wore a gold cross around his neck, his elbows were encrusted with eczema or psoriasis, and he gave off a slightly salty smell.

I told him to lie down on the medical bed on his side with his knees raised to his chest, but these instructions were confusing to him, so I slid my helping hand under his puffy knees and guided them in place. I'd seen Angel administer an enema in exactly the same way. I had no idea whether, medically, it was the best position for receiving an enema or if it was just her style, but when I saw him as he was, curled up in a foetal position, I couldn't help but notice how vulnerable he looked. It was then that I realised that such simple things as physical placement, nudity, my gaze, my costume, and the setting could have compounding consequences. I saw something else; I felt it as well: the gaping disproportion between what Mistress feels and client feels.

I filled the enema bag with 500ml of lukewarm water, put on a latex glove, lubricated the nozzle at the end of the tube, and inserted it an inch into his ass. He gasped as I penetrated him, but I believe it came from a feeling of violation and surprise rather than discomfort – the nozzle wasn't quite a finger thick. Meanwhile, I focused wholly on the technicalities of the job, trying to get it right, watching to see what happened, and how he'd react. With one hand I held the bag above my shoulder, and with the other hand I twisted the lever near the spout of the nozzle and watched as the water flowed down a clear plastic tube and into his bowels. Meanwhile he held his belly and moaned. It took about ninety seconds for the bag to empty and then I closed the lever and extracted the nozzle.

I put the contraption in a bucket on the floor and told him to turn over onto his back, and to my surprise, which I disguised, he had an erection. It was alien to be in the presence of an aroused man when first, the cause of that arousal was so mysterious; second, it was so distinct from my own lack of arousal; and third, I wasn't offended or put-off. I was even a bit flattered and encouraged by his stiff penis because it meant things were working. But I was confused about how to address his erection and arousal. Tease him or mock him about it? Punish him or not mention it at all? Not knowing, I said nothing. Instead, I did something I'd seen Angel do; I pressed my hand down on his bloated belly and stared him in the eye. He looked frightened, like he was happy to be frightened.

'I have an obsession with cleanliness,' I told him. 'I like everything to be perfectly, perfectly clean. No mess. No spillage, not a single drop or speck. I think it's just about the only thing that makes me angry. Mess.' And then I smiled generously and applied more pressure to his belly. Actually, I had no idea how long someone could hold an enema; it could have been five minutes, or it could have been twenty-five minutes – but then what happens? I hadn't thought to ask Angel. Could he rupture? At what point would he tear for the toilet against my wishes? Or would he wait until it was too late? In which case, what kind of fetid mess awaited the medical bed and floor? After three minutes he began to whimper. After six tense minutes he pleaded to go to the toilet. 'Not just yet,' I said. I was gambling. I increased the pressure on his belly and together we waited. At eight minutes he began squirming in panic, or he was pretending to panic, I wasn't quite sure which. But after nine minutes his desperate pleas rang truer and coincided with my vision of a ripping colon. I released my hand and he tore for the toilet.

Outside, I lit a cigarette and thought about having just tormented a corpulent fifty-five-year-old man with water. Simple and technical as it was to administer an enema, it had given him an erection. And what would happen when I told someone what I'd just done in that little white room? How would what I'd *done* distort in the telling? Who would I tell? I'd go home after work to a four-storey Victorian house we called the Brixton Massive, where I lived with a young English diplomat, a radio producer and puppet maker, a twenty-one-year-old Japanese violin prodigy who'd studied under Yehudi Menuhin, and an actor/screenplay writer. It was Wednesday. It was scrabble night at the Massive. So, most likely it would be over a game that I'd gently corrupt them with highlights from my day . . .

Natsuko's bedroom was directly beneath mine and I woke up every morning to the violin vibrating up through the large cracks in my floorboards. When she took a break, I used to make her my fancy porridge and then she would lend me her body so I could practise my rope bondage. In the cathedral-like common room-kitchen on the top floor of the house, I would tie her to the vertical beam in the centre of the room. They knew me as a Canadian chef, a part-time builder, one-time juice-maker, enthusiastic games player, tidy flatmate – and now, the dominatrix bringing back evidence and anecdotes from an arcane sexual world. And in the act of telling, those nameless things that had occurred within the seal of the cottage would acquire all sorts of adjectives, flavours and textures in the imagination of my listeners.

I was waiting for the sound of the toilet flush while it was dusk in suburbia, the dinner hour. I could smell family and food, moist air and moss or mulch, and I heaved in nostalgically for Canada. I remember looking up at a tie-dyed, indigo-blue sky and thinking: nobody sees me here in this gap between worlds. And then I heard the toilet flush, and I went back inside. He was standing in the centre of the medical room looking sheepish and limp. First, I saw him, and then I was assaulted by a foul stench that came wafting from the toilet because he'd neglected to shut the door once he had done his business. If I'd been more experienced, I would have known how to use the offence against him, seeing as he was into humiliation, but as it was, I pretended not to notice and was edgy throughout the session.

11:37 a.m.: *Bernie had just undressed and was lying naked on the tiled floor, his head on a rubber pillow. When I entered the room I was almost punched by the sharp tang of his sweat, whereas he appeared oblivious to his odour and the challenge it imposed upon me. After all this time I've never had the tact to mention it. But within minutes I've become immune to his particular pungency, and soon I'll stop recoiling from the rivulets of snot and saliva that run from his mouth and nose onto the front of my rubber skirt.*

CHAPTER 4

Shame

The cottage kept meticulous files of the regular clientele. All newcomers were obliged to complete a four-page questionnaire detailing their likes, dislikes, perceived pain threshold and fantasies. At the end of a session, the questionnaire was filed along with a follow-up report, written and dated by the Mistress, describing what happened in the session, what equipment was used, what worked, what didn't and why, and overall comments and suggestions for future sessions.

In Adam's file it said: enjoys a wide range of bondage and pain. In the questionnaire under nipple torture he ticked off tweaking, clamps, electrics, needles. Under cock and ball torture he ticked off bondage, cock rings, needles, electrics, clamps, weights, squeezing, pulling, yanking. Under anal play he ticked off dildos, electrics, plugs, vibrators, strap-on dildos and anal torture. Under corporal punishment he checked off bastinado – caning of the soles of the feet.

On 17 July Olivia, who no longer worked at the cottage, tied his cock, clamped his nipples, electrocuted his nipples and penis, hung weights from his balls, and used a spiked dildo on him as anal torture. She wrote 'hand relief to finish', which means she masturbated him at the end of the session. But of course there was no record of dialogue, nor a comprehensive recipe for making the session flow.

On 25 March Angel had recorded that he passed out when sitting upon the fibreglass dildo that was screwed onto the bondage chair, but she didn't explain how she coped with the frightening incident. Did they carry on with the session after that? Did she refund him his money? What do I do if there's a medical emergency in the dungeon? The answers weren't to be found in the files.

The records said that Adam liked slow-building pain administered sensually. In the questionnaire he said no to biting, pinching, scratching and hot wax. It was no to sharp and sudden pain. No verbal abuse, no humiliation, and no marks or redness lasting longer than a few hours.

On 13 May Vivian, who no longer worked at the cottage, wrote: can take a medium amount of pain on his nipples and genitals. Very responsive nipples. Not submissive, but polite.

Angel wrote: takes medium pain on C&B, loves all types of bondage, not submissive, very quiet, nice, shy.

But it's what his file didn't say that I found shocking. On the cover of a salmon-coloured dossier it simply read: Adam/ masochist. On the questionnaire under physical description it said: tall, slender, fit, handsome, mid-thirties, dark hair, green eyes. But let's be accurate here: his eyes are sometimes glacial blue, sometimes aquamarine, and sometimes like the white foam off a breaking wave. They were the most aquatic, tempestuous, supernatural eyes I'd ever seen. I was instantly shaken, instantly in trouble. I needed time to look at them, while instinct warned me not to.

When he spoke, the words were leaden and unequivocal, but then he wasn't a talker – which only seemed right considering his almost audible, somehow screaming eyes. At first I didn't notice the full, feminine design of his mouth: the thinner, inset lower lip, and those distinct and full twin peaks of the upper. The exquisite calligrapher's line drawn from his pressed lips that tapered and then twirled upward at the corners like whirlpools, the confident angle of his jaw, and the serious chin were among the treasures I discovered only later. At the time, I opened the door to greet a shy, polite, non-submissive masochist, and instead I met with Beauty's blue eyes.

He put down a battered briefcase, took off his shoes, and followed me into the medical room. I asked him if there was anything he particularly wanted to explore that day, or anything he wanted to tell me before we began, but he said he'd leave it up to me. Then he handed me £150, a lot to pay a novice for an hour, and feeling the implicit pressure to perform miracles, I took the money and left him alone to get himself undressed.

I took refuge outside, where I was hidden from the neighbourhood by a grey stone wall, a tall wooden gate, and a wild mesh of shrubbery. So it wasn't for disguise that I took the trouble to lower myself onto the single, narrow doorstep of rotting wood. I was wearing a tight rubber dress and thigh-high boots, which made bending awkward and risky, but I felt unsteady and nervous and I needed the ground. With my heels digging into last season's leaves, I lit a cigarette and tried to collect myself. Funny how I'd tried to prepare myself for absolutely anything, be it unusual, bizarre, gruesome and perverse, yet it hadn't occurred to me that I'd squirm under the challenge of extreme physical attraction.

I thought of Adam alone, getting naked, preparing to place himself at the mercy of a young woman who was going to see to his pain, his pleasure, and his orgasm. I imagine he found those first few minutes uniquely thrilling and terribly exciting: not knowing me, not knowing what I was capable of, not knowing what he'd be tempted to endure. And then there was I, thinking I'd have to pretend that he wasn't the first masochist I'd ever tortured, and a beautiful one at that.

We had fifty-five minutes together. When I opened the door to the medical room he was standing naked in semi-profile, looking at a medical poster on obesity. I'll have seen a thousand naked bodies, maybe more by the time this serpent's tale is told, but his stands as an ideal, an epiphany in the shape of a man.

Yes, he was astonishing, but I was just as astonished to be so wholly affected by the masculine perfection that lay before me. His shoulders, collarbone, and upper ribcage were almost grotesquely defined and wide. His long, lissom limbs were like a painter's strokes, and his legs like those of a preying mantis. As I followed a bulging green vein along the inside of his arm, I felt an intense compulsion to wrap my fingers at least halfway around the thick of his wrists. He had enormous hands, a wedding band, and badly bitten fingernails. I was restless. It wasn't enough to look; I desired to *do* something with his beauty.

I told him to lie down on the gynaecological chair. Then I

fixed his legs in stirrups. I fastened in his chest, his upper arms and thighs, his belly, wrists, and neck. The whole procedure took four minutes. Next, I tied a shoestring around the base of his scrotum and around each testicle, finishing with a knot near the tip of his penis. That was at least three clumsy minutes because I hadn't yet acquired the dexterity for genital bondage. Reaching self-consciously for a pair of nipple clamps, I stood outside myself, watching my stiff awkwardness and embarrassing uncertainty. What was my face doing, I wondered, as I felt his eyes piercing me. How did I look? What did he see? She is clamping his nipple. He is wincing. She is clamping his other nipple and he's grunting. It's obvious he's not happy. And I think: what *kind* of pain does this masochist want? How is it done? What's the trick? What's the recipe for making some elaborate, erotic dessert out of honest pain?

Eleven minutes into the session and neither of us has said a word. I keep an eye on his impressive erection because it reassures me and helps me believe that the mysterious force of his masochistic nature is taking care of his pleasure all by itself, despite my inexperience and insecurity. I tugged at the clamps because it was something to do, and because I knew from his file that he liked pain to his nipples. While I tugged and tweaked, I watched the lines deepen around his squinting eyes and his mouth stretch as wide as it would go. He looked like a portrait, a caricature of pain.

Suddenly, I knew with humble certainty that whatever it was he wanted or needed from me was not mine to give. I wanted to give him something exceptional; a platform for that beauty, but I didn't know what or how. What should I say? What do I do?

The more I analysed, the more I was paralysed. What a waste of money, and such a sham to be paid to control him when it was painfully obvious and disappointing to us both that I couldn't. The desire to surrender and terminate the session was intense. I didn't need to do this. No one is forcing me to do this. I'm stubborn, self-flagellating, and afraid of giving up or giving in. But then I told myself that bad sessions were inevitable in the beginning. Did I really expect to appreciate the subtleties, complexities, and psychology behind erotic pain and sadomasochism after half a dozen sessions? So I braved on, resigning myself to trial and error, and a baptism by fire.

I put on a latex glove, lubricated my finger, and inserted it into his ass. Should I have been gentle or rough? Again, what did a masochist want? I put a condom on a rubber butt plug, lubricated it, and pushed that into his anus. It was something, it was definitely something, and I think he agreed. After all, his nipples were clamped, and that in itself was something. Plus his penis and balls were so tightly bound that they shone and the veins bulged along the shaft – and that was something. And if I had done no more than strap him down naked, spread and suspend his legs in the seductive insulation of that white room, then that would have been something. But now, on top of everything else, there was a plug up his ass, and another thirty-nine minutes to fill. So there and then I decided to electrocute him.

I wasted several minutes, almost £10 worth, just sorting through tangled wires and attachments, setting up the electric box, and avoiding his eyes. Before doing anything else, I needed to remove the clamps on his nipples. He groaned with unrestrained displeasure when I removed the first, which made me dread removing the other. But I did, and he growled with redoubled displeasure. Next, I fastened a metal ring around his testicles and wired it up to the box. Finally I clamped his nipples with wired prongs and took the electric box in hand. I set the dials at a low intensity and a slow pulse and for a few seconds I might have appeared to know what I was doing. Then I turned on the switch.

Nothing happened. I increased the intensity by minuscule degrees and hastened the pulse. Still nothing happened. I thought maybe the box was broken, and yet the light was flashing. The silence in the room was overwhelming and I could feel the sweat trapped inside my rubber dress. I continued turning up the pulse until finally he jerked and grunted, unimpressed. But it was working. Something was happening. I increased the pulse and with that I felt my own pulse increasing. But when I checked his cock for consolation, what I saw was the crude, unequivocal symbol of failure – his penis was shrinking! In a desperate spasm, I turned it up some more, and suddenly he erupted in a wild, contemptuous, 'NO!'

It was terrifying. *He* was terrifying. I was terrified. I didn't know him. I didn't know what he was capable of. I switched off the electrics instantly, and at the risk of my personal safety rushed to undo the straps around his neck, wrist, and upper chest to set him free. It all happened with such alacrity and urgency, me unstrapping his ankles and thighs, he tearing the clamps off his own nipples, undoing the strap around his belly, removing the ring around his balls, and finally pulling out the anal plug himself, that I had no time to hide my shame, my shock, and my fear. I backed up out of the room and shut the door behind me.

I felt that I was to blame for showing my weakness. He was frustrated, maybe embarrassed for himself, for me, and his power pounced upon my vulnerability. Shamefaced, I returned to the room and handed him back half his money. He was buttoning up his shirt and didn't bother to look up; he just waved the money away, preventing me from easing my guilt. It was then that I committed my final *faux pas* by saying I was sorry. His head shot up and he glared at me with glacial disdain. 'Don't take it all so personally,' he snapped. But that is exactly how I took it, and I wanted him to leave. Leave – and never come back!

CHAPTER 5

Welcome

I know exactly when he's here by the creak of the gate. I take a deep breath, and as I exhale there's a knock at the door. I don't know him and there's no point in trying to imagine. I only hope he's not too handsome. Let him be polite, engaged and responsive. Let him see my beauty, power, and intelligence; let him see what he wants to see. Let's hope he's not too passive and unimaginative, or too easily enamoured. Let me see the very thing in him that he needs me to see. Let us connect, and then see where we can be.

I know you first by your eyes. I note the speed and discretion with which you enter and shut the door. I look at your clothes, smell your aroma, catch the slender length of your fingers, or the thickness of your eyebrows, and the bulge of your Adam's apple. I gauge your age, your height, your weight; guess if it's self-love or hate, and I ask you to take off your shoes. I notice your shoes and then the shape of your foot. In the reception room you sit down on an embarrassingly low stool and, with deliberate slack,

I make my way to the tall chair and turn to face you. I cross my legs, remember my posture, grip the pen, and enjoy those silent, suspended seconds. With the clipboard and a blank questionnaire on my lap, I take comfort in my role and the structure of the next four to six minutes. You won't shock me. I have no taboos. I'm a professional. Judgement is reserved and discretion preserved within the safety of these arcane walls. You can see that I'm attentive and sympathetic, and I want to know more.

Who is he? He is sixty-two, forty-eight, early thirties, late fifties, mid-twenties. He was only seventeen and he wanted to wear a collar and be forced to do humiliating and degrading things. He's retired. By his own admission, he's too old for this sort of thing. It's his first time seeing a Mistress. He stopped counting the number of Mistresses he's been to see. He visits once a fortnight, once a week, once a month, or whenever he's not shooting a movie. It's a treat for birthdays, bad days, or holidays. He's single and lonely, married and lonely, engaged and content, 'practically divorced' or recently bereft. He wears a suit. He wears a beautiful suit. He drives a limousine for a living. He's a philosophy professor who climbs mountains, and professes to be madly in love with his wife – and he's seventy-eight. And he wants to be lorded over and tortured by a sophisticated sadist. He's a soft-spoken veterinary surgeon with fruity breath and wavy hair who brings along a mask, a tank of nitrous oxide, and a sack of ether so he can re-enact his first dental visit, which was also his first erotic experience. There are dentists, and chemists, and businessmen too. He brings me Haydn CDs, coffee-table books, Swiss chocolates, and bad flowers from the kiosk at the tube station. He buys me shoes, stockings, figs and herbal teas.

His company builds cranes. He manufactures greeting cards. He's the carpenter, the landowner, the lodger, the estate agent, the gardener, the surveyor, and the solicitor. He's wealthy. He's poor. He's fit, he's fat, he's got bad breath but a healthy demeanour. He's the guy in the brown slacks and the checked shirt, reading the *Evening Standard* on the train home to a roast chicken dinner and a glass of white wine, a tense wife and a widescreen TV. And you'd never know, never guess that he likes to spin a wheel and roll the dice.

It's so tempting to say that he's anyone. He's kind, charming, endearingly stressed out. He's lonely, neurotic, timid and post-traumatic. He's unbalanced and bold. He knows it's a game. He knows what he likes. He's not afraid to seek it. His needs are so simple, and so highly sophisticated. He has shifty eyes, livery eyes, and a thoughtful brow. He has a scar, a strange wound, a birthmark, a twitch of madness, a crease of weakness.

I ask him what he's interested in. 'What would you like to explore?' And he says: warm water enemas administered by a cool rubber nurse. He says: angora, pretty feet, ball-squeezing, a brutal whipping, bondage and teasing. He wants to be caned so that he welts, so that he's marked, so he melts. He wants a trophy, a memento of his trial. He wants to stare at my shiny cat-suit and thigh-high boots through the bars of a cage. He wants the tight embrace of latex on his flesh. He likes the smell of rubber, the 'swoosh' sound of a rubber mackintosh, the scratching of nails, the click of high heels, a chorus of ladies' cackling laughter. He wants me to wear tan-coloured tights, seamed silk stockings, shiny black hold-ups, an army uniform, a pencil skirt, a graduation robe, a cape, a smirk and a snarl. He wants me to be caring and cruel, just caring, just downright cruel. He wants me to be sly and sexy, mysterious, psychic, psychopathic, suggestive, intuitive.

He needs to hear certain words spoken over and over again: 'worthless', 'wanker', 'selfish', 'slut', 'stupid', 'sex', 'sissy', 'cock', 'cocksucker', 'clock', 'ass', 'Charlie', 'fag', 'fuck', 'bad boy', 'naughty boy', 'for ever, for ever'. For ever.

He pays me to slap his face and spit on his cock, chastise him, laugh at his genitals and mutilate his manhood. He wants to be tested, challenged, humiliated, penetrated, and pushed to his limit. He wants stimulation, transformation, and transcendence. Will I stick tomatoes, dildos, or nylons up his ass? Drive nails through his scrotum? Brainwash him to give me all the money in his wallet? Make him cry? Make him worship me? Will I suture his foreskin, shave his chest, pierce his nipples with needles, suspend him upside down, and shock him with a series of contrasting sensations? And the answer is yes, I will. I nod as if to say I've done it all before.

He wants to be dominated however I see fit. He wants to submit. He wants to feel overpowered, overwhelmed, and bombarded with sensations. He fantasises about slavery, about being locked away in a closet, sense-deprived and frightened of his fate. He wishes to be hog-tied and gagged, a stocking forced over his head. He brings stinging nettles and wants them rubbed into his genitals, and then he wants to be wrapped in cling film or bandages, and sat upon. He wants to be taught to walk like a lady, talk like a lady, dress like a lady, and behave like a slut. What do I know about dressing like a lady, talking like a lady and behaving like a slut? Apparently more than I thought.

When he says, 'tied and teased' he means for me to be sexy, swivel, flash some flesh, tie his lust in knots. He means stroke him, tease him, play with his penis and do all the work. He wants my pleasure. He wants his pleasure. He doesn't know what he wants. He wants me to be inventive, imaginative, credible, and kind. It's not *what* I do; it's *how* I do it. I could torture him with a spoon, or a scary suggestion, and make him quiver with a well-timed tickle. He wants something special, exceptional – of course he does. He wants something new, something different, something naughty and subversive. An hour or two to realise his fantasy. An hour of guiltless, exclusive attention. Adrenaline. An orgasm. He wants to forget about himself, be someone else, relinquish control. He wants to go to the extreme. He *is* extreme. He wants to relieve the pressure, to play out his desire. He wants to endure, he wants to be rewarded for his pain, and he wants to know his limits. He wants, he wants, he wants . . .

Like a wagging dog, that's how Bernie arrives. But just before he enters, he pauses at the threshold in comic deliberation. He looks up and looks uncertain, so I smile back. That moment of hesitation is him at his most honest and endearing.

'Quickly, Bernie, and shut the door, quickly.' He knows to take off his shoes. After he does so it's the usual shtick; he bends over, points to them and says, 'Stay shoes, stay' as if he were commanding a couple of canines. And then he turns to me, beaming with mock pride and says, 'See, they always do exactly what I tell them to do.' He's being cute and playful, I know, but I can't help reading between the lines; in a matter of minutes he'll either be the obedient dog or the implacable trainers. He might be mocking himself or parodying my pretence

of power. Never mind, his joviality's contagious and I play along. 'Wow, that's one impressive command you have, I can see you've trained your trainers well.' We're both in good humour as we pass through the padded door of the dungeon.

He takes off his coat and hands me a wad of notes that come folded in a clear plastic sandwich bag. I've never asked him about this. Just before I leave him alone to get himself undressed, I do ask if there's anything he wants to tell me before we begin. He treats the question with extreme suspicion. He tilts his head, knits his brow, and squints at me as if I'm insinuating something. Given that I've considerately asked him this question at least fifty times, his reaction irritates me. I could have saved us both from that minor flaw in our greeting by simply not asking, but it's become a point of obstinacy to do so. On the rare occasion that he submits a request, it's along the lines of, 'You can go really far with the suffocation this time.' He says it as if it's a fresh inspiration, today's special splurge, and instinctively I shirk and stiffen in objection – I already go as far as I feel I can safely go. What's he asking me to do? Perhaps he says it out loud as a way of generating excitement and verifying the fantasy, and really, I should just play along. I should say: 'Bernie, you said it, you took the words right out of my mouth because today is the day I'm going to push you like you've never been pushed before.' And then just carry on as usual.

Bradley gave me the unsavoury impression of someone who talks with his mouth full and tracks mud on clean floors, unaware. In a lazy, effete whine he asked me not to hurt him, shout at him, or humiliate him in any way. His delicacy was in risible contrast to his leviathan physique. He was about thirty with puffy eyes that made it look like he'd been crying all his life.

When he took off his street clothes he carelessly tossed his Armani jeans in a corner instead of hanging them up, and paid me for the hour as if he were buying a burger.

In a sultry yet commanding voice I told him to come closer, closer, and then I began explaining how I'd dress him up then strap him down and have my way with him. 'Can you listen? Can you learn? Can you do exactly as I say, nothing less and nothing more?' But he was having none of it. Bobbing his giant head up and down and snorting as he laughed was his subtle way of telling me that domination and submission weren't his game. I laughed with him just to stay in the game. What he paid for so lackadaisically was a pampering, a psycho-sensual massage. He wanted to be dressed up in ladies' lingerie, wig, shoes, corset and stockings, then gagged, blindfolded and tied down to a bed for the remainder of the hour.

The ordeal of fitting him into a corset, yanking, tightening the strings and then helping him to fasten the now dwarfed stockings to a suspender belt was comical, but when it came to fastening a nylon stocking around his small cock and balls, he was surprisingly erect. If he so much as caught a glimpse of himself in the mirror – the long black wig, the red satin corset with the black lace trim and those huge, hairy calves in the stockings – he turned away and giggled almost girlishly. He wasn't interested in how he looked; it was how he felt. And I imagine he felt those satiny textures, the thrill of transformation, and the anticipation of bondage and abandon. I brushed the fur on his chest and teased his nipples with the tips of my fingers, but he was so ticklish that the most innocent caress sent him into a fit of jitters and giggles that killed any possibility of a sensual start.

It was a lonely, mechanical hour. Once he was blindfolded and gagged, I guided him onto the medical bed and stepped out of my heels. I tiptoed around him, beginning without design, tying his left wrist to the handle on the side of the bed, and then dragging the rope across his belly and around the other wrist, criss-crossing ropes until a pattern emerged – and I followed it. I took my time because there was nothing else to do. This was all he wanted. Whenever I tugged and yanked to reinforce the rope work, he purred in agreement. Whenever I swept my hand across a bound testicle, along the inside of his thigh, or around a nipple or toe, deliberately or incidentally, he giggled through the gag and twitched in his coil. Otherwise he was perfectly still and silent, and if it wasn't for his erection, I might have thought he was sleeping.

Ten minutes before the hour was up I put on a latex glove, lubricated it with baby oil and masturbated him. No sound, just close-ups of a gloved hand moving up and down a slippery, circumcised cock. For a second I thought: this is cheap. For a second I felt empty. For a second I wondered if there weren't other things I ought to be doing . . . but then silently, he came. It was seven minutes before the hour and I reached for some tissues, wiped his belly, dabbed the tip of the corset, and began undoing the ropes to set him free. When I said goodbye, I assumed I wouldn't see him again.

In the beginning I dressed Bernie in a leather hood that laced up at the back with a zipper across the eyes. I'm surprised that he was silent for so long. Only after months did he admit that the zipper cut into his face unpleasantly whenever I sat down upon him. So we switched to a rubber hood that zipped up at the back and had holes for the mouth and the nose. But at the end of the session when I removed the hood I was shocked to see him nearly drowning in his own sweat. Through a process of elimination we came up with the perfect seal: my favourite rubber skirt that flares like a ballerina's tutu, folded over my groin and pressed against his breathing holes. Since then we have always made do with just a blindfold.

So it caught me off guard when, having seen him for more than a year, I asked him if there was anything he wanted to tell me before we began, and I was halfway out the door when he said, 'I'd like to see.' He'd been thinking about it, he said, and he thought it might be even more powerful and tormenting if he could see what was coming (i.e. my groin, my heel, my fist) while being powerless to prevent it. For a moment I was impressed; I hadn't thought of it that way before. Maybe because I wanted Bernie blindfolded. I didn't want him to see my eyes on the clock and the mirror, or my sandwich, and my rising and falling crotch. For two hours his eyes would be gazing up at me and I preferred my privacy. But he wasn't really asking, he was requesting, and this is a service for which he pays his hard-earned teacher's wages, or depletes his inheritance. It wasn't my place to refuse. Except, I did my best in subtle ways to sabotage the session. I took too much time tying him up, I left the room a few times, hardly talked to him, and didn't push the limits. I wanted him, subconsciously if not directly, to equate seeing with bad session. And I think the tactic worked, or he got the point, because since then we've always used the blindfold and he doesn't complain.

With 'Trousers' Dan it's always exactly the same. He enters like a crowd, like a whirlwind of worry, panting, frazzled, and harried.

He perspires. Beads of sweat shimmer in his sandy brown hair. He speaks with shallow breaths and repeats himself. 'Oh hi Anna, hi, Anna, hi, hi how are you, hi, oh, Anna, how are you?' he says as I hand him a glass of water. 'Oh thank you, thank you, oh Anna thank you, you remembered, you're so clever you remember everything, oh thanks, you're so kind, it's so nice to see you. How are you?' And he hands me eighty pounds in tens and fives, and sometimes coinage, for a twenty-minute session. He begins undressing even before I've taken my leave.

The name Anna was an accident. When working at the mansion, on those rare occasions when Mr M addressed me, he always got my name wrong. Instead of calling me Susan he called me Susanna, and the way he said it made it sound sexy and sibilant. And for a second I saw myself as a saucy, exotic maid.

When Angel let me stand in on one of her sessions at the very beginning, she caught me off guard in front of a blindfolded client. This is Mistress . . .' And she turned to me, enquiringly. The first thing that came to my mind was Susanna, which I whispered in her ear, but Anna is what she heard, and that's what I became. I thought: understated Anna, Anna Freud, palindrome, Anne Frank, Anna, this girl in Toronto who I have never met but who is apparently my doppelganger.

What's Trousers Dan's rush? Why so flustered and panicked? He's in his mid-fifties, wears tailored, pin-striped suits, cufflinks that I help him with at the end of the session, classic shoes, subdued, silk ties. Underneath he's always got on silly underwear: ballooning boxers with polka dots or flashy stripes, parrots and palm trees, or puckered lips, and even sillier socks like Bart Simpson and Mickey Mouse. He's English, was educated at

Eton, and it seems he was beaten, perhaps teased, by classmates and now probably by his colleagues and his wife. I think he said he had a wife. He's a banker or a stockbroker, I can't remember which. I can't remember if he told me so, or if I've made some things up. I only know for certain that he's kind and that he personifies stress. Anyway, he's very proper, not so much submissive as effusively polite. I like his quirks, his pace, his nervous disposition, but then, I only have to know him for twenty minutes at a time. I wish he'd orgasm more quickly at the end of the session. He pushes it, he pushes the twenty minutes. Sometimes he can't ejaculate under the pressure and I start talking nonsense and repeating myself until finally, finally, twenty-seven minutes later he comes.

I return to the medical room with a chair that's the right height for putting him over my knee. He stands naked, his hands covering his genitals while I casually take a seat and look him up and down. I'm wearing pin-striped trousers, a suit jacket, and high heels. And right away it begins, because of the time constraint. It's practically scripted, choreographed, always exactly the same.

'Well, so it's you again. Couldn't keep those wandering hands to yourself, could you? Trying to grope the young ladies. Is that what it is this time? Naughty boy. Too much testosterone, that's what I say. You're teeming with it and it's nothing but trouble. Time to fix that.'

'Why, what are you going to do about it? What do you mean?'

'Don't get snide, it's the wrong place for that. Come here. Come here!'

'What? Why? Why should I?'

'Sit down on my lap.'

'I'm not your little lapdog, I won't do it.'

He does it. He faces me and I bounce him up and down on my lap.

'Is that it? Is that all your weight?'

'No, no it's not, I'd hurt you.'

'Try.'

He adjusts his weight. 'Come now, that can't be all of you, you're just a delicate little thing, aren't you?'

'No, don't say that. I'm not.'

'Aren't you? Could have fooled me.'

'Stop teasing me.'

'Get over my knee.'

'No.'

'Get over my knee!'

And he does, making sure his penis is pressed against my woollen thighs.

'Now who wears the trousers around here?' Half-heartedly, I start spanking him and he flays his leg in a feigned effort to make an escape. I wrap my right leg around him and lock him in.

'Are you trying to escape?'

'Yes.'

'And that's the best you can do? You're like a girl.'

'I'm not!' He revolts and tries again to escape, whereby I squeeze even harder.

'You're so strong. You're like a man.'

'Yes, and call me "Sir" from now on. Got that?'

'Yes, Sir.'

'Louder.'

'Yes, Sir!'

'Say it in your highest, girl voice.'

'Yes, Sir.'

Meanwhile, I continue to spank him and he continues trying to wriggle himself free.

'I can see this is having no effect on you.'

He stops wriggling. 'Yes, yes, Sir, sir, it is. I'll be good, Sir. Sorry, Sir. I'll be good.'

'More drastic measures are in order.'

'What do you mean?'

'Get up.' He rolls off my lap and drops to the floor on his knees, and puts his face into my woollen lap.

'No, no, I'll behave, Sir, sir, I will,' he says in muffled melodrama. And then he looks up at my face. 'Don't smile like that . . . why are you smiling like that? No, you're so cruel. What are you going to do?' And he burrows his face in my lap again. What is it about the face in the lap? It's always in the session.

'Nothing I haven't done to others before. I'm about to fix you once and for all. No more raging testosterone, no more defiance. You'll thank me. Things are going to be different from now on.'

'What do you mean? What are you going to do to me?'

'Call me "Sir".'

'Sir, Sir, what are you planning, what are you going to . . .'

'Practise saying "Sir" with a higher pitched voice.'

'Practise for what?'

'Get on the medical bed. I'm going to get rid of those balls.'

'Castr–'

'That's right, I'm going to castrate you. And I'm going to smile while I do it.'

'You wouldn't dare.' And he sticks his tongue out at me. I smile back as I grab his balls and give a good squeeze.

'Ouch. That really hurts. I'm sorry, okay, I'm sorry. Ouch, that's quite a grip you've got. Okay, okay. So you say you've castrated, that you've done this before?'

'Countless times.'

'You're lying.'

'Let me explain; it can be quick and relatively painless, or slow and excruciating. And I think I know which it'll be.'

'You wouldn't.'

'Roll onto your side.' I hold his testicle in my hand and squeeze.

'Cough.'

'No, why? My doctor makes me cough when he examines my testicles. Why do you have to check them? You're not a doctor. You're not my doctor.'

'I'm making sure you're fit for an operation. And I just wanted to squeeze them one last time.'

'No, you're a sadist!'

'The long painful operation, now it's decided. Cough. Good. Both balls feel bursting with health to me.'

'I can see you enjoy this. You enjoy tormenting me!'

'I am enjoying myself, it's true. I'm enjoying myself because I have every confidence that I'm doing the right thing, doing you a favour. Turn onto your back.'

He says 'No', but then he turns over. 'Are you going to shave me first?'

'Of course I'm going to shave you first. You're going to be smooth and silky down there.'

And then, with unavoidable awkwardness, I get up on top of him, resting on my knees, facing his feet, with my bottom in his face just close enough for him to kiss it. I remembered to bring the baby oil with me, and now that I'm in position I drizzle it all over his groin and his penis. And then I tickle and stroke the pubic hair and the left side of his oily groin region under the pretence of shaving him. But in reality he finds the gentle tickle most arousing and comforting.

'Are you going to make me kiss your bottom?'

'All the time. You better get started, start practising, you're going to be doing it enough.'

'You mean you're going to make me kiss your bottom every day?'

'So often you'll have counted the number of stripes in my trousers and you'll be dreaming about my bottom shoved in your face.'

'So I'm going to be in your office every day?'

'Every morning and every afternoon. I don't feel you kissing, and what about "Sir"?'

'Sir, Sir, you have such a strong bottom, Sir. More oil, Sir, more oil.'

It's never enough oil. I pour more baby oil on his groin region and keep rubbing it and tickling it with one hand and masturbating him with the other. It's been twenty-five minutes, the session's over.

'Oh, that's good, that's perfect. What's going to happen to me afterwards? How are things going to change? How are you going to dress me? Will I dress differently? Oh, that's so good, Anna, Sir. What if I'm bad? Are you going to punish me? Oh, that's really good, Anna.'

'What I'm going to do is dress you up in pink frilly dresses and take it upon myself to mould you into a docile, submissive creature. You're halfway there once I get rid of the things, but training will complete you.'

'You're not going to cane me? You wouldn't do that.'

'Wouldn't I? The cane's what I use on all the naughty girls. I'm going to pull down the lacy knickers that I'll have chosen especially for you and I'm going to cane your bottom, ten, twenty times . . . in public if need be.'

'In front of others, in public? You wouldn't.'

'Wouldn't I? With relish I would.'

'You're sadistic! What are the most strokes you've given?'

'Hundreds.'

'You haven't. I don't believe you.'

'Fine. Get up, and bend over.'

'No, Sir, Sir! I'll be good. Please, more oil, Anna . . . softer on the side, the side, up a little more . . . that's it, that's nice, that's it, I'm really close . . . so you'll take me out, take me out in public with you?'

'Call me "Sir"!'

'Sir, oh, Sir, Sir, get rid of it, get rid of it all, get rid of it all . . . aaah, oooh.'

'Every last drop of it.' And he ejaculates. And then I hand him some tissues and he lies there a moment, drained, recovering, and then it's, 'Oh, Anna, oh, Anna, wow, Anna, that was amazing, wow. It just came up at the last minute, didn't it? Thank you, Anna, I feel so much better. It's so good seeing you.'

I leave him alone for a minute so he can get himself together. When I come back in the room, I ask him if he's busy at work – which he always is, but mostly he asks after me. He's interested in all I have to say. In dribbles over the years I've told him where I live in London, where I stay in Scotland, my background as a chef, my reading and writing habits, what I studied at university. He's not interested in discussing his life outside the Cottage. And at last he's calm and relaxed. That will change in a moment and he'll start winding up. After he dresses, he makes his way to the door but turns back and scours the medical room, puts his hands in his pockets, checks his wrist for his watch, looks up at me, then scans the room again.

'I haven't forgotten anything, have I? Got my glasses, my umbrella. Did I bring an umbrella? I didn't, did I? No, I didn't. I guess that's everything. Okay.' And then he takes another step towards the door but stops.

'I feel like I've forgotten something. Have I, Anna? Let me just look. No, I guess I have everything.'

'You're fine, Dan, you have everything. You haven't forgotten anything.'

'Okay, well, thank you. Thank you so much. It's really great to see you, Anna, really wonderful. I mean it. I hope you know it, how much I like you, and respect you. Do you know? I always enjoy seeing you, so thank you. Good. There. Okay, take care. Bye.' And then he kisses me on the cheek, kisses my hand, and with reviving nerves he scurries out the door.

He calls me twice, three times a month, usually at about eight in the morning or earlier. He wants to come along that evening at six, six-thirty, or seven. He's just as breathy and nervous on the phone. 'Hi, Anna, hi. How are you? Do you have the trousers? Oh good, I just wanted to make sure.' Sometimes he calls *just* to ask about the trousers, to make sure I still have them, and to check that I'm still in London.

It happened just once. Bernie was barely through the Cottage door when he declared with an obvious build-up of courage and resolve that I could do anything I wanted to do to him.

'Anything?' I asked suspiciously.

'Anything,' he beamed back.

'What do you mean by "anything"?' I pressed.

With the impatience of a man about to lose his nerve he reiterated, 'I mean you can do anything you want to do to me, anything at all.'

It was a paralysing and infuriating request. What I wanted? I've heard that one before but I know it's not what he means. Strictly speaking, it's never been about what I wanted. I don't 'want' to suffocate Bernie and flick his nipples with ten-pence coins for two maniacal hours. Nor would I prefer to give him an enema, hang him upside down blindfolded, and lower his head in a bucket of ice water. Come on, at the end of the day, I'm doing my job, which is to facilitate his want. And sure I get satisfaction from giving him his wants, but what I want? Ha! What if it's to share a couple of pints of Guinness at the pub instead? What if I really want him to scrape the candle wax off the tiles, massage my feet, staple the questionnaires, file the folders alphabetically, organise the stocking drawer, pay me for two hours and leave after one?

It's not really about what I want, and he doesn't really mean 'anything'. It's a word for me to interpret. It means: create an experience, something different, something I want him to enjoy or something he would enjoy if only he knew it. I'm supposed to know because I'm a dominatrix and trained to decode and extract the sexual desires of men like him. Was I being lazy? A man I've grown to care for, a man that trusts me with his life is asking – no, paying me – to do anything I want to him, and it feels like a chore. I suddenly realised how comfortable and cushy it had been knowing exactly what he wanted and what to expect from our sessions. It was such different work coming up with 'anything'. How do you choose from 'anything'?

Besides, I was shocked. After all this time, I thought I knew Bernie. I was sure that nipples and suffocation were intrinsic to his pleasure . . . and now a session that could forgo the two – it was extraordinary! What drove him to this? Simple curiosity? Did he want to know what others experienced? Or was the experience of complete surrender £300 worth of excitement? In the end I reasoned that if 'anything' meant exploring something less life-threatening, and almost anything was less threatening than suffocation, then that could only be a good thing.

So 'anything' it was.

CHAPTER 6

Improvise

Start with a simple dish and then make it one hundred times. With time and repetition come a golden, capable confidence, devotion to detail, and the freedom to improvise. You begin to know by the steam on the window, by the way the sauce coats the spoon, the vigour of bubbles, the changing, deepening hues, an aroma, and a crackle in the pan. Every facet of your skill and knowledge will be called upon. Your aesthetic, ingenuity and intuition will be put to the test. A sense of timing and order are required in the preparation of a deceptively simple spaghetti Bolognaise.

What's the season, the mood, the time of day? Who will be eating? You've learned to handle the tools, to chop finely, quickly, safely, and work without waste. Make use of every second. Learn to tidy as you go. You're always making decisions: when to slice instead of chop, how thick, how big and how small. How long to cook, because shape and size respond differently, and when to turn up the heat.

The onion: what kind, what strength, how sweet, how much? As for the saucepan – which one will you choose and why? Warm the pan before adding the oil.

Have a sense of how much oil to splash in the pan. Know the different oils, their flavours, their smoking point, how quickly they perish in the heat, their nutritional value and fat content. How can you tell when the oil is hot enough? By its fluidity when you swirl the pan, by the way the light reflects off its surface, or by sticking a wooden utensil in the oil. When a froth of tiny bubbles dances vigorously around the wood, it's hot enough to add the onions and the grated carrot. Carrots add a sweetness, which balances the acidity of the tomatoes and red wine.

Wine for depth of flavour and colour. You need to peel the tomatoes. First slit the skin with a sharp paring knife, make a small x, and then blanch them in boiling water for about nine seconds, or when the skin starts to leave the flesh. Then quickly shock them in a bowl of ice water to stop the cooking. Peel, quarter, and roughly chop. Garlic now or later or not at all? Kosher salt or sea salt – what's the difference? When do you add the salt, how thick do you grind the peppercorns? If you add rosemary, if you add cloves, if you add chilli pepper, how will they affect the final flavour? Did you first taste the sauce in your mind? Was it something you first tasted as a child? The ingredients are simple but the decisions, the variations, the poetry and possibilities are endless. One learns by doing it, again and again.

One can only get good at it by doing it again and again. After learning the basics: how to use a whip, handle a cane, tie a tight knot, set up the electrics, truss testicles, insert dildos, how to construct a beginning, middle, and climax, then it's time to edit and refine the act. And I relished the flexing of my voice, using it in seductive and poignant ways. I learned how to cause a tremor with a whisper, to assail and assault through my tone, to recognise and hypnotise a man in the dark. It's through attentive application and sensitivity that you learn where to lay the stress, how far to push, when to back off, and when to turn up the heat. Finding the look, the balance, the very spice that makes the meal – that is a thrill.

I learned the dominant grammar, rhymed and chimed my taunts, was paid to play with words, to spin them, and spew them however I chose. The most hideous, vile, shocking soliloquies poured out of me like splashes of paint. I could preach and pry, persuade and pirouette around adjectives.

The power of words. The power of silence. The eloquence of the body. I could tease the testicle of a bound, blindfolded man with the heat off my body. I learned to walk across the room with enigmatic confidence. I listened to his body, read the creases in his face, heard the fear in his throat, waited for that telling note.

When I enter the room he's either standing naked, or he's kneeling. Either way, something's being said. Is he eagerly submissive, an experienced slave, or does he lack imagination? Why is he kneeling? Does he have an erection? Does he look me in the eye? Well, what are the vibes? What do I sense? Those first few minutes are full of information and first impressions. I need to set the tone, reassure him and make him trust me right away. It's what I'm wearing, it's my confidence as I breeze through the door and walk across the room, it's my energy, it's my presence of mind as I sit down and cross my legs. I am performing in the theatre of the dungeon.

'I want you to go low. I want you to go as low as you can possibly go.' It's one of my opening lines when it comes to submission or obedience training. He never drops that low on the first go. It usually takes three increasingly enunciated repetitions of 'I want you to go as *low* as you can possibly go' before his nakedness is pressed against the floor, his nose and mouth breathing in the disinfectant. In such a position, he's visually impaired and I become an omnipotent voice raining down from above. A physical pose will affect the psyche; how can he not feel as low as he goes?

I'm studying his manly shape, the curve and prominence of his spine, the tightness of his ass, the patterns of freckles on his back. Maybe I admire his strong, elegant calves, the span of his shoulders, and the courage of his submission. He has a mole, a middle-aged waistline, or a scab on his ankle. I introduce myself. I tell him about my exacting nature, that I'm a perfectionist, that I want him to strive and obey, to listen and learn, and do exactly as I say, nothing less and nothing more. I say, 'I'm always watching you, evaluating you, looking for proof that you're striving. Even if you can't see me, I'll be watching you. I want you to put all your focus, all your effort into listening, obeying, doing exactly as I say, nothing less and nothing more. I believe in punishment and I believe in reward. If you're striving to please, it will not go unnoticed. If you slip, if you don't put forth one hundred per cent of your effort, I'll notice. Do you like a challenge? It's no fun without a challenge.'

If he was into cock and ball torture, perhaps I'd start by

instructing him to put his hands behind his back and come close, even closer, and then cup his balls in my hand, maybe fondle them, maybe yank them or squeeze them.

'What are these? Balls, yes. And aren't balls for sport? I mean, don't you have sport with balls? You do, don't you?' And I smile sweetly. 'Today, I'm going to play sport with your balls.'

I might continue to squeeze and fondle and tug at his balls with gradually increased force, testing his testes and tolerance while gauging his reaction. On a couple of dozen occasions, with ever-growing conviction, I've said, 'There's something I've always wondered about balls. I want you to tell me what you think, and help me to clarify: if I squeeze them very hard, I mean as hard as I possibly can, do you think they'd *implode* or *explode*? Tell me, which do you think?' Gruesome images, both of them.

Now, if it was corporal punishment he wanted, I could spend long, lazy minutes engrossed in the minutiae, the rhythms and endless variations of touch and tempo. I'd put him over the whipping bench or over my knee and begin stroking his bare bottom, teasing him, warming him up. I magnified my caresses, stroked, strummed, kneaded, and slapped in soft staccato. When done to music, the whole room vibrated to the act. The slaps get louder, harder, sharper; and my hand burns. He's my instrument, and I play him and compose.

For the first six or seven months I read only work-related material when I was at the cottage. I was looking for wisdom and instruction. I worked my way through fetish magazines, rope-tying manuals, butch lesbian stories, the folkloric tales of Masoch, Stanislavski's *Building a Character* and *An Actor Prepares*, old case studies compiled by Krafft-Ebing a century ago, erotic literature, of course de Sade and Bataille – all the philosophers, psychologists, and authors of aberrant sexual behaviour. I even studied fashion magazines to improve my make-up technique and read a bona fide military torture manual printed between a sickly yellow paperback that Angel purchased off the internet . . . until I felt stuffed and unpleasantly gorged on platitudes, theories, formulas and myths.

It finally occurred to me that I was actually discouraging my understanding of domination, sadomasochism, fantasy and fetishism with over-intellectualisation. I had privileged access to unmediated, unbiased, empirical knowledge; it was for me to experience and improvise. Thereafter, I read only for pleasure and company in those lonely suburban hours.

I composed hundreds of letters to friends and family, mostly in my head, and ritualised my smoking to one cigarette while my visitors were getting undressed and I was deciding what I'd do to them, *or* one just before they arrived, a cigarette to mark their departure, and one to draw a close to the day. Once or twice a week, when there was enough time between sessions and the whim and weather permitted, I blotted out the black liner around the corner of my eyes, slipped my jeans over my stockings and a jumper over my corset – or removed my rubber top – and strolled through quiet, pale stucco land until I came to the high street and Saul's falafel deli.

Bernie trusts me. He trusts that I'll push him to extremes and release him at the crucial moment. He trusts that I know that moment – and that's where he's wrong. Only Bernie knows the whereof and wonders of that dangerous edge. There are days when I feel the most urgent need to speak the unspoken. I say, 'Bernie, let's be honest, you know I can never be certain.' Or morbidly, and more to the point, I joke about how bad it would be for business if he were to die.

For at least a year I'd been acting purely on instinct. My knowledge of suffocation was empirical, born of first-hand experience. So when Angel handed me a medical report on strangulation, suffocation, and oxygen starvation to read before seeing Bernie that day, I was shocked. In the case of suffocation, if a problem becomes apparent, it's already too late. And more terrifyingly, something could go wrong at any time. The science is unequivocal: there's no safe way to suffocate a man. The scissors by my left side have been a ruse, a token, a pretence. I remember a sudden sickness running through my body; it felt metallic and acidic, and my temples throbbed. Retroactive fear, I thought, for the dozens of times we'd cheated death. It was obvious I had to quit while I was ahead. He was booked in at three o'clock and I intended to tell him how I felt.

3:02 p.m.: *He had just taken off his coat when I waved the science in his face, but he dismissed me and brushed it aside. In fact he was practically insulted. There was nothing he didn't know, and know better than almost anyone else about the risks of suffocation. And as far as he was concerned, we'd never come close to that truly dangerous edge. He was trying, and not exactly failing, to make me feel like the dupe, and the betrayer of both my role, and him. If he'd come back to me week after week, it was largely because I'd appeared not to judge him, had never admonished him or made him feel foolish for his inarguably dangerous pleasure. He snidely assured me that he didn't have a death wish, and that he had no intension of dying in some cottage in the suburbs, and there I believed him.*

I could see how the needs of his nature distorted his reason. But me? Why would I do such a thing, knowing what I know? What did I do it for? And what did I know for certain? How was I to reconcile our combined experience with a cold, clinical report? I knew it was dangerous, but minus a few seconds a round, it didn't feel dangerous. Seeing sixteen men that week might have had something to do with it. Did three hundred pounds have something to do with it? When I thought of Bernie's sessions, I thought of seventy-two thousand seconds, a hundred and twenty minutes of repetition, millions of flicks, the challenge of surmounting the boredom. The danger of our session was only an aesthetic consideration. When Bernie leaves, he's giddy, euphoric, and completely satisfied. He'd be even happier if he could stay and talk and share his rapturous glow, while I'm just so relieved to have survived the trial of time that all my morbid doubts are forgotten. After all, it was only two hours and he's always been fine, and I've earned a month's rent in a day.

It happened one quiet evening in May that Bradley was about to arrive and I was feeling especially relaxed and focused. I clearly remember resolving to get *into* the hour, and not just *through* the hour. And that decision, that subtle shift in attitude made all the difference. I slackened my pace, followed the rhythm of his breathing, his tiny undulations, and my own with equal concentration. Everything was magnified. I felt a more subtle language open up to me. I tried to imagine I was him and imagine how it would feel to be coiled in ropes and blindfolded. How does it feel to be touched when you can't touch back, when you don't know where or when the next touch comes? I could just about imagine the pleasure of relaxing and embracing the silken softness of a fibrous cocoon. I could just about imagine his pleasure. It was a revelation to me that the simple act of tying a man in knots could provide such a wealth of possibility.

When I removed the blindfold and gag I expected something from him. I expected confirmation that we'd made a connection, that the session was different, more substantial and intimate, but he said nothing, and left in the usual impersonal way. I was sore, still, I felt I'd learnt something.

Once summer arrived, Bradley was visiting in tennis shorts and sweaty T-shirts. The day he sprung in eating a falafel that I recognised from my favourite local deli was the day we broke the ice.

'You got that falafel from Saul's, didn't you? I love that place. That's the best falafel I've had since Israel.'

'You were in Israel?'

'Yes, I lived and worked on a kibbutz in Israel when I was seventeen. I was one of the fishermen. Me and fourteen men.'

Well, it turned out he knew the very kibbutz; and had close friends in Israel. I'd been dressing him up, tying him down and masturbating him for months, but that was our first conversation, the first time he saw beyond my professional persona, and the first time I opened up to him.

Twenty-five minutes into the session my corset strings brushed against his side in passing and he thrust out his hand and gripped the corset's trim. I froze. He let go but he continued to hold out his puffy hand, palm up, and it confused me. He had never tried to communicate with me in our sessions before. He reacted but he never initiated, never reached out to me as he was now literally doing. What was he trying to tell me? I made a generous guess and gave him my hand, which he instantly took, gripping it rather firmly. I was touched by the soft gesture, even more so because of the many months it had taken.

CHAPTER 7

September 5th

I've never asked him why. Why did you call back after such a failure of a session, and why did you wait two hundred and forty-two days to do so? At first I thought he had made a mistake, so I told him that Angel wasn't doing sessions any more, only me – which was true. But he said it was me he wanted to see. It was just after ten in the morning. I was leaving my flat for work when my phone rang and a voice from some great depth said, 'Hi, it's Adam.'

And that memory returned like the fresh sting of a slap: Adam the masochist. Adam's eyes. I'd seen at least a hundred and fifty different men since that aborted session, but none had his beautiful, dangerous volatility. I remembered the explosive, 'NO!' What was 'NO'? Was that to me? Was it no to the moment? Or was it a revolt against his nature? What was 'No'? That was a storm behind the calm façade. That was danger, that was beauty . . . and I knew I should leave him alone. And I knew that I wouldn't. Eight months had changed me. This time I'd be confident; I'd give him everything he wanted and even more than he could fathom. I'd make him regret how he behaved in the past. He'd feel he got me wrong. I'd show him what I was capable of, and so I booked him in at four o'clock that very afternoon.

The day began like any other. At seven I rolled over in my bed and read a book for three quarters of an hour. When I got out of bed, I raised my arms to stretch, and then folded over and pressed my palms into the floor for sixty, fifty-nine, fifty-eight, fifty-seven seconds. I felt my tendons lengthen, the burn in the backs of my legs, and the blood race to my head. It felt good. A friend once said to me that stretching was like accelerated growth. I did thirty sit-ups and twenty ballet pliés, ten in first position and ten in second, and five sun salutations. It wasn't even a ten-minute routine but it always proved to me that so much can be done in a minute, an hour, a day.

I drank my morning cures of green tea, aloe vera juice and warm water with a squeeze of lemon while listening to talk radio. But really I was building courage and/or stalling. It was precisely because I found jogging such a struggle and a bore that I forced myself to do it every other morning. It was my way of suffering consciously, overcoming myself, and battling laziness.

I walked along my serpentine avenue lined with old acacia trees, Victorian houses, and rod-iron fencing. I blinked one hundred times in rapid succession. And then my eyelids ached. I focused on objects in the far distance: the fading white trail of an aeroplane, a copper-coloured steeple, a bird perched on a chimney. And then zooming in, I read the words of approaching street signs, licence plates, house numbers . . . I was stretching my eyes. Living in London, looking at close-ups: text, computer screens, and the dilated pupils of a client was limiting my field of vision. When did I last look in the distance and study the shape of the landscape? I am too enmeshed in the details. When I reached the lilac-painted house, number eighty-six, I began inhaling for four seconds and then exhaling for four seconds. Inhaling, exhaling . . . And then six, and then eight until I reached the park gate and started jogging.

I jogged past rhododendron bushes and, beyond them, a murky pond with ducks, Canadian geese and two weeping willows. I pretended it was a lagoon, a Louisiana swampland. But after a short bend I came to the base of the hill and the beginning of my trial. It made no difference that I'd run the route two hundred times; it was always difficult, the ascent too steep, my breathing all wrong. I kept my head down, gazing at my pounding feet because if I had to face the sharp incline and the summit, I would have lost my courage. My breathing was irregular; I couldn't find my rhythm. Definitely shouldn't smoke. Phrases I'd thrown flippantly in the face of clients came back to taunt me: 'It's no fun without a challenge. I'm going to push you, I'm going to make you suffer for your pleasure.'

Even when I saw the wooden bench that marked the summit, relief was not instantly forthcoming. I jogged past the wagging dogs, tennis courts, and green open field. I jogged beyond that threshold where one is injected with the feeling that one can jog for ever.

After fifteen minutes I was more bored than tired. I'd reached my goal, overcome my resistance, got out of the house, and up over the hill. The last stretch of the course felt redundant, which was yet another challenge: carrying on when I could see nothing more to gain.

Finally, I stopped at the park gate and allowed a couple of minutes for the chemicals of pleasure to course through my body before walking back home, fortified and flowing with triumphant well-being.

After showering, I prepare my favourite meal of the day. In a sequence of swivelling motions, I take the leftovers out of the fridge from the previous night, which I'll incorporate into the meal, fill the kettle with water, put a pan on the flame, a vegetable steamer on the other, take a mug from the cupboard, a filter from the pantry, and coffee from the freezer. I try not to waste a single movement or motion in this dance of economy. The kettle boils as I crack an egg in the warm, oiled pan. The greens steam as I chop shallots, slice a lemon in half, rip mint and parsley leaves, crumble feta, and quarter tomatoes.

Sometimes I take a photograph of my breakfast, so beautiful and bountiful it appears to me, in the kitchen, beside the window, on the chocolate-brown plate, gilded and garnished with sunlight.

The fifty-yard radius outside Brixton tube station is a pocket of claustrophobic hell. Crowds of blurred, angry, muttering, screeching people move in all directions. It's a wasps' nest. You can't walk in a straight line; you must zigzag, weave around, jostle and be jostled. There are too many layers and textures of sound and sight, too many stories, too much tension and frustration for such a small, concrete space. In a single glance I saw a leathery old lady sitting outside a frozen food shop playing a comb and tapping her swollen knee, a man with dreadlocks selling incense, incessantly chanting 'incense', three rough, burly men selling diverse and delightful flowers beside a bickering couple and a newspaper stand, and a middle-aged Korean man selling paper fans and other useless trinkets spread out on the ground on a terrycloth towel. Someone was yelling 'batteries, ten for a pound' out of tune with a female evangelist, all flaming red hair, spindly body and feverish eyes, shouting 'Jesus will save Brixton' through a loudspeaker that wasn't switched on. Boys were hissing, 'skunk, skunk, ganja, marijuana' to anybody within earshot, a young homeless woman was petting her sleeping dog. Mothers and pushchairs, congestion at the bus stop, tiny T-shirts, tight jeans, slick and complicated hairdos, grey, unhappy faces and vacant eyes.

I saw polka dots of bubble gum paving the sidewalks and streets beneath a colony of marching shoes, and my eyes moved up to greet a haze of bosoms, bags and backpacks. Just as I caught sight of a mother slapping her two-year-old on the head, I was jostled by a lady running for the bus which in turn caused me to graze the shoulder of a teenager on my right. A couple of strides later I heard her hiss 'bitch' behind me. Bitch? *Bitch?* Why bitch? Why me? And then she said it again to a girlfriend beside her. 'That bitch just stepped on my foot and she didn't say sorry.' I tensed with anger, choking my hostile impulse to respond. I'm on my way to work, to expertly intimidate and abuse men, and still I feel vulnerable and incensed by the impersonal provocations of a rude teenager. Frustrated and exasperated, I whipped around and raved like a madwoman, which blended in nicely with the scene. And then I ran, shoving people on my way down the stairs, past the ticket barriers, flying down the escalator and onto a train that was waiting at the platform. For the third time that morning my heart beat violently.

Regardless of season, it always felt cold, dank, and musty in the cottage first thing in the morning. But no phantoms. No fossils. No screams trapped overnight in the standing coffin. No scent of semen. The cottage had forgotten everything, and so had I. I took off my shoes, turned on the lights, put on an Ernest Ranglin CD, and began the big clean. I swept the tiled floor of each room, and the rubber-floored entrance area before filling a bucket with warm water and detergent. I put on latex gloves and got down on my hands and knees to scrub. I did the entire cottage, twice, before rinsing the floors with hot water and drying them with towels. I cleaned in order to clean my mind and prepare for the workday. I love cleaning.

I made it my point to apply my make-up as quickly as possible, and I had it down to four minutes. Make-up has never suited me. I wore mascara, eyeliner, lipstick and blush, but looked pretty similar to how I look outside the dungeon. It was the lighting, the outfit, the context, and my attitude that radically transformed my appearance in the dungeon.

At 11:28 I sat down in the reception area with a fresh questionnaire and clipboard on my lap and waited for the creak of the gate. A stranger named Joe was booked in at 11:30.

At 11:32 it seemed that one of the most irritating anomalies had struck again – the man who books an appointment with no intention of showing up. Could it be because he got cold feet, or does he get a thrill from screwing up a Mistress's schedule? Or was he in a terrible accident? Well, certainly it happened often enough.

At 11:36 I was relieved. Never mind the money, never mind that I'd dressed up and psyched myself up for nothing; I had over an hour to sit in Angel's wild garden and finish reading Daphne du Maurier's *Rebecca*, which had somehow escaped me as a young adult. I took off my boots, my spiky collar and my stockings, threw a jumper over my rubber top, and went outside.

At 12:50 I took off my jumper, fixed my make-up, brushed my hair, put on my stockings, my boots, my collar, and a heavy, black rubber mackintosh. Gideon was booked in at 1:00 for an hour.

At 1:11 a twiggy seventy-five-year-old man with fine auburn hair, a red nose and the weathered face of a passionate gardener was standing naked in the centre of the dungeon, his ribs shaking in their cage, his cloudy eyes set deep in their bony sockets; he is well into his fantasy. He looks the part, so slavish and medieval-like, a heavy metal collar locked around his neck, shackled ankles and wrists, thick chains joining everything together. From his stretched scrotum hang four and a half pounds of lead weights. My rubber mackintosh brushes provocatively against his thin, trembling body as I tease his nipples and paint a picture of life as my slave.

'I'm never going to let you go. You know that, don't you? You're here with me for ever and ever, kept here as my slave. Have you ever slept standing in a cage? Ever been punished for doing nothing at all? Been beaten with a whip? So many things to do, so much time. I could show you off to my girlfriends, let them have their fun with you – some of them aren't as kind as me. One of them's positively vicious when she gets excited. Ha! What a treat it'll be for them. Later. There's time for everything. I might even take you out for a walk when you've been extraordinarily good.'

'Would I be wearing a mackintosh as well?'

'Matching mackintoshes, absolutely. Only yours will be disguising your nakedness and several kilos of chains wrapped around your feeble body . . .'

'I'm pathetic, I know. I'm sorry. I'm just a slave, that's all I'm good for . . . but I'll wear a mackintosh and you'll wear a mackintosh?'

'And we'll go walking in the rain with you dragging along behind, trying to keep up, trying not to embarrass me.'

Towards the end of his sessions while he's masturbating, I talk too much, trying to help him to climax because he wants that so much and it's difficult for him. He invariably stops at one point to say, 'Forget it, it's not happening, it's useless, it's hopeless.' But he starts up again and so do I because I don't want the session to end without him coming. I don't want him to feel disappointed.

'. . . and I'm going to make you sleep standing up. I'm going to leave you in a dark closet for hours and days and by the time you get some human contact you'll be so grateful, I'll be able to do anything to my slave.' And eventually he sputtered into his hand, and dripped onto the tiled floor.

At eight minutes past two he was dressed and combing his hair in the medical room. He was thinking out loud, muttering angrily, 'Stupid. Idiotic. I'm such a bloody fool, aren't I?'

He's talking to my reflection in the mirror. 'I'm too old for this, Anna. Do you know all the money I've wasted and the pathetic lies I've told my wife these past fifty years? Dear me, I don't know why I do it. Bloody curse. It's perverse.' And then he turns around to face me, and here we go. With milky eyes he asks, 'Why do you do it? Why would you want to touch all these dirty men? And why do you have to be so kind to me? I don't get it. You're so capable. Why are you wasting your talents on old sods like me?'

It was the same harp every time, and I didn't like it. 'I've told you what I think already; your fetish is a gift, it's interesting, fascinating. Okay, I agree that it's expensive, but once a month, five pounds a day, the price of a tube pass, and it's relatively harmless. Just think of the unique pleasure you derive from a word, the texture and swoosh of a rubber mackintosh, the weight of chains, the fantasy of enslavement. It's not your fault; you didn't choose your fetish and it's never gone away, so why not accept it, and enjoy it? Besides, I see a lot of older men, very intelligent, well educated, respectable like yourself, so you're not alone. As for me, I happen to enjoy giving pleasure and facilitating fantasies. And I'm good at it. I get paid well to do it, and what else do you think I ought to be doing?'

I didn't tell him that he was spoiling a perfectly good session. But I was thinking, why does he sulk? Why doesn't he keep his guilt and shame to himself? Why hasn't he worked through these feelings after so many decades? Why does he try to make me feel ashamed?

2.13 p.m.: I was on my hands and knees, wiping semen off the dungeon floor.

2:17 p.m.: I was eating a hummus sandwich in the garden, and answering the telephone to a man who was interested in catheters and other medical procedures.

2:30 p.m.: I answered the door to a stranger named Robert. Corpulent, pale-faced, thin feminine eyebrows. Submissive, was my guess, sensual, wants feminisation, likes anal play, probably into verbal humiliation, no pain. I guessed right.

3:38 p.m.: Robert was gone but I could still smell him on my hands. It was harder than I thought. He wasn't very vocal or responsive, pretty limp in fact. He kept looking at me with those empty eyes, waiting for me to entertain him, giving nothing in return. I filled in the follow-up report, what we did in the sessions, what worked, what didn't, suggestions for the next session – because he'd probably be back – and then I filed it along with his questionnaire.

I retrieved Adam's file from the cabinet and thought about him for the first time since the morning. I stood in front of the wall of mirrors in the medical room, staring at myself, inventing myself, bolstering myself. I told myself that I was beautiful, that I was great at my job, that I cared . . . and that that ought to be enough. It's just an hour, and he's just a man, and it doesn't take that much to please a man. It'll be fun. I'll enjoy myself. It's a performance. It's nothing. It doesn't matter. I heard the creaking of the gate and then a firm rap at the door.

He entered like a strong gust of wind and swiftly shut the door behind him. He put down his briefcase and undid the laces of his black leather shoes that had just been polished but were plainly falling apart. I guided him into the medical room and he took to his seat like an adolescent who was testy with authority. 'That's not very attractive behaviour,' I thought, 'but it will change.' I held my posture, conscious of concealing the rapping in my chest.

I took a deep breath and asked, with practised casualness, 'What would you like to explore today?'

'I'll leave it up to you.'

What I said next was not something I'd planned to say. I hadn't even formulated the problem when the solution left my mouth. 'I want you to wear a hood.'

'Actually, I'd rather not,' he said.

So, there you have it; three seconds after saying, 'I'll leave it up to you' he was taking it back.

'I'd really prefer that you wore a hood to start. I'll take it off in a short while.'

'No thanks. I prefer to see.'

'Trust me,' I implored. 'I'll take it off in a little bit, and it'll be worth it. I've got something in mind, wait and see.' He wasn't pleased, but reluctantly he agreed and handed me the money.

While he got undressed I stood outside, trying on the one hand to calm my nerves, and on the other to conduct them towards a useful end. Nervous energy usually resulted in my best sessions, kept me focused, kept me on my toes.

Back in the medical room I caught him poking a huge jelly dildo on the shelf. When he turned around to face me, I avoided the trap of his eyes by heading straight for the leather hood – the one with a zipper around the eyes – and slipped it over Adam's handsome head. I laced it up at the back and took his mammoth hand in mine, guiding him onto the gynaecological chair. The relief I then felt from his facelessness was palpable, and wonderful.

He was just a naked man, any man, and all the power and freedom were mine. I could look, touch, and make music with that body. It was a melodic moment. There were violins in the background, and one beautiful instrument in the foreground, strapped down and cloaked in silence. I came so close to him that my hair fell in the slope between his neck and shoulder, and I could smell his biscuit coffee breath beneath the hood. My eyes wandered down the taut planes of his body and then halted at the sound of that huge manly totem; now his cock was the loudest thing in the room.

From the outside it was nothing spectacular, just me bending over his chest, putting my mouth to his left nipple, taking the nipple between my lips, and applying my pressure. But between us something spectacular had occurred. An electrical, chemical explosion. Who could say what it meant? Was it in our combination, or did he exude something that I was able to receive? Or was it his response to me? I merely licked, sucked and then bit his nipples and yet the most eloquent dialogue was unfolding. I remember how he reached out with his large fingertips, and given physical limits and blindness, he stroked what he could find. He found the ball of my shoulder, the wavy ends of my hair, a slender wrist, and with caresses so delicate they seemed to stroke the air just above my flesh, causing ripples to pass through my body with hot force.

And then I noticed, and there was no mistaking the connection: the harder I bit, the more I hurt him, the more tenderly and passionately he responded.

There came a powerful point when I felt I could do no wrong. I tied his cock, squeezed his balls, stuck a dildo up his ass, but I always returned to his nipples with my mouth. It was such a simple act but I don't think he expected it. A mouth on a nipple is probably more intimate than most Mistresses are willing to get. But the mouth is a perfect tool. Near the end of the session, I removed his hood and stared him in the eyes while I squeezed his nipples between my fingers, and he masturbated . . . and like that, with giant force, a soft shriek, then a swallowed weep, he came.

Just before departing, he knelt down in front of me to tie up his shoelaces. Then when he stood up at six foot-two, I noticed that his shirt was tucked in too deeply, and his trousers were slightly too short. He looked awkward in his clothes. Was that because I knew what they concealed? It occurred to me then that he didn't possess even the faintest clue about his beauty and the power it contained. Perhaps I was one of a handful, maybe the only one, who recognised it. Neither of us had smiled or spoken more than a dozen words since the session began; we simply shook hands, and then I shut the door after him. I felt good. I felt triumphant, and aroused. I was still vibrating from that current, that chemistry he'd triggered in me. It was new, it was the brink of discovery, and yet the feeling had nowhere to go.

I'm sitting on Bernie's face, flicking his nipples to Mozart's The Marriage of Figaro *and locking eyes with the woman in the mirror. Who is she? But of course – she is me. But do I like what I see? I do, I like what I see. I think the role suits me. My dark eyes are lined with kohl and my black hair shines a shade of blue in the red light of the dungeon. I'm wearing a spiky leather collar around my long slender neck to striking effect. My cheeks are healthy and flushed, my lips red and plush, and the texture of my olive skin is like powder or porcelain. I look doll-like, spectral and beautiful.*

My eyes return to Bernie, his compact frame, those solid calves and tiny feet. I'm impressed with my bondage job and feel a pang of regret for never having brought my camera. Sixty-six or ninety-nine photographs of Bernie in various bondage installations over the years would have made an amusing retrospective. But I remind myself that I've deliberately resisted the temptation to replicate the moment. My challenge is to accept and embrace the impermanence of our sessions.

It's a concert in a vacuum. A man is suffocating. I'm suffocating a man. How can something so dangerous be so banal? A man is suffocating beneath me, drooling on my rubber skirt, bleeding from the nipples, keeping an erection while we gossip and banter and wittily spar with one another, whenever he catches his breath. A man is paying me to suffocate him for pleasure's sake in a small vault-like room of a cottage, situated in a North London Jewish suburb. And if I drag back the telescope six hours, then I'll be in the ballet class that I attend three times a week, wearing pink tights and pink slippers, dancing with my secret, correcting my posture and pointing my toes . . . and nobody there knows what she knows. In eight and a half hours I'll be making dinner – whatever I conjured up while sitting on Bernie or transport back to Brixton. In ten hours I'll be in bed, alone with a book.

On the bench, on the outdoor platform, waiting for the train, at the end of the work day, that's where and that's when I let go of those hours and episodes, those characters and the brief yet penetrating connections. The train arrives. The next one's not due for thirteen minutes. I decide not to move. I decide to wait. The air is so fresh and misty in North London, almost tropical at times, and the blue ceramic rooftop, the fan of succulent foliage, and the huge expansive sky are enough to transport me.

CHAPTER 8

Beauty

Now Adam visits me every Thursday for an hour, the most erotic hour of my week. Every time I open the door to him I catch the rays of those supernatural eyes and my heart convulses, my skin tightens, my retinas shrink, and I have to turn away. He's a shock to the system. His beauty, his intensity, his combustibility frighten me – and I'm right to be afraid. But I'm just as mesmerised by the dangerous flame, and by my own capacity to be so captivated by the myth of a man.

We wear our poker faces before and after each session – or at least I do. I treat the starched, formal greetings and farewells as a stylised joke, a sexy game we're playing for tension's sake and irony. How interestingly it frames and enhances its opposite – the thing that is about to, or has just, happened.

But I had yet to learn how shy and silent he was outside the grammar of extremes.

As it stands, a beautiful man, a client, a masochist, enters into an airtight accord. There will be no 'sex' as it's understood. It will be my job to administer pain erotically and expertly. Thus he finds his release. When he leaves the sealed container of the cottage there'll be no telltale marks on his body for his wife to detect. If he never calls again, I have no way of finding out why. Whoever he is, whatever he does outside the hour is not my business, and *this* is exactly how I want it; a symphony in the background, a range of sensations assailing me, the brief connection, the spice of anonymous intimacy, the distilled, concentrated moment. I respond to detail and subtlety, rules, roles and melody. This is theatre, finitude, an utterly otherly experience.

Yesterday, while waiting for a train on the underground platform, I spotted a young woman standing near the platform exit, her shoulder and temple leaning lazily against the wall. She appeared withdrawn, oblivious to the scores of people that passed her as they spilled onto the platform. But those that caught her face – and a split second was all that was required – would have been struck by her exquisite beauty. I was struck, so was a man nearby me who stopped a dozen paces down the platform, as did I, and then turned, as did I, to steal another look. How could we resist? Nobody wished to be rude or indiscreet but no more did we want to deny ourselves – what, exactly? I wasn't sure. It seemed that there was something to be gained from looking longer. Curiosity to satisfy or a hunger only her beauty could feed. What is my thing with beauty? I'm sure I didn't imagine it, I'm sure it was so; the tension of not-looking surrounding her was thick and palpable.

As the train pulled in I looked again, and still it was too marred a glance to seize on her features, but long enough to grasp structural perfection. It was in the wingspan of her eyebrows, the width of her forehead in relation to the space between her eyes; it was the height of her cheek and the angle of her jaw, and I truly regretted having to turn away.

I took a seat, the train doors shut, the people settled, and as I was thinking about beauty, beauty itself sat down right beside me. How ironic it was that her proximity was its own impairment. I couldn't turn to look at her because she was too close. The train sped through the tunnel and I noticed the people around us shied away from her beauty. I could just make out her double-glazed reflection beside my own in the dark window opposite. Those were my slightly imbalanced, dark eyes, the slope of my nose, the shape of my forehead, the oval of my face. My beauty was not structurally perfect; it was contingent upon the angle, the lighting, my attitude, my state of mind.

After Enema Larry ejaculates and the rubber-nurse-enema fetish spell is broken, he sits on the toilet with the door wide open while I take turns leaning against the gynaecological chair in the adjoining medical room, smoking, and passing the cigarette over to him. The nicotine stimulates his bowels in case he has anything left inside of him. We invariably laugh at the absurdity of just that: sharing a cigarette and a laugh while he sits on the toilet after I've given him an enema and an orgasm in the essential shiny black hold-ups, rubber nurse uniform, and long black rubber gloves.

I'm so fond of that short, skinny forty-five-year-old and his saggy-assed jeans, his orange-toed socks and stylish spectacles. He's happily married, lives in Kent with two teenage kids, plays in a band, and drives a black cab in London. But he's not so happy to find his greatest arousal and release from a tube stuck up his bum by a certain kind of woman in a nurse's uniform. He would so much prefer to find that great sexual pleasure in having intercourse with his wife. He'd rather not be robbing the family holiday kitty to satisfy his fetish, but what should he do? He's been to therapy. He swapped one therapy for another, but it didn't work. He blames his overbearing, Jewish mother for obsessing over his bowel movements and forever sending him to hospitals to be poked at, prodded, and cleaned out by matronly nurses as a child.

Just before leaving one evening he went to kiss my cheeks goodbye but I backed away just in time. 'I don't want you to catch my cold, Larry.'

'Oh, but, Anna, I *want* your cold,' he instantly volleyed. It was the kindest thing anyone had said to me in the cottage. A beautiful thing to say. I loved my job for moments like that, for unexpected intimacies born of strange circumstances. True, they weren't my orgasms, my shrieks of pain, or my paroxysms of pleasure, and it wasn't my secret revealed, my shame being faced, my fantasy fulfilled, but I drew nourishment, power, and a deeply human thrill all the same. It was the joy of cooking all over again: striking the balance, that attention to detail, the time constraint, the elaborate preparations, variety, sensuality, spontaneity, improvisation, the delight and power in giving, feeding, and pleasing the palate.

*

He wasn't due to arrive for another ten minutes but I already knew exactly what he wanted done to him. Angel, who stopped doing sessions just as soon as I was willing to work full-time, gave me some tips on the telephone from her house across the garden but when it came down to it, it was he who would guide me throughout the procedure. It was my first time. I tried to help him through the door but he sort of shoo'd me aside, and we made stilted introductions. In one way or another he'd make it clear that *he* was in control of the session, not I. I got the sense that he regarded his extreme and unusual penchant with great pride and connoisseurship.

When the time came, I hoisted him onto the gynaecological chair, strapped his dangling legs in stirrups, and set aside his stainless-steel crutches. He had cerebral palsy. I was so keen and curious to explore his twisted naked body, but he was abrasive and cold and insisted on keeping me at bay. So, like a nurse would do, I removed the rings on my right hand and put on a thin plastic glove that was like a bin-liner, except there were channels for the fingers. On top of the first, I put on a tight fitting, powdered latex glove and reached for the tub of lubricant. I caked my hand, in between my fingers and up my wrist just as far as my elbow – which was as far as I could fathom.

He lay on his back with his legs spread apart and hoisted up in the stirrups, while I stood in between his legs, facing him, and slid one finger inside his ass. He sucked in his breath and then, softly, he exhaled, which was very encouraging. He felt warm and pleasantly silken inside. There was nothing dirty or scatological about caressing his entrance with my fingertip. I could feel his sphincter relaxing and him opening to me, so I pushed my finger deep inside him. And then two fingers, and my reward was an unctuous, gurgling, angelic score of groans.

I stretched him. I spread my fingers apart and pushed against his rectal walls. I wasn't rough, I was following a rhythm, sliding my fingers in and out of him, and causing this transformation. His mouth drooped half open, his cheeks blushed like a fevered child, and he lost his stiff abrasiveness. It was so simple, so satisfying and thrilling to provide such extreme pleasure. So I pushed on, curious to deliver, curious to see how far I could go. I squeezed four fingers together so they overlapped, tucked in my thumb to make my hand as slender as possible, and pushed myself inside of him. I got as far as the joint in my thumb, and that was as far as I could go.

'Push harder,' he urged, but as much as I tried, bone, muscle and cartilage resisted. With my right hand halfway inside him, I paused for a second. If it didn't happen, if I didn't get my fist inside of him, then we'd both be disappointed. I leaned my elbow on my stomach and used the weight of my body to push my arm into him. He cried, 'Yes, yes, yes, I can take it' while I pushed and pushed, and then something startling happened; in one, involuntary vacuum motion, his rectum swallowed my hand. What an amazing breakthrough! It was exhilarating to be suddenly in the firm clutch of a man's internals, my hand among his organs, my mini ripples causing tidal waves inside him. Or what? What did it feel like? I studied his glassy eyes, his fiery cheeks, and those deep, ecstatic whimpers for clues.

'There's nothing like it. I can't describe it,' he says. 'It feels incredible . . . go deeper . . . deeper, I can take more.' So, with care I curl my fingers to form a fist, trying not to poke him, and then by touch, by degrees, by listening and feeling, I found my way along a fleshy, narrow tunnel. There was no mistaking the connection: the more I pushed, the more intense and fulfilling was the pleasure that he craved, a pleasure very few have enjoyed. I was awed and envious of so much pleasure, mysterious as it was to me. Here is a man whose cumbersome, challenged body, most certainly his daily grief, has compensated by offering him profound sexual fulfilment. And I'm a part of that.

I got as far as midway between elbow and wrist before I felt I could go no further. I stayed there for a couple of minutes to give him time to rest and absorb the experience before slowly withdrawing my cupped hand. It slid out like a birth, my hand, and it was encased in a shock of thick yellow slime. I hid my hand and took care he didn't see my surprise or the unsavoury aftermath in case it broke the spell when meeting his gaze.

I don't remember him having an erection; I don't think he did. He must have made it known that he either didn't want to or couldn't ejaculate at the end of the session. And I understood that he'd achieved climax in another, far more profound way. Before he took his leave, he kissed my cheek, shook my hand and thanked me for more than I felt I deserved. He was a changed man, affectionate, relaxed, and very charming. I saw him to the door, where Angel was waiting to help him into a taxi.

I shut the door behind him and floated to the toilet, glowing with satisfaction. I'd made his day, fisted a man, done the extreme, and found it an easy, natural, and surprisingly beautiful experience.

I washed my hands and dried them. And then, out of habit, I

sniffed them. Whether his palsy had contributed I couldn't say, but the rare reek of fluids and organs that had seeped through two gloves to my hand was more than I could handle.

I was in the medical room, standing in front of a wall of mirrors wearing a white rubber nurse's uniform and black high heels, and I held up my tainted hand and shook it as if I was wringing the air, and screamed. And watched myself scream – which was all I could do in revolt.

I washed my hands obsessively all week until the trauma of that stench subsided, and *that's* when I first felt the fore notion of limit, and seriously wondered how far I'd go, where I would draw my line. It would be something simple and sensory like a smell, but it would be something.

The third, fourth, fifth and sixth session didn't make it through the hour. Adam would be standing in the medical room in his extreme nakedness, erect, silent, anticipating the exceptional. He would crouch down and I would stand behind him to lace up the hood at the back. I would always begin with a hood because it gave me confidence. As I laced it up I admired the way his neck so elegantly flowed into shoulders, blades and back. I invariably felt the remarkable fission between us, the implosion of possibility.

I touched his nipples. I always began with his nipples. I pressed them between my fingertips. I touched them with my mouth, crushed them between my lips, licked them with my tongue, bit them with my teeth . . . when suddenly he ejaculated, eighteen minutes into our third session, thirty minutes into the fourth session, and thirteen minutes into the fifth – I've recorded it in his file. The incredible thing was he climaxed each of those times without any genital contact. It was proof that extreme forces were at play. It was him; he seemed to feel more than others, or feel more of me. He was more responsive than others, more passionate, more alive.

As soon as he ejaculated, the session ended. It was understood that to carry on administering pain after orgasm would have been something else entirely, and I wasn't prepared to go there. I tried to refund him some of his money but thrice he refused. He showed no signs of embarrassment, frustration or regret that his session ended prematurely, but neither did he express surprise or appreciation for these spontaneous, orgasmic experiences.

And if he never called again, so be it. My hands were full of twelve to twenty men a week, and full of the solitary hours in between when I was either waiting for a stranger who might not appear, a punctual regular who wasn't due for a while, or I had just shaken hands, patted the shoulder or kissed his cheek and sent him on his way. Sometimes I reclined on the gynaecological chair but mostly I curled up on the rubber floor in the reception area, surrounded by cushions, with my feet on the electric heater, and then off the heater when it became too much for my feet, and then back on the heater in two minutes when my feet got cold, while reading and answering the phones. Back and forth, reading *Daisy Miller* and responding to enquiries: do I do equestrian scenarios, hard sports, is there a baby service, a wet room, a stretching rack, can I come along in an hour?

On 21 November, our eighth encounter, I recorded in his file that Adam made his first request. He was wearing a dark-blue suit that day, looked devastatingly handsome, and was more animated than usual. He even made a charming effort to suppress a smile – the first of its kind. There was something he wanted to show me so we moved into the medical room where, from his battered briefcase, he pulled out two packages of wooden clothes pegs, sixty pegs in all. And it *was* funny; those innocent domestic aids carried around in his briefcase and about to become the principal tools of torture for months to come.

Mostly it was sheer abundance that made the clothes-peg ritual so effective and impressive. Sixty pegs applied one at a time were like words in a sentence, spoken slowly and then quickly, enunciated, and spiked with his response. Starting with the loose flesh of his scrotum, I drew a fan of closely spaced pegs across his testicles, and then a second and then a third, until there was no more flesh to pinch. At which point I worked my way up the shaft of his thick, long, stiff penis. There was only enough loose flesh to clamp a single row of nine. When every inch of skin on his genitals and groin had been pinched – about forty pegs – I began working on his chest, drawing arcs from armpit to breast. I left the last four pegs for his nipples. Already I could see how I'd improve my designs and technique in the future, with him, or with other clients.

After twelve or thirteen minutes I stood back to view the result – it looked tribal. It was an aesthetic of abundance, and I thought, this is exactly the kind of pain he likes: slow, mounting, polymorphous, primitive and excessive. He can take it because of how sensually I administer it, and because it makes him feel powerful, and because it makes me feel powerful, and he feels my power, and because I've made him feel. I thought, this is exactly the sort of pain I like to administer: slow, simple, yet full of possibility, variation, and complexity . . . and intense, immense visual impact.

He couldn't see, so I unzipped the eye slit of his hood and let him look in the wall of mirrors, but first he turned upwards and looked at me. And I looked at him, at his eyes. When he finally looked in the mirror, his exclamation was half laugh, half guttural, sensual rasp. I wondered how seeing himself as he was, naked, hooded, spread out, a bush of wooden thistles hiding his genitals and tattooed across his chest, affected his pain. I stepped in between his hoisted legs and planted my gaze on the slit for his eyes while I inserted a rubber plug into his ass.

Once I re-zipped the hood, undid the straps, and lowered his legs from the stirrups, I took his powerful hand in mine, and led him to the dungeon. I put him inside the rubber-lined chamber that resembled a standing coffin, and fastened his wrists and ankles with the leather straps fitted into the chamber. Just before closing the coffin door, I brought my mouth up close to his, so I could smell his distinctive breath, and I pressed my body against his pinched flesh in a bittersweet embrace. And then I left him alone.

I walked outside into unsuspecting suburbia just as the light was beginning to fade, and breathed in the autumn. The sky was huge, hemmed with trees in silhouette, and the clouds were peach and wispy. I would have looked across at Angel's kitchen aglow behind the Venetian blinds. She was my friend, the Madam, and an increasingly absent and unreliable receptionist. She spent more and more time hiding in that filthy house, harbouring a secret. For every minute I stood there dragging on a cigarette and admiring the sky, he suffered alone in the dark, and I got paid two pounds and fifty pence.

Back inside, I washed my hands, brushed my teeth, refreshed my make-up, and remembered myself in the mirror. When he heard me re-enter the dungeon, he rattled in his cage and moaned a sort of greeting. And I thought: my presence has instantly changed the nature of his pain, now he has a witness. I moved towards him to relieve him, but then I changed my mind. Instead, I took a seat on the bondage chair and sampled the silence and the tension. I caught myself in the mirror and there was no one in the world to see that I was smiling. A couple of minutes seemed like a very long time and then I said, 'Hello.'

'Hello,' he answered through cast iron walls, and even in those two muffled syllables I could hear his distress, and a yearning for attention. The click of heels on the tiled floor, the snap of the padlock, then the metal door whining open – those were the sounds that filled the tiny room. And there he was, a beautiful serpent, wriggling in pain, but still erect.

'What were you thinking about all that time, alone?'

'I was thinking about you, and suffering for you,' he answered right away and I was sure that he meant it.

For the first time, I really heard those words and their romantic, dangerous ring. In a single, careless sweep, I ran my fingers through the bush of wooden pegs, which caused him to wriggle and cry out. So the longer the pegs were on, the more they hurt. But apparently it hurt most when taking them off. I was a concentrated surgeon, a courageous lover, and a cruel tormentor as

I slowly, sometimes quickly, pulled the thorns from the lion's foot. I removed all but the last four pegs from his nipples and rewarded his stinging flesh with my soothing, cooling caress. I cupped his balls in my hand and could feel their ache. I gripped his sore cock, because I could, because it felt powerful to grip his sex and reward his suffering. I slid my hand down the slickness of his chest and removed the final pegs. Finally I pressed his throbbing nipples between my fingers and felt his piercing pleasure, electricity and ripples.

Actually, it was the very last act that strikes me as extreme: the caning of the soles of the feet. Maybe it's because feet, unlike the anal glands, the testicles, the penis, and the nipples aren't related to reproduction and sexuality, as far as I can see. Feet have so many other connotations, cultural, spiritual and personal. Feet are sacred and foundational, and it felt deviant and especially cruel to take a cane to those soft soles and beat them, five, ten, twenty times.

He's facing the wall of mirrors. He's bent over the whipping bench, and the soles of his feet and bottom are facing up. When I remove the hood, he can see me standing behind him. I have the cane in one hand and, with the other, I reach underneath his chest so I can squeeze one of his nipples and inflame him again. His body is pressed against the bench and my thigh is pressed against his ass. When I feel him on the verge of climax, I stop abruptly, and get up.

When the first stroke struck the pad of his foot he inhaled his scream and moved with the pain by thrusting his genitals against the leather bench. I struck once, twice, three times, and the thin cane whistled as it cut through the air, and snapped as it bit his flesh. But it left no marks. I watched myself in the mirror, raising my arm, wielding a stick in prelude to a brutal act; and it was such an arresting sight that I looked twice before turning back. I struck fast and my aim was precise and we fell into tempo. His undulating body and my flicking wrist were one continuous motion.

When I undid the straps and set him free, he simply, quite beautifully spilled to his knees. From the low leg of the whipping bench where I sat up close to him, I squeezed his nipples one last time while he looked up at me and masturbated. I pressed as hard as I could, and it hurt, but he never took his eyes off me, not even when he opened his mouth to cry out in ecstasy. And then it was over. I smiled, or maybe I sort of winked at him, but no words came forth. If we talked, I was afraid that spindle of magical thread would snap. I handed him some tissues to wipe the semen he cupped in his hand, and then I left the room.

I'm thinking of all the money Bernie could save if he were to suffocate by himself – but it's a terrible idea. Aside from the exponential danger, the interplay, the psychodrama, the witness that I am, the sparring for control, the tango of two; the coin flicking and the stomach punching would be amiss if Bernie were to suffocate alone. The correct balance of real danger, safety and fantasy requires intervention. I can accentuate his helplessness with blindfolds, bondage, surprise attacks, and by the roles I play – any variation of competent, challenging competitor who is playfully cruel and dangerously frivolous towards his fate. He knows it's not true, but it's my job to make him doubt or forget what he otherwise knows.

Amid an honest gasping fit, I might ask him if he heard John

Humphrys on the radio that morning. If he's disconcertingly quiet under my groin, I might say, 'You're so quiet under there, Bernie, I can't hear you struggling, and I want to hear your struggle.' It's true – the hampered movements and muffled sounds assure me that he's conscious. If I see a finger wiggle or a leg twitch, I tease him and ask what all the commotion's about. 'Is that your idea of a rebellion? Is that you exercising your little bit of freedom?' And then I make a mental note to tighten that bit of rope, not immediately, but in a little while when he thinks I've forgotten.

Adam is in the closet with a hood on his head and eighty clothes pegs on and around his genitals, his inner thighs, his sinewy sides, his armpits, and his muscular arms. This time I speak to him before closing the chamber door. I say, 'I want to reward you for what you're about to suffer. And I'm curious, if you could have any reward, what would it be?' I was surprised by his reply.

'For you to take off your skirt while I'm suffering in the closet.'

'What would be the point of that? You can't see me.'

'But I'll know.'

'No,' was my impulse, whereby I shut the chamber door, and escaped to the medical room to blush in front of the wall of mirrors. I knew why I said no. I wasn't sure I wanted to give him permission to think about me in the nude. It was crossing a line. A good Mistress does not succumb to that easy trick – but then, why not? It was a seductive and cerebral proposition – and I wish I'd thought of it myself. If it was my body he desired, why shouldn't I make use of that desire? I was his focal point, the purpose and the plot, the reason and reward for his pain. I unzipped my rubber miniskirt and it sprung open in my hand. I was overcome, in a good way, by my slender half nakedness, looking as I'd never looked in the medical room, or anywhere else.

On entering the red haze I sizzled with mischief, walked straight to the chamber, and opened the door.

'Are you suffering?'

'Yes.'

'Are you suffering for me?'

'Yes.'

'Suffering, and imagining me?'

'Yes.'

'Imagining me with my skirt off?'

'No.'

I brought my skirt to his enormous hand and he gripped it with his fingers and understood immediately. 'Oh, thank you,' he swooned in elation. I could have left it at that, seeing that this surprise was enough; and his being blind, bound, in pain and excited by what was so close and so elusive – that would have been enough. But I let his bound hand stroke the hem and trim of my panties and the bare flesh of my inner thigh. I let him touch me for the first time ever. I twirled around while his finger stayed in touch with my body and he felt the contours of my bottom and the flow of my hem. I continued to twirl until he was touching my belly, and the way he touched me was an art. I savoured that simple, sublime moment, even with its limits, possibly because of those limits. And for him, touching the hem of my panties and the warmth of my thigh was the ultimate reward for his pain, well worth suffering for. And here is another tableau: me kneeling down in front of him to remove the pegs from his genitals while his fingers rest lovingly on the crown of my head.

And what he'd suffer for a kiss! I didn't think it possible, but each session was more intense, and inched closer to a seductive unknown. The first kiss was hampered by the hood and the small hole for the mouth, and so was actually a breathy, juicy tangle of tongues – and the breaching of yet another boundary. It was fantastic. It had the taste of his peaty, coffee, cigarette breath, and it lingered in my life while he was at home with his wife. These were the most electrifying hours of my week, and they had nowhere to go except to evolve or revolve, expand and collapse within their own contained universe. It took strength to let him go.

At the end of one of those magical hours, he dropped to his knees and pleaded to suffer more. More? More! There was a plug stuck in his ass, ninety pegs had been snapped off his flesh, his hands and the soles of his feet were raw from the cane, his nipples had been tortured to their bloodied limit, but he wanted to suffer more! Then where would it go?

'I'll do anything, anything,' he said. 'Let me hurt myself for you,' he said.

The thing is I heard violins in the background, and a beam of natural light had entered through a corner in the black velvet curtain. He looked unnaturally beautiful and wild-eyed, on his knees pleading to endure more, wanting desperately to endure more; and I wanted to give him what he wanted.

I put a pair of clamps on his nipples, clamps that were attached to each other with a chain.

'Hurt yourself then.' And he nodded. 'Put the chain in your mouth and look up at the ceiling.'

So he lifted his chiselled chin that gives me a chill, which caused the chain to yank the clamps on his nipples until something had to give – the clamps, which snapped off his nipples and made him scream through the chained gag.

'Do it again,' I said.

CHAPTER 9

Revelation

I'm praising the profession that brings down barriers, and brings me into contact with hundreds of naked men: men I might not have known had they kept on their clothes. I found the short cut to an honest appeal. Now I wonder: are all men the same? So vulnerable, needy and grateful for some undivided sexual attention; so transparent and so complex, so built for pleasure and easy to please?

In theory I could do six sessions a day, six days a week, and earn a yearly income of a hundred and fifty thousand pounds, then retire a millionaire after eight years. In practice, my threshold was four or five sessions a day, five days a week, for a few months, and then it was time for a holiday. One day six men all want to come along at once, and three of them are named John and four of them want humiliation, and you do it, push it if you can because, sure enough, the next day there'll be three cancellations, a newcomer that doesn't show up, the phones go quiet, there's a tube strike, it's a bad-weather day, or the end of the month when everyone's broke. The reality was I never knew how the day or the week, let alone the month or fiscal year, would pan out. I couldn't plan ahead or budget with any certainty, but that didn't stop me from calculating constantly. If I did two weeks where I made two thousand pounds, then in seven weeks I could put away five thousand – that's ten before the New Year. I always over-estimated, but at my peak of industriousness and miserliness, I had thirty thousand saved at any one time. But it was funny money, slippery, easy to spend. Those glossy pink salad bowls, the giant candles, the shaggy rugs from Habitat, the white truffle oil, Borough Food Market on Fridays and Saturdays, the organic blueberry juice, the cinnamon-scented vinegars, Aztec grains, white teas and Fiji water were paid for by lashing and bullying, lewd, lascivious tirades, spitting on faces, mastering the face-slap, stamping my feet, sticking them in someone's mouth. A session with Bernie was my rent and phone bill, plus my tube fare for the week. Every time George visited me I made a point of buying flowers for my flat, roses en masse, heaps and heaps of happy tulips, as well as a house plant, a lemon tree, or a bonsai. Gavin's three-hour medical session more than paid for my red velvet coat.

He began visiting me a year after his wife died. He was still doleful and weepy with grief. His voice was so soft that I had to crane my neck, strain my lazy ears and hold my breath at times to hear the story of his loss through a cloud of halitosis. He was bearded, moustached and Irish, and in his fifty-six years he'd never visited a Mistress.

I can't remember whose idea it was to feminise him but it was exactly the thing. He was so eager once he got started, so keen to lose himself in the role. I dressed him up in a black thong, high heels, stockings, suspender belt and bra, and a long black wig: with some guidance and encouragement, a tart was born. When he saw himself feminised in front of the mirrors, me standing behind him teasing the tops of his stockings and his nipples through the bra, it was a revelation – and it was just the beginning.

I put him over the whipping bench and pulled down his panties in one jerk, like his pimp. How sinful and salacious it must have been for him. I felt around for his penis, and it was wet and erect. That always boosts my confidence. I groped, pinched and manhandled his bottom while flattering him, saying things no one had ever said to him: 'That's a perfect, perky little ass just asking to be touched. I like you half naked, half dressed, it suits you; you look willing, wanting, you look like you want to be touched, you look like my slutty, horny, wanting girl in your high heels and bra, and silky stockings . . . irresistible. I'm going to warm you up. Watch how it warms me up to warm you up. First I'm going to warm up your ass then I'm going to open it up.'

I spanked him very lightly and told him I could see he was going to be my very special girl. 'Would you like that?'

'Oh, very much, my Mistress. You're my Mistress. You really are. I want to please you,' he cooed, passionately. He cried at the end of the session, on his knees in his thick, ribbed corduroys and blue woollen jumper, hot, indulgent, elegiac tears.

Once a fortnight we embarked on a full slut-training course that began with transvestite transformation. He fell in love with a pair of open-toed, ankle-strap sandals, and began appreciating the way stockings emphasised the contours of his legs, lifted his buttocks, and made him feel sexy. He had a thing for fancy panties and started buying them for himself. I dressed him in spaghetti-strap dresses, corsets, PVC mini-skirts, and pink feather boas. He lapped up my encouragement and strived desperately to please. We worked on poise and balance. I prescribed ballet exercises for grace, shaved his genitals, taught him to gyrate his pelvis, wiggle his bum and thrust out his silicon-padded chest. We worked on batting eyelashes, looking coquettish, and *feeling* slutty and salacious. Sadly, he slobbered quite a bit whenever he tried to run his thick tongue across his lips, and it hung out of his mouth in an apparent aid to concentration when he was instructed to parade around the room like a prostitute in his sandals. The beard and moustache didn't help.

After five months I was gagging him, flagellating him, beating him with a heavy wooden paddle and sodomising him with a strap-on; and he'd become a pro at sucking dildos, and I'd become a pro at slut training and pimp speak. In the end it was a very sweaty, feverish affair. In the end he found his ecstatic abandon.

He was always very reluctant to leave. He had become enamoured with the one who'd helped him lose himself in wild, rude desire; helped him lift the grief off his breast. He tried, in vain, to extend the boundaries of our relationship by inviting me to his place for dinner. I returned the gesture insofar as I told him something personal: 'Perhaps someday, thank you. It's nice to get a dinner invitation: as a chef I rarely get them.'

One day as he was about to leave, he paused, turned around

and said, 'You once told me your previous occupation; now I wonder if you could tell me my previous vocation?'

'Why?' I asked, somewhat irritated. His devotion and faith in my 'higher powers' had become too much for me, and I was about to fail his test. 'I really couldn't know a thing like that, and I don't want to guess.'

'Oh, come on, just try, please. I know you'll get it.'

It was ludicrous but I stared at him and pretended to be looking into his soul . . . but he looked like a vet, an architect, a curator, a librarian, a book dealer, and many other things as well. I opened my mouth to tell him that I didn't know, but to my own surprise, that's not what I said. I was staring at his neck and wool jumper and the light-blue collar underneath, and perhaps to chide him, I said, 'You were a priest.'

Sombrely he closed his eyes and slowly nodded. And then he kissed my hand very – well – religiously, and added, 'Don't tell anyone.' But hell, why not? As soon as he left I rang up Angel, and when I went home that evening I told my flatmates that I'd raped and sodomised a priest.

I'd probably been seeing Trousers Dan for a couple of years when one day, while rubbing the left side of his oiled groin, masturbating him, and talking the usual spiel, he suddenly called out, 'You're not going to put me in a wheelchair, are you?'

Huh? I had no idea how a wheelchair figured into a castration fantasy and wool trousers: Helplessness, disempowerment, emasculation . . . Okay, I get it, maybe. Or is it a memory, a real memory?

'Why, you bet I am! I'm going to strap you in it and then leave you outside in the rain.' Thereafter, the wheelchair was added to the repartee.

But then, several months later, he surprised me again. He'd entered and greeted me as usual, paid me in five-pound notes and change, and was already undressing when I left the room. A couple of minutes later I returned to the room and found him, not naked as always, but wearing an M&S rosebud-patterned ladies' nightgown. Once upon a time I mistook Dan's fantasy for something simple and straightforward. Once upon a time I thought those wool trousers were invested with the nostalgic power of a fetish. Now I didn't know. Was it the trousers themselves, or was it the statement behind the trousers that excited him? Was it a castration fantasy specifically, or the underlying experience of humiliation, torment and emasculation in general? Or did those things – wheelchair, nightgown, wool trousers, the threat of castration – refer to real events? Was it fantasy, or had such a twisted schoolmaster really existed?

After so many months of seeing Adam I was served a cautionary reminder. He was in the standing coffin, hooded, wrists and ankles leather-bound to the inner walls of the chamber. He'd been in that spot a dozen times before, yet this time I sensed something was different. I felt he wasn't enjoying himself. None of my actions were provoking the usual response. My thought was to remove the pegs off his groin region as quickly and painlessly as possible, but when I took off the first one he roared with such bitter blame that I was loath to remove the others. I braved the third or fourth or fifth peg when, suddenly, he jerked with such savage strength that he ripped the straps off the chamber's inner wall and freed his arms.

I backed up towards the door, towards safety, and got a glimpse of something ugly and beastly before I left the room. My heart throbbed in its cage, and all I could think was: he's violent and volatile and out of control. It happened before and it could happen again. And it was unacceptable. Yet when I went back to the dungeon, he was calm and unrepentant.

'I don't like your hostile behaviour. Don't do it again,' I said.

But I don't remember him making any promises.

12:45 p.m.: *I'm desperate for it to end and finally the end is near. I get a second wind for the grand finale. When I've thought about it beforehand, I've tied him up in a way that makes it easy to free his right hand without disrupting the rest of the bondage. He knows it's time so he grabs his penis between his thumb and finger, milking it like a teat. I reach for a tissue and let it drop so it floats down and lands discreetly on his belly. I'm trying to protect the ropes from being soiled without him noticing. I don't want to draw attention to his masturbation in case it makes him feel self-conscious. I take my place on his face and begin rapidly flicking his nipples. After just twenty seconds, I lift and let him gasp for a breath before dropping back down on his face. I do this several times in succession in order to work him up. And then I sit on him for longer. Thirty-five seconds, I lift, he gasps. Forty seconds, same. It's been tacitly agreed that we'll try to coordinate the climaxes: the peak of suffocation with ejaculation. Twenty-six, twenty-seven, twenty-eight seconds . . . and he comes.*

It takes another five or six minutes to untie him. I work quickly, assuming that what was once so exciting and meaningful has instantly become unpleasant and cumbersome. Unless he gets there before me, I remove the blindfold last. The contrast of light assaults his eyes and he makes a show of rubbing and blinking. He looks like a man waking from a deep sleep. I hand him a tissue so he can blow his nose – suffocation makes the mucus flow.

He's rejuvenated and giddy as he descends from a great high, and he wants to talk about anything and everything – except what we've just done. He talks about his delinquent students, the book he's reading, or some campus rant, and I'm thinking I've had enough of Bernie for one day. There's something about him having just bought two hours of my time that makes me a bit restless about the time he takes for free. But he doesn't seem to notice, and now he's working himself into a difficult yoga pose. Sometimes, out of the affection I feel for Bernie, or the pity, I demonstrate how I do the pose and allow him to correct me if I get it wrong.

When I'd been seeing him for a couple of years, and he was leaning against the whipping bench putting on his sock, out of nowhere I asked him why he liked suffocating or how it all started. I remember he paused for dramatic effect, and then slid on his second sock before looking up at me and smiling like he was about to tell me an irresistible joke – and indeed, he was.

'I was born this way.'

'But how do you know that?'

'I told you, I was born this way. I was born with the umbilical cord around my neck. So I was born suffocating.'

Can you imagine anything tidier? We both laughed, cautiously at first, neither of us knowing exactly why or for what. Naturally, I didn't buy his explanation, and maybe I laughed thinking that he was laughing for the very same reason. He couldn't really believe that? What about all the blue babies that aren't into erotic suffocation and all the people who are into erotic suffocation that weren't born blue? And maybe we laughed because it didn't matter, it really didn't matter; something hysterical was gaining momentum, something beyond all reason that made us laugh for a full few minutes.

It was my last session with Adam, only he didn't tell me so until he was hooded, and strapped down in a bondage chair in the dungeon with a plug up his ass and dozens of clothes pegs pinching his groin. And for Pete's sake, why did he choose that moment to tell me? What a slap in the face! It proved he had all the power in the end, the fact that he could just walk away. I must have thought things would go on indefinitely. I don't know what I thought. Perhaps I thought that we were coming to something, building towards something meaningful – but not any more. Then again, how long would I have carried on without wanting more, without wanting to take pleasure as well as give it? How long until he wanted more than I could give him in an hour, in a tiny red room in suburbia? He was a married man, a client, a stranger; he'd shared his soul with me for sixty minutes, but that was only 0.0059 per cent of his week. And now, even that minuscule amount of time was being taken away without warning or resolution.

'Why is it our last session?' I asked casually.

Actually, the whole thing was based, at least in part, upon a misunderstanding. He was going away for the summer, and he had the impression that I'd be gone when he came back because, for several months, I'd been hinting to my regular clients that my departure was imminent, and that I *might* not come back. I needed a break from domination. I'd been working four, five, six days a week for about two years and my world was shrinking where once it seemed to be expanding. And Angel had been threatening to sell the house. But no dates had been set for any of this. It was just Adam's imagination, or lack of it, that turned the moment into a self-fulfilling prophecy. And ultimately his decision was to go away at the end of the hour and never see me again. Cold and cowardly, I thought. How could he?

It was a blow to accept I was so dispensable and inconsequential. I felt powerless, and sick. A wave of nausea and futility washed over me and almost drowned me when I thought: *this is wrong!* I had a childish, raging impulse to make an impression, lash out and revolt. He was blind, immobilised and defenceless, even if he did have all the power. He never knew what hit him. I gave him no warning just as he had given me no warning. I kicked him sharply in the pegged groin – and regretted it even before my heel had made contact. But then it was too late.

It was truly awful the way he sprang – but didn't, because he couldn't. His involuntary wail, inhale, whatever it was, was horrible. I was afraid of what damage I'd caused. I was afraid of what he'd do. Our first session, the explosive, shaming 'NO', the ripping of the leather straps in the chamber. Fear and guilt flooded my mind as I rushed to remove his hood, before unbinding him and removing the pegs. It was a painful shock for me to see his beautiful face so bloodless and anguished. And there were tears in his oceanic eyes. I went to get him a wet face-cloth and, while I waited for the water to run cold, I reviewed the unhappy symmetry of our story. It ends with indignity, volatility and violence – the way it began. Only this time, it's my rage that has caused the rift.

And I *am* angry. I have difficulties in public. Strangers and their cold conduct, crowds, cheap floral perfumes, all varieties of loud, aggressive noise upset me disproportionately. I feel compelled to speak out in public in a very un-English manner. As a result of my verbal compulsion I have frequent hostile confrontations. The question for me is not *do* I say something but *how* do I say it? If someone's eating stinky food near me on the bus or tube, I'm likely to tell him or her so. Just last week a young woman, trying to get her child in a pushchair through the aisle of a bus, screamed at an old lady to move her 'goddamn ass'. A couple of dozen onlookers sat mute and passive, so why did *I* feel compelled to intervene? What am I, some kind of urban samurai? I told her to stop her shouting and stop being so rude and obnoxious. Predictably, she flung her head around and aimed her vitriol at me. 'Who the fuck asked you, you nosy, smug bitch?' My question is, how does one respond to that? Because, as it usually goes, it escalated to the ridiculous point where I was shouting – *shouting* – 'Stop shouting already', which, if I didn't actually imagine it, caused a hushed giggle throughout the bus. Well it *was* ridiculous. I got off the bus at the next stop and she kicked me in the back of my right thigh as I did so! Oh, how I wanted to turn back and fight; the desire was so hot and wild in me. I didn't, probably because the doors were closing. I limped home instead, and it took me a long time to calm down. The chemicals circled my system before finally settling at a stable, molecular sadness.

How I wish I could find a better recourse for the bus drivers in their half empty buses that ride right past bus stops of people just for the hell of it. Hundreds of thousands of Londoners must know what I mean. Impotently, very unattractively, I chase the bus down the street, screaming 'fucker' or whatever; or I punch the bus if it stops at a traffic light, or I memorise the vehicle's ID number. But I've never lodged a formal complaint. It's not immediate enough. But if a waiter asks me if I enjoyed my meal, I will always offer an honest response. Sometimes they take it on board, but usually they couldn't care less. Then I wish they wouldn't ask.

When I wait twenty minutes at High Street Kensington for the Circle Line train and the notice board says 'no delays', I will approach a tube worker and request an amendment to the board or an information announcement. If I see someone littering, I tell him or her to pick it up, and they tell me to fuck off. Once I did achieve my goal diplomatically. I happened to be looking out the window of my flat just as a teenage girl walked past my gate and discarded her chip cone, that thick white greasy paper, onto the pavement. I stuck my head out the window and called to her.

'Hey, hey, you. Hello there,' I shouted down with extreme cheerfulness, 'you forgot something.'

She stopped and looked up, very confused, but I smiled even bigger and she retraced her steps.

'Hi there, you dropped something,' I said, pointing to the chip cone, as if I were doing her a favour. She looked down at the paper and then up at me, and I was nodding and smiling as she bent over and picked up the cone, still confused, and walked off. I followed her from the window and to my sheer triumph I saw her drop the rubbish in someone's bin along the street. But that's rare.

Why *am* I raging? What's hurting so much? Is it the inconsideration of others, or is it that I feel invisible? Why am I so critical and intolerant? I'm ranting and raving and totally misbehaving.

Until now, why did none of this anger find its way into the dungeon? What does that mean? Of all places to channel my anger . . . Instead, I feel tolerant and compassionate at work. I'm tactful and effective, accepting and empathetic, and my subjects are keen and receptive to my influence. I counsel and encourage, give pleasure and distribute my love. I forgive them their unsavoury odours, their abjectness, their weakness, their clumsiness. Even when I'm spitting in their faces, slapping their balls, humiliating and verbally abusing them, flogging them, suturing them, hammering nails into them, I find that I'm almost never angry in the dungeon. I control what goes on in the dungeon, I make things happen and connect with strangers in the most intimate way. When one of us speaks, the other listens. There are umpteen hoods and blindfolds, nonetheless we attempt to cast off our masks. So, off with the mask. Why am I angry? It's because there's something I'm needing; it's not enough, these brief, magical, collapsible moments in a vacuum. I want something lasting. I want to be more to Adam.

I went back to the dungeon with a wet cloth, prepared to apologise for my aggression, ready to calmly end the session. But upon entering the dungeon I saw he was sitting exactly as I'd left him, the pegs still on his body, only there was colour and forgiveness in his face.

'I'm ready to continue,' he said.

I hadn't anticipated that. I had to think. I handed him the cloth and a glass of water and confronted his eyes for one of the last times.

'Please, can I touch you just this once?' he asked.

And I couldn't think why not. For years he'd been denied the power and pleasure of giving, of seeing me and touching me. I'd denied myself for just as long. Nobody touched me in that room. But just this once I'd forgo control, the restraint of my role. I'd lost it once when I kicked him; now let's see what happens.

First I kneeled down between his legs and removed the pegs from his groin. He didn't scream, didn't make a sound, but kept stroking my head, whispering, 'Anna, Anna, Mistress Anna.' When I stood up, I looked down into his face, and he looked up into mine and, without breaking his adoring gaze, he raised my flared rubber skirt, my favourite skirt.

I let his fingertip touch my thigh, then traverse along the hem of my panties. That single stroke was more electrifying and satisfying than the applause of a million dove wings . . . I stood there with my flesh on a precipice while his finger traced the lace and memorised my face. I almost fainted from the closeness of his finger to my sex. It was then that he discovered the truth, and I think it really took him by surprise that I wanted him, because there was surprise in his eyes. He touched my sex and felt that I was wet. Confidence and confirmation, an invitation, our last meeting . . . what had been withheld until now was finally free to proceed.

It was like the breaking of a wave: CRASH, exalted foam, silver spray. The entire structure, years of restraint, collapsed and a tide of passion poured forth. We kissed like starved, parched animals, feeding and drinking in a fever, in a freedom feast. No constraints, no hood, no pegs, no leather straps, no rules. Every look, every touch was the succulent taste of liberty.

I kissed the back of his neck. He kissed my shoulder and my armpit. I kissed his hair. He kissed my stomach and my ankles. I could kiss anything I wanted, because for the remains of the hour he belonged to me. I kissed the eyes that had me mesmerised. I kissed his eyelids, his long lashes and his thick eyebrows . . . and they tickled my lips. I felt his mouth and his hands, their joy discovering all of me, and without wanting to spoil the word, it was ecstasy. His hands were curious and yet they seemed to know my body better than I did.

And then we broke the final rule by having sex on the dungeon floor.

When it was all over, I was trembling, sweaty, dizzy, shattered and euphoric. I stood up to change gears, and caught myself in the wall of mirrors. My hair was wild and the make-up smeared across my fiery face. My favourite rubber skirt was ripped and I'd have to throw it away, but I had consumed and been consumed. We said nothing, having communicated everything, and I walked out of the room. It was the end. But it was also the beginning: we had made a date for the early autumn.

PART TWO

CHAPTER 10

Home

Naturally I'm not perfect. I have no desire to dominate you in 'real life'. I want you to challenge me, inspire me, nourish me, and let me be vulnerable. I want to look up to you, love your mind, and learn from you. I want us to be equal. We share the same intensity. We have this rare chemistry. We're of a kind. I want you to love me, and not some fantasy of me. I want the ordinary. I want the extraordinary.

And I'm so romantic.

I remember walking through the common, swinging grocery bags and coming home to him. The savoury details, I recall, like what I'd planned to cook for dinner. I was going to peel and quarter parsnips and toss them with whole garlic cloves in their skins, shavings of raw ginger and cubes of butternut squash in peanut oil, cinnamon, maple syrup, rice vinegar, crushed pepper, star anise, and a dash of soy sauce. I was going to roast the mixture in a hot oven for an hour or so, and meanwhile prepare two tuna steaks and salad. I didn't make the salad, or any of it in the end, but the vision was complete: bitter frisée lettuce, crispy sautéed shallots, paper-thin slices of pear, and crumbles of praline that I'd make from scratch and then crush to crumbs with a rolling pin; and a simple dressing of grape-seed oil and sherry vinegar. I saw dinner served on black plates and salad mounted in the red ceramic bowls I'd carried home from Japan in a backpack.

The meal was meant to nourish, to taste of comfort and balance, and please the palate. I was going to plug in the flower lights, put on Pat Metheny, and afterwards we could watch a film, or if he was tired (sleep was a passion, a pastime, and an escape of his), then maybe I'd read to him in bed, because reading out loud was a passion of mine.

I remember everything about that insufferable evening. How the light fell like timber on the grass of the common a couple of hundred yards from my flat. The orange and pink clouds, the quiet, closing sky, and the air that smelled damp from an earlier rain were mixed with the warm taste of roasted squash and cinnamon. It was early springtime then and I was feeling its fever and promise. I was going home to him, the man that I loved and, incredibly, the man that loved me. I could deconstruct and doubt it later, and I would, but for the moment, that fecund and hearty moment, I was deliriously happy. As I inhaled, my chest expanded and I envisioned the warm meal that I would make, and the person who'd be waiting to receive my love.

And then, next stride, I felt something nagging me, a sense of the familiar. I actually stopped and tried to place it. I felt the crush of plastic in the sweat of my palms, the weight of the groceries, saw the neon moon above and the footpath below, and then I knew what it was, why the moment felt so familiar: it was reminding me of an underwhelming painting, which had nonetheless beguiled me. And I was the woman in that painting.

It was a windy afternoon in Istanbul. I had to chase a wrapper or a piece of paper that I'd accidentally dropped and it went spiralling and twisting like a dervish dancing before I finally caught up to it. All of a sudden the smoke-coloured sky tore open, accompanied by a clap of thunder and a flash of lightning, and then came the downpour. I ran for shelter in a small art gallery where a corpulent lady in a lime-green dress sat smoking at a desk near the entrance. I had entered a white room and a storm of colour. I was wet, my fingers cold, so I turned left and went towards the one painting that glowed warmer than the others. I was drawn to its woody browns, hypnotic crimsons, and mellow yellows because it comforted me, that scene, those colours.

The painting was of a street lined with tall brownstone houses and autumn trees. There was light from the dining-room windows and moonlight reflected in a puddle, and a street lantern was casting an elegant shadow off a slender woman who's seen from behind. Who is she? What face does she wear? She's walking in the middle of the street, grocery bags hanging from each hand, and one gets the feeling that it's her neighbourhood, that it's dinner time, and that she's going home to cook for someone.

I had an unexpectedly poignant reaction to such a simple scene. I felt nostalgic – but for what? When? Something about that painting made me long or grieve – I couldn't tell which. That warm, autumn scene depicting home and hearth, stability, simplicity (or was it ordinariness?) – was that what I wanted? Was I staring at the thing I most wanted or something I'd forfeited? After all, I was in Istanbul, writing, wandering, seeking, and single. My homes were many, I'd cooked for hundreds, but I ate alone and gave my love to plenty; I was *not* on that woman's path.

Now on the common in Brixton, I'm the woman in the painting with her grocery bags in hand, going home to him! I crossed the road, walked a block, and turned a corner.

With impatience I climbed two flights of stairs and felt the burning in my calves as I unlocked the door to my flat. I kicked off my shoes, passed the living room, the dining room, headed straight for the kitchen. I put down the bags filled with food and a tomato rolled onto the counter and then dropped to the floor. I didn't even bother taking off my coat before I went searching for him.

And there he was, asleep on the living-room sofa.

My first impulse was to wake him up with dozens of thoughtful kisses. Make every kiss an event, a statement, a question, a daring investigation. But his breathing was so even and his face so at peace that I stopped myself from disturbing him. Instead, I stood there studying his beauty, trying to work out the power it had over me, why it meant so much to me, how it was that the slope of his nose, for example, could bring me so much pleasure and inspiration. Meanwhile, his chest rose and fell and he made that whistling sound like air passing through the reed of a concertina. 'Giant lungs', the doctors said. I did not disturb him and I didn't start dinner as I'd planned to do because just then I had an idea.

I backed out of the room just as he stirred in his sleep. I assumed he was on the edge of waking, so I swiftly hung up my coat, and began unbuttoning my top as I climbed the stairs. On the landing, I stepped out of my jeans and my underwear, removed my vest, my socks, even the silver rings on my fingers and thumbs, and then I stood naked, wondering if there was anything I needed – and there was; I needed the clock.

At 6:39 I got down on all fours, parted my knees, hung my feet over the top stair and dipped my back, which raised my bottom. I felt my palms and shins pressed into the hardwood floor, the draught on my flesh, and without moving so much as a hair, I waited for him to wake up and find me there.

CHAPTER 11

Courtship

When Adam and I made love on the dungeon floor at the end of our final session, I crossed a line, blurred the boundaries, and broke the 'cardinal rule' . . . but then nothing happened; the whole summer passed with him away. When September came around, we arranged to meet at a pub in Soho.

I did not dress up for the occasion. I wore my favourite black corduroys, a brown turtleneck, a pair of flat red shoes, a turquoise scarf, and a cream coat that I'd bought second-hand. It was how I always dressed and I was determined to avoid pretences. I wore my hair down, my eyes were lightly lined with kohl, I wore mascara, and my cheeks were hot and blushed from an earlier shot of whiskey, the present excitement, and the autumn breeze along the Old Compton sex tease. I felt confident and slightly reckless. I was thinking that it was a one-off, that there was nothing to lose. On the contrary, I would not have passed up the occasion to meet the man whose eyes had hypnotised me for the last two and something years. It didn't matter whether I liked him or not; I had no expectations. I was meeting Adam the Masochist for the thrill of disclosure, and the aesthetic of closure.

I'm sure I wouldn't have been so confident meeting Adam that evening if he'd been the first client I'd met outside the dungeon, but in fact, he was the last.

Melodic Mike called me at suppertime on a Saturday. I was at home cooking and he sounded drunk. He said he'd seen my picture in a fetish magazine, said he was looking at the picture as we spoke, that I sounded as alluring and attractive as I looked, and that he needed to see me right away. 'You have this deep, dark, bewitchingly thoughtful look in your eyes. I must see you tonight.' The voice he used to bribe me with one thousand pounds was distinctly, seductively velvety – but it didn't work.

'Oh, come on, a session's not worth that much money. Besides, how do I know you'd show up? You're drunk. You shouldn't be driving, and I'm in the middle of my dinner. But your voice is so musical, so melodic and unusual, do call back.'

And he did, the following day. I bowed to his chivalrous voice in the end and agreed to see him on a Sunday evening, a day I never work. He entered the cottage wearing these gorgeous square-toed patent-leather shoes that rose to the ankle. Jerome had worn those shoes.

Mike had boyish good looks, sandy brown hair and canine eyes that deliberately avoided my gaze. He kept his head low and I felt he was hiding his face rather than behaving submissively. Then he was very firm about wanting to wear a hood throughout the session, or at least a blindfold, and he wanted to do away with the preliminaries, meaning the questionnaire and a conversation about his likes and dislikes. Instead, he handed me a folded piece of lined paper on which he'd jotted in black pen all the things he felt I needed to know before we began. It read: hoods, enema, genital bondage, dildos, strap-on, a severe caning with slow build-up and gentle encouragement, bite-gag and bondage for the caning. Extremely sensual nipples, no humiliation and definitely no verbal abuse. Cross-dressing?

When I returned to the dungeon he was on his knees, head bowed low, and I got the sense he was already deep in role and yearning for something powerful to occur. I teased his nipples between my fingers and it was true, they were extremely sensitive. He gasped with passionate surprise and swooned into submission. I knew from these first two minutes just how it would be, as I so often do, and I knew I had him, knew it would be an intense session, that I'd surpass his expectations. He needed to be sensually, almost maternally taken through pain and punishment.

'I'm yours, Mistress,' he whispered, and I could tell that he was scared. 'Oh God, I'm all yours. Please hurt me. I'm ready. Make me suffer. It's just what I need.'

I tied his cock and his balls with a thin leather lace and then strapped him down over the whipping bench. I remember his pedicured feet, his shapely calves, and his smooth, firm bottom. He had an athletic build, a nice back, and was large and erect. I could feel his tension, his fright, and the sensual aura of a rite. Sex and possibility were in the air, and I began to cradle the power he'd invested in me. I saw myself in the dungeon mirror in profile, my strong slender arm, my curves wrapped in rubber, my hand gripping a cane and I was struck by the artistic, dangerous appeal of the pose. I gagged him and then I caned him ten, twenty, forty, sixty times, starting slowly, building gradually, awaking the endorphins, finding a rhythm, and guiding him to a place beyond pain.

Afterwards, I touched the wet tip of his cock, and reached my hands underneath him to caress and squeeze his nipples. I was moved by his courage, by what he'd endured. When I undid the straps and he stood up, he held out his arms and we warmly embraced.

We finished the session in the medical room. I'd given him an enema and he was now on his back with his legs raised and resting on my shoulders. He was wearing a blindfold, and I was facing him and penetrating him with a dildo that was strapped over my skirt. While we rocked back and forth, I gently squeezed his nipples and got into the motion of fucking. Meanwhile he was masturbating. Suddenly, judging by the sounds he made, he had one enormous orgasm. I rolled my eyes because it seemed slightly exaggerated. 'Oh come on, how can it be *that* good?' I felt like saying. I was jealous and embarrassed by such gaping discrepancies in realities. I took off his blindfold and he grabbed me and held me to his chest, rocking me, kissing the crown of my head so graciously, and whispering, 'Oh my God, Anna, Mistress Anna, whoever you are, where have you been? You're so wonderful.' He was pulling at my hair by accident and squashing my face, and it was awkward. How far I felt from wonderful. I was tired. I wanted to go home. He offered to drive me back to Brixton.

When he pulled up outside my flat in his black Land Rover,

he turned to me and asked, 'You don't recognise me, do you?' He looked so self-important and serious suddenly. 'I have to tell you something. I probably won't see you again and I don't want you to think it has *anything* to do with you. I'm going away for three months. I travel all the time for work. Besides, I only feel the need to be caned once a year, and then I never return to the same Mistress. I've been seeing Mistresses for twenty years but I've never seen the same Mistress twice. Maybe I'm paranoid but I'm sort of a celebrity, you see.'

'An actor?' I asked, less impressed than maybe he'd hoped.

'No, TV presenter.'

'Well, I don't have a television so I haven't seen you.'

'I also write for the --- and I used to be an --- and I'm saying no more.'

I didn't invite him in, but he reached over to me and we kissed goodbye.

He called me up a few months later and we had our second session – the best session he said he'd ever had. Afterwards we went to a fish restaurant in Lambeth where the interiors were decked out like a ship, the waiters dressed like sailors, and the sound of seagulls and foghorn filled the room on replay. He thought it was fun. Over rare tuna steak with olive and caper caviar, and mussels for starters, he told me about the first time he flagellated himself.

He was eleven and at boarding school. His father had died the previous term, and he can't forget the look on his mother's face and those words, 'Now you're the man of the family.' Around that time he would escape alone, deep into the woodlands of the school grounds. When he felt certain nobody else was around he took off all his clothes and ran about wild and free. With branches he collected off the forest bed, he beat himself. With pinecones he gathered, he penetrated himself.

'I don't know why I did it or how it related to my grief, if at all. It felt like a passage into manhood and it was glorious and ceremonial. After beating myself and penetrating myself, I would masturbate, stinging with pain, roaring with pagan excitement, and have these powerful, unbelievable orgasms. When I was twenty-four and in New York I came across a fetish magazine purely by accident and I was shocked to see pictures of women whipping men! It was a revelation that you could actually pay someone to beat you, that there was a service for that sort of thing, and that other people had the same desires.'

I was enchanted – lifted and saddened – thinking then of centaurs and cedars, and a young boy dancing naked and discovering an ancient sexual beat.

That night he slept at my flat. He couldn't quite get over the bemusement of being in the flat of a dominatrix. Look: she reads, she has a blue fridge and cupboards, a tennis racket in the corner of her bedroom, a worn pair of ballet slippers by the fireplace, a cute pillow on the bed embroidered with a different name. All the evidence of daily existence seemed to upset his imagination. He wanted to spank me. He said that he had a long-term girlfriend, they were on the rocks, but she loved being spanked and he was rather good at it. There was something sexy and sassy about pulling down my own pretty knickers as if to say, okay, let's see what you can do because I can take what I give. So he spanked me, not once, twice, but three times too hard. It didn't arouse me, but I could handle it. But when he unbuckled his belt and pulled it off his trousers, I thought: I don't really need to do this. And pulled up my knickers.

And then I remember how he pulled down his trousers, and presented me with his proud, hard member. He lay back on my bed like some kind of prima donna, tweaking his own nipples. 'Come on then,' he said, 'suck my cock,' like I owed him one for not taking the belt. Oh, I don't know. It all seemed so dissatisfying and selfish, that is, before the shellfish. Selfish shellfish was all I remember before dashing to the toilet. Two days later I was still violently ill. He had to be up at the crack of dawn because of an all weekend booking at a spa outside London. Our goodbye was on the terse side, with him looking less than impressed by my fey, sickly state and the sexless flannel pyjamas that I'd slipped into during the cold sweats of the night.

He visited me a third time a few weeks later, and again he could only see me on a Sunday. Now I see that the third session was pushing things. I made my way to the cottage after ballet class and Angel, who was always home, came outside to sit with me in the garden on her picnic blanket. It was a lovely summer afternoon and while eating the sushi that I'd brought for us, I told her about Melodic Mike. And then, together, we came up with a plan.

It was dusk when he arrived. He wanted to talk for a few minutes before we began. He asked me for a cigarette. He was going to have his one cigarette before bedtime now, instead. He was stalling, nervous and worried that he wouldn't be able to lose himself in the role after having seen me out of context. I wasn't worried; I was a professional, and I had something very special in store.

It was dark and quiet in that North London suburb by the time he was naked, gagged and blindfolded. I tied his cock and balls with a shoestring and put clamps on his nipples after I teased them and seductively squeezed them. And then I told him to face the wall and spread his legs. First I had to guide him to the wall because he couldn't see. And after I pulled on a latex glove and lubricated my finger and the tip of a small rubber plug, I worked the one and then the other into his ass. He was aroused and in role when I led him to his shoes and instructed him to slip them on. By the time I opened the cottage door and he felt the evening air, he'd figured it out and began shaking in resistance as well as muttering through the gag.

'Trust me,' I whispered soothingly in his ear. 'No one will see you and no one will hear you. We're alone in the woods.'

I had, with fading confidence, to shove him, gently but firmly, across to the garden towards a tree. I tied him to the tree, his back facing me, and tried to ignore his jerks and trembles. We kept a birch in the dungeon. Not until then had I had the occasion to use it. I warmed his bottom with the tips of the twigs before I raised my right arm to flagellate him.

I thrashed him a few times without satisfaction, for his shivers had intensified to the point of crisis and I stopped. I untied him and got him back indoors as quickly as possible while whispering words meant to reassure. I shut the door behind us and removed his gag and blindfold. Without looking up, like a petrified child, he made straight for a corner of the room, faced it, and heaved quietly.

I felt pretty awful and pretty stupid. He had malaria, but how was I to know? More that I'd trespassed into his past for the sake of aesthetics and style without carrying a map. I apologised, and it took another cigarette and a shot of cognac, which I keep in the dungeon, before he felt ready to resume – indoors.

We met for lunch twice after that – rare occasions that he was in London and could spare a couple of hours – but he admitted he was worried about his public persona and my profession. And seeing as he was fourteen years older than me, married to his work, and a selfish lover, there was no pain in not seeing him any more.

So Mike was the first client I saw outside the dungeon. Bradley was the second. It was 12:43 p.m. and he was thirteen minutes late.

I was leaning against a post on the corner of Old Compton Street in Soho, watching the people, thumbing my phone, and wondering what he'd think of me. He had only ever seen me wearing make-up and skimpy fetish wear, and on that midsummer's day I was in my favourite corduroys, thinned to threads in patches and stretched out of shape, and yellow trainers. He didn't even know my real name. After months of perseverance he'd finally broken my resistance and I agreed to meet him for lunch. It was an inverted way of getting acquainted, starting from the inside, working outward. Starting with his naked hairy body, his sexual penchants, his orgasms, and moving on to jobs, family history, goals and ambitions.

I imagined him leaving the family mansion every morning, a wide foyer with French mustard walls and grey marble floors, wearing his trainers. I could see an overbearing mother in the background, big-haired and plump, a faded glamour queen clutching her first gin of the day. I saw him getting into a soft-topped sports car and cruising to the gym or the tennis courts. I knew it was a trite, celluloid scenario, yet I felt no desire to replace my fables with the truth. So why did I agree to see him? Because I'd already agreed to see Bob Rosenberg from New York in a hotel lobby at sunset, so I turned that day into a blurring of boundaries, professional and personal.

I saw Bradley turn the corner across the road, a giant among the crowd, wearing tennis shorts and a grey T-shirt with a darker grey 'v' of sweat across his apish chest, and talking on his mobile phone. As he flicked his head in some emphatic gesture, he caught me watching him. There wasn't even a twitch of surprise in his expression when he recognised me – and I was on the lookout for it. He kept to his pace and motioned for me to cross the street. He was still talking on the phone when I followed him into an Italian restaurant. His large, sloppy frame parted its way through waiters and clientele alike as if he owned the place, and for all I knew he did. He chose a booth in the back, and instantly a friendly, moustached waiter appeared, slipping us two menus.

I ordered potato dumplings in a cheese sauce, a green salad, and a glass of red wine. And then he ordered: salad Niçoise, no dressing, olive oil and a slice of lemon on the side, 'a glass of carrot juice – no? All right then, freshly squeezed orange juice and a bottle of sparkling water.' When at last he gave me his full attention, he treated me like an old friend he hadn't seen in ages. Was it because we knew something intimate about each other that he thought we could bypass the formalities?

He explained that it was his business partner on the phone. Could he trust me? He thought out loud, staring boldly into my eyes. 'I trust you,' he affirmed. 'I feel comfortable around you. I feel like we're of the same cloth.' And so he divulged his current business plan in meticulous detail. He was about to open a boxing gym, something big to compete with the Detroit original. He told me everything I didn't want to know about boxing and then said, 'But now I want to talk about you, and the cottage, and what's the story with Angel? And how'd a nice Jewish girl like you get into torturing men? And what do other clients ask for? Give me all the gossip.'

I couldn't think at that moment what it was I wanted to hide and what I wanted to share, but the feeling of comfort was mutual and so it ended up that I opened up to him, and tried in earnest to answer all of his questions. I even told him about my engagement later that day with a stranger named Bob.

Bob Rosenberg from New York had seen my picture in an international fetish directory. Compared to the thousands of voices I'd heard over the years, his was by far the most enthralling. He'd had a dream about me and awoken with a very 'unearthly feeling'. He was coming to London next week, and he wanted us to meet. After I hung up the phone I realised we'd never got around to discussing his fantasy. We arranged to meet on a Saturday. He called again the day before his departure to London and I was just on the verge of asking him his fantasy when he asked if we could meet in the lounge of his hotel for a drink to first get acquainted. 'I have gifts for you, jewels, and a suspicion that we'll fall in love.' And I was wooed.

A final call came on the eve of our meeting. He was nervous, he confessed. He'd been to a gallery that afternoon and seen a portrait of me. Did I know there was a portrait of me in the National Gallery and a postcard version that he held in his hand as we spoke? It was confusing and creepy for a moment, then I guessed what he meant. It had been said before that I look like a woman in a Modigliani painting.

'And how will I recognise *you* in the crowd?'

'Well, I'll tell you, people often mistake me for Michael Caine. I told Michael to his face once, and I teased him, of course, about being the better-looking one. He didn't like that very much.'

So he was on joking terms with Michael Caine. Who *was* this man with the voice of a prince of promise, planting seeds of love and romance?

At half-past six, two doormen welcomed me into the gorgeously tasteful hotel lobby at Claridge's. Chandeliers, beige leather and silver salmon-coloured walls. I gave a cursory glance around me, and then a more thorough inspection, but there was nobody that fitted Bob Rosenberg's description. In fact there was nobody about at all except for an elderly, bespectacled, toadish little man with his trousers pulled up too high, and who was, by some coincidence, walking my way with a twisted grin on his ungainly face. Could it be Bob? Sure enough, it was.

I took it in my stride. He wasn't apologising for misleading me, and I wouldn't give him the satisfaction of seeing me made the fool. However, he was still the same smooth talker and in ten minutes we were drinking excellent champagne, and there were jewels on promise.

'Wouldn't you like your gifts?' he asked after the second glass was poured. I most certainly did. With his dentures beaming at me, he presented me with a large and promising blue velvet box.

'Open it,' he urged.

I did, and the necklace, no wait a minute, I believe it was a waistlet, a gaudy plastic trinket with Christmas-coloured gemstones. I was speechless. Was I supposed to thank him or throttle him?

'Would you like your other gift?'

Frankly, I wasn't sure that I did, but he insisted. The second 'gift' was a red apple key chain that I felt certain came from a duty-free shop at JFK airport. And the third gift was a poem that he'd composed, something he was very proud of; something I felt compelled to shred right away when I got home.

By the third glass of champagne, I was terribly eager to leave when he pulled out an envelope of snapshots. A cut-out of me from the fetish magazine among the pile of snapshots of attractive, smiling young women, one looking playful in pigtails on a swing, one of a woman, her boyfriend and Bob on the beach. They were mistresses he knew on a personal basis, 'friends', he called them. And I guess I was being interviewed to be next in the snapshot.

I was drunk and I was maudlin. I had to ask though. 'So what did you want to explore in a session?'

'Oh God, nothing. I'm too old for all of that. I can't even get it up. No, those days are gone, my child.'

I went home shortly after sunset, very drunk and very maudlin.

*

The following day Bradley called to ask about the prince and we laughed about the toad. He'd invited me out later that week and over onion soup and endive salad with apple, crumbled Roquefort and walnut pieces for me, and sea bass with caviar, new potatoes and samphire for him, he told me his amazing story.

He was an only child who grew up poor. His parents died within a year of each other when he was still a teenager. He dropped out of school when he was sixteen and spent his time between his three surrogate families: a street gang, the community centre's judo club, and a clothing stall at Ladbroke Grove where he made his money selling textiles. He was proud of his street savvy, his photographic memory and his IQ, which he claimed was 149. He had a natural sensibility for textiles and cloth, and was judo wrestling competitively at twenty-one, when he surmised that there was no money to be made that way. He shifted all his energy to textiles and made a name for himself travelling all over Asia and the South Pacific buying fabrics. He started his own company with two friends and it thrived. He claimed millionaire status at twenty-eight.

Then he discovered what he described as a loophole in his banking transactions, a mathematical anomaly that allowed him to duplicate his money and effectively steal ten million pounds from the bank. As far-fetched as it sounded, to his credit he launched into such complicated and technical detail that I was sold on his story. He swore he would have got away with it too if he hadn't been sloppy when selling the business. He was arrested, and months later a scandalous court case ensued. His face hit the newspapers but he never flinched in the courtroom.

He stuck to his story, whatever story that was, and while his collaborators got eight years apiece, he got off with a suspended sentence. He has no official identity, which means no credit and no passport, but a criminal record. He was stripped of his money but managed to retain some property. He became best friends with his lawyer in the process, and they're now in business together.

Bradley drove me home in a soft-top sports car, just as I'd envisioned. But that was the only thing I got right about Bradley. Compared to some of my other clients, his love of feminine features, and the silent hour of bondage made him unspectacular. I had to get outside the dungeon to find out if he was a bank robber or a brilliant liar.

When I met Tullis he was thirty-seven years old, a bachelor, and a missile and aviation lawyer. Inspirationally happy, optimistic, fit, and full of spirit, he was new to domination. I was his first Mistress and he was like an excited puppy whose paws I was forever tearing off my body because, actually, he never got it, never got the boundaries. Besides the negligible nuisance of keeping his hands in check when they weren't tied behind his back, I enjoyed that he let me spank him, cane him, and anally penetrate him. His nipples, like those of so many men, were extremely responsive, and one skilled squeeze sent him to his knees, promising total submission in a throaty, theatrical voice – which was an act really, because the very next minute he was putting his hand up my skirt. I slapped his face, which he loved, and his orgasm was so loud, so over-the-top, that I found it quite alienating.

He came back to see me a few more times over the months

and then, one evening before leaving the cottage, he asked if I was interested in seeing the most beautiful thing.

'Well, of course I am.'

'You need to come outside for this.'

So I put on the rubber mackintosh that I kept for Gideon, and peered over the tall fence onto the street where he was leaning against a rhino-grey S-type Jaguar.

He drove me home in it and I still remember the sensation, the cocooned exhilaration of speeding over Waterloo Bridge with the view of the London Eye, the Houses of Parliament, Bankside, the brown river water like stale cinnamon, the city lights, and driving into Brixton. I invited him into my flat, a block down the road from the Brixton Massive. There we drank white currant tea, platonically.

The following day Tullis used the word 'dastardly' in a text message, and I liked that, and we went to see a play together. We ended up back at his flat in Marylebone where he had a giant painting of a purple plum above his fireplace and an oak treasure chest full of costumes, fancy dress, hats and masks for his amusement. We drank champagne and stood on the sturdy table like children or newlyweds, beaming at each other, singing and bellowing in tone with Nina Simone. We sang about being free, breaking the chains, and removing the bars that keep us apart. I was dressed in a black and gold Japanese kimono, Tullis in a purple velvet smoking gown, and it was wonderful.

And so, and so . . . by the time I met Adam in Soho, waiting with his arms akimbo, I'd done this sort of thing before. That's what I thought, until he looked me straight in the eye, and smiled with the left side of his mouth. I felt something large and heavy, like a truck had run over me, and then I knew that I hadn't done this sort of thing before.

I'm certain he was as beautiful as ever, perhaps more so, but that's not what I remember. It was his dark-blue turtleneck with the snag in the sleeve, and the black hair and eyebrows contrasting with the whites of his gold wedding band and eyes. When he got up to get me a Guinness, I saw he wore the trousers that were slightly too short and the very polished pointy leather shoes that I really disliked.

He told me he'd been in a car accident that afternoon and my first thought was that I caused it, indirectly, and I still believe it.

'But you don't look injured or upset.'

'That's because I'm fine and it's hardly the first time I've been in a car accident.'

That was the first hour of a monumental twenty-hour date. Hour twenty: my flat, on my bed, he said, his expression like a knell, 'There's nothing else to tell.'

His mother was eight months pregnant with him when a tree in a storm fell on the roof of the car. Miraculously she walked away without a bruise or a scratch, and then died of cancer eighteen years later.

'Five, maybe six car accidents, and even more brushes with death since that time in the womb. Had I picked you up in Brixton, it would have been the first time back there since I was sixteen. I was stabbed eleven times at a club there, and I lost four pints of blood. A double miracle, the doctors said, for the knife to miss my vital organs and then to survive such a loss of blood. Susan, I will grow old. When the time comes for me to die, I'm convinced it won't be a surprise. I don't want to die, don't misunderstand, but I'm not afraid of dying.'

I thought: who says this sort of thing? Who's not afraid of dying?

He'd made dinner reservations at the OXO Tower overlooking the Thames, and when it came to crème caramel and coffee I knew that he was thirty-six, that he grew up in North London in a housing estate and that he'd never lived anywhere but North London. He left school when he was sixteen. 'Not for me,' he said. 'I was a rebel, and angry. I liked to fight. But don't worry; I'm not like that any more.'

He got a small job at a big, corporate company where he stayed loyal, and upwardly mobile, for twenty years. It was a long way from a poor childhood and school drop-out to a six figure salary, a four-bedroom house, a BMW M3 sports car (in repair), long vacations, a wife, a three-year-old son, and weekly pain sessions with a dominatrix. His sales job, outsourcing, or whatever it was, was never made clear, but it meant he had a flexible work schedule, spent days away, and nights in hotels, mostly in Birmingham and Leeds. He could work from home or from any of the offices all over England because he did most of his work over the phone. He'd been with his wife for exactly half his life, it transpired. She's seven years older than him, it transpired. A nutritionist and alternative health care consultant. She and I have the same birthday.

Amazing, I thought, that a man of such intense beauty, power and passion could be so ordinary, so routine and conventional. He wears a suit, he wears a handsome suit, he drives to work, he has a son, he has been with the same woman for half his life, the same job for twenty years, same neighbourhoods, same childhood friend, mortgage, gym pass, an Alsatian dog . . .

He ordered sea bass, rocket salad, and something else. I forget what I ate. But I remember that he made me laugh quite unexpectedly. I was grateful for that. On the surface all was calm, but stormy scenes from the dungeon were bubbling beneath. He used to practise yoga, and so do I. He didn't eat salt or refined sugar. He tries to take care of his body, and so do I. He seemed shy, centred, and arrogant. One look at those enormous hands told me he could fix and build things and, in a single blow, destroy them. He would survive catastrophe, thrive in war, and move smoothly and lucidly through emergency. He seemed to possess more power, and be endowed with more gifts, than he knew what to do with.

His talkativeness that night was an exception. Normally, if he wasn't submitting and suffering and speaking a bewitching litany of love, he was by far the most silent, impenetrable, mountainous void of a man I'd ever met. I must remember that.

It wasn't until we were in the cab on the way back to his hotel room in Holborn that we kissed. It was ripe, succulent, timeless; our finest words all evening. My head was full of his perfume when we walked into his hotel room. We made love, or had sex for six, or seven or eight hours, interrupted twice. Once by a text message at midnight from his wife wondering if he was all right.

'I left her a message about the accident. That's her getting back to me, what, ten hours later? I don't think she gives a damn.' And then he laughed, bitterly and sadly.

Another break came at four in the morning, when we left our lair for air, and I bought a vegetable samosa at the petrol station.

We were a perfect match, physically, constitutionally, and

chemically. Entwined, tangled, locked, braided, coiled, side by side or overlapping – we fitted in every way. As if our cells were in celebration, his pelvis rocked with mine, his moans sounded like a sacred cry, and I noticed, even marvelled, how his fingers could trace designs in my imagination. With Adam, every touch, every caress, be it his or mine, was a budding revelation; a seed, a sprout, a bed of possibility. Was it sadomasochistic? It was more than that, but yes, it included that. There was time and appetite for everything. I squeezed his nipples, which caused him pain. I gripped his cock with confidence because I knew exactly what he liked, but the pinching, the tugging, the ball-gripping, side-scratching, lip-biting, tongue-sucking, hair-pulling, ass-fingering, squeezing and slapping were simply born of intense attraction, and what anyone might have done.

On the fifteenth hour, having devoured and been devoured, we lay there digesting and spooning under the covers. The daylight was intruding through a crack between the heavy curtains and I wanted to get up and seal the room for one more hour, but I was too self-conscious and shy to walk naked across the room and have him stare at me, to be so exposed. So I lay there with his breath on the back of my neck, his finger stroking the dip in my waist and the pool of my belly button. 'I feel we've lived out fifteen years in as many hours,' I said. 'I feel the thing's complete. It can end here. Is there anything left to say or do?'

And he squeezed me hard and replied, 'Oh no, Susan, no. These are only hours. Relationships are long and slow; they last years. I hope this is just the beginning.'

When he said it, then I knew that I'd longed for my lover to say it.

We checked out of the hotel at 11:20 a.m. The maid had already knocked twice. I'd fallen asleep for an hour but he says he had none. His manner with the women at the reception desk was intimidating, laconic, almost rude. So that's how he conducts himself with people, I thought. He wasn't very charming, wasn't friendly. I passed through the glass doors of the Holborn hotel into the clamour and razor-sharp daylight feeling tired and lustreless. He'd see it all, my unbrushed hair, my face unwashed, the smearing of yesterday's make-up, my neighbourhood, my flat, my bedroom. I was wearing last night's clothes and I'd missed my morning rituals of reading, stretching, tonics and potions. Frankly, I was relieved to have missed my morning jog. We took the tube to Brixton. I was surprised that he didn't have to work but happy not to let it end. We ate an English breakfast at a café where we found we had nothing more to say. Wait a minute, that's not yet true.

Walking through the common, back to my flat, I asked him what he did to keep so fit since he was no longer practising yoga.

'Have you heard of freediving?'

'No.'

'Have you ever seen the movie *The Big Blue*?'

I vaguely recalled that irritating actress Rosanna Arquette, but what resonated was the word 'diver', whereupon my mind went adrift with aquatic references: the way his body rippled like a dolphin when he took the brunt of pain, his waxy sleekness, the broadness of his shoulders, the tan lines, and those oceanic eyes . . . well, *of course* a diver, a merman . . . water, water, creature of the sea!

*

Freedivers train themselves to dive on a single breath, without an oxygen tank, but why, I don't exactly know. For centuries, women and men have been freediving for pearls as their livelihood. But the extreme sport has evolved, sans pearls. He could dive sixty-nine metres on a single breath, and hold his breath in a static competition for six minutes exactly. It suited him: the silence of deep waters, submersion, subversion, danger, pushing limits, the poetry, the futility . . .

I thought of Bernie and his fifty-five seconds.

CHAPTER 12

Tipping Point

6:54 p.m.: *He's still asleep on the sofa downstairs. I've been silent and motionless for fourteen minutes, only moving from one thought to another while intensely aware of the stiffness in my body, strong emotions and boredom. It troubles me that there's but a few feet separating us, and yet he can't sense my presence. If we were really as connected as I so wanted to believe then wouldn't he feel me suffering for him? But I'm not just doing it for him, I'm also doing it for me, in the belief that conscious suffering will make me stronger. I want to know if there's pleasure to obtain beyond the pain. I'm desperate to stop but my desire to overcome my desperation is still stronger. This is a case of mind over matter. If I stop now, then the last fourteen, now fifteen, minutes will have been for nothing. And I will have discovered nothing. So I stay where I am, and for no particular reason I start thinking of tomatoes.*

How could I do without tomatoes? I tried growing them in the garden. My mother used to slice them and sprinkle them with dried dill and salt. My twin brother can't stand them. Jerome and I used to dry them in the oven at the mansion overnight. I dropped one this evening when I put the groceries on the counter top. And we crushed thousands of them into pulp that summer at a fusion restaurant in Montreal. It was my first job after chef school.

The restaurant was a trendy, Mafia-owned establishment. The waiters were all models, with names like Athena and Jean-Luc, and the head chef was a doe-faced French Canadian whose moods swung between melodramatic melancholy and boyish bursts of creativity. Some said he was an artist and others called him a fool. He favoured radical combinations like peanut butter and butter beans, and semolina cakes with grapefruit-infused corn kernels. It was summertime and I loved it. We made cold tomato soup with watermelon, crushed ice, sherry vinegar and parsley oil. I peeled apart the segments of a lemon, peeled off the thin white membrane until I was left with only yellow, tangy meat, which I added to the Greek salad.

We painted the plates indigo and olive green, dark brown and summer shades, using edible emulsions of beetroot, parsley, blood oranges, pink grapefruit, mangoes, raspberries and blueberries. You mix, say, the blueberries in the blender with a spoon of Dijon mustard until smooth. And then you introduce a light olive oil, one drip at a time, into the purple as it's blending until you have an emulsion thick as desired. We also reduced balsamic vinegar in a shallow pan until it was the consistency of molasses, and transferred all our edible paints into plastic squeeze bottles. Come service time we drew abstract designs, Jackson Pollock and Mondrian-style on enormous white plates that were then carefully stacked with food. The most elegant chocolate-brown ink could be achieved by simply mixing olive oil and cinnamon. We deep-fried the bones of skate fish, which are edible because they become brittle in the hot oil, and stabbed them strikingly into the potato mash. We stacked all the wonderful creations into tall, tenuous towers that teetered – and sometimes toppled – on the way to their destination. Sadly, the looming, hovering, frowning Mafia became convinced the chef was a fool, and strongly recommended he include some traditional staples, such as pasta, on the menu.

Towards the end of summer, dozens upon dozens of crates of Quebec-grown, organic plum tomatoes arrived twice a week, along with an industrial crank-and-pulverise machine that was hand operated and designed to separate the peel and seed from the juice and meat of the tomato, but only after we'd pared the nipple off each tomato and then hand-fed it to the mouth of the machine, one at a time.

For weeks the ripe tomatoes were loaded downstairs in the cellar, and stacked up high. Tomatoes as far as the eye could see in a space that was at least a thousand square feet. If pasta it must be, then the chef was going to preserve only the finest, ripest tomatoes, as well as his integrity. He'd be known for the best home-made pasta sauce. And naturally we made the pasta; beautiful turmeric yellow, parsley green, beetroot rose, and squid-ink silver. If you weren't nimble that day, if you browned the butter or burnt the croutons, or if there was nothing else to do, instead of repose, you were sent downstairs to deal with the tomatoes.

One summer evening, I was made redundant and sent

downstairs with another chef to join the tomato brigade. It was me and Benoit, the three porters, and a slaughter of tomatoes, whole and in purée form that were stored in two enormous barrels. Finally the purée would be poured from barrels into mason jars, sealed with basil, and stacked on the shelves for the winter. The cellar was full of crates of plates, glasses, old cushions, broken chairs, rolled carpets, a chipped toilet seat, and an grimy cement floor. The only way to clean the floor was to hose it down and sweep the water with a metal broom into a drain the size of a tennis ball that was situated in the centre of the room.

I was happy to get away from the kitchen, the summer heat and the chef's sulking mood. Benoit was telling me his plans for the future. He was twenty-two and he wanted to marry his girlfriend next year, work in a hotel kitchen where he could get a pension, and have five children. One of the porters was showing me a wallet photo of his girlfriend in Bangladesh, and the radio was on. I remember it was Bob Marley's 'Don't Rock the Boat' playing when it happened. One of the porters swung around, perhaps he was dancing, but he tripped and fell against the barrel, which toppled on the second barrel . . . 'cause I don't want my boat to be rocking', and what looked like fifty gallons of red liquid flowed like a river, seeping into far-reaching corners of the filthy cellar floor, carrying flotsam and food, and staining the hems of our chequered trousers. It was a bloody mess, an apocalyptic vision, murderous and glorious, and for a moment none of us could do or say anything.

Then, 'We're going to lose our jobs, I'm going to get fired, he's going to fire us!' cried the guilty, panicked porter.

'Try to salvage it!' I ordered.

A flurry, a scattering in search of mops, cups, flour scoops and dust pans – anything we could lay our hands on to skim off the top layer of liquid and return it to a barrel.

'Oh my God, we're going to be fired, we're going to be fired.'

'No you won't,' I assured, although, who knew, maybe he would be fired. 'It's an accident. You just need to hurry up, move it!'

But it was hopeless; bits of food and grime had soiled the winter sauce. How could we serve such filth? No, we needed to changed tactics.

'Stop!' I suddenly ordered. 'Get rid of it. Don't save it; there's no point. Let's just clean it up before the chef comes down!'

In a new wave of panic we dragged the thick sauce into the centre of the room and fed it to the tiny drain. I was crouched down low, busy sticking the handle of a wooden spoon down the hole to prevent blockage and speed up the drainage when we heard the voice of the chef at the top of the steps. Cravenly, bizarrely, we ran back to our stations, me and Benoit to the paring table, the porters to their corner, and resumed as if nothing had happened, as if maybe he wouldn't notice, I don't know.

I remember the following in freeze-frames: the chef's black shoes on the stairs, his thick thighs, his royal-blue initials embroidered into his white jacket, the pouting mouth – then the expanding whites of his eyes. He reaches for an invisible support, then he leans back into a doorframe, raises his hand to his contorted face, opens his mouth to speak, whimper, or scream . . . come on, out with it, please . . . we all freeze . . . but nothing happens, not even a peep. Time has frozen, nobody flinches until Benoit twists his knife into a tomato and the nipple is flung a few inches. I turn to look, and when I look back the chef has disappeared.

We discovered later, after we'd cleaned up the cellar and found the courage to resurface, that the chef had left the building during the dinner service peak, not to be seen again that night. They said he looked drunk or dazed or in pain and he hadn't said a word.

7.00 p.m.: *That makes it twenty minutes. Every minute makes it more unthinkable to quit, and more unthinkable to carry on. Insufferable paradox. I call to him in my head. In my head I say, 'Hear me, if you love me, hear me calling you, feel my discomfort. Wake up and be my witness! See me, see what I've done for you, and release me!' I wait, I wait, and there's nothing.*

And then I start crying. And realising that I won't even wipe away the tears that are tickling my cheeks make me cry that much harder.

When I was ready to work full-time at the cottage, Angel resigned from doing sessions. All her regular clients she palmed off onto me, unscrupulously. Those that were sore about being dumped on a novice didn't return, but Adam the Masochist, Enema Larry, Nuisance Michael, Electrics Bob, Blood Bob, Bald Lez, Whining Wez, TV Mike, Trousers Dan, Mountain Greg, Plastic Man, and others went on to become my regulars instead.

Still, Angel used to greet me every morning. She would walk across the garden in those brown felt slippers of hers, carrying two warm mugs of Earl Grey tea and the diary under her arm. She seemed so together, so organised then. We each kept a diary, and ran a very tight ship. Among other things, I maintained the files and stapled the questionnaires, as well as doing the sessions. She did the laundry, changed the batteries in the vibrators and electrics, bought the toilet paper, the surgical equipment, the lubricant, latex gloves and other supplies. We had two telephone lines, the landline which rang through to the cottage and through to Angel's dark house, and my mobile phone. We ran two advertisements in dozens of magazines and, between us, we received four or five dozen calls on a busy day. I was dedicated, hard-working, and diligent. I answered my mobile twelve hours a day, and worked five, six days a week.

We were back and forth between house and cottage, and spent a lot of time in the garden in those halcyon days. She used to greet me in the mornings in that long, brown, loose-knit cardigan of hers, hair in a rumple, or a new shade or style. We'd consolidate our diaries. Sometimes I brought her a Tupperware of last night's dinner, and we were more like friends than Madam and Mistress. The initial phase of friendship passed like a schoolgirl crush. Everything seemed to culminate in a fit of giggles and side-splitting laughter. We talked while I did the cleaning – she didn't like to clean yet I was a bit obsessive about it. She used to tie my corsets for me. I used to take more trouble with my costume until I ripped a number of outrageously overpriced rubber outfits, and realised that my clients didn't mind or notice when I repeatedly wore the same two or three as long as I still made an effort, and as long as I felt good.

Angel helped me with my make-up while I talked about the client I was about to see. 'He wants something new, something scary, what should I do?' She had experience and some clever ideas. She listened, and supported me in those early days while I talked through my first impressions of domination, submissive clients, cross-dressers, men who wanted to be humiliated, how to make the session flow, how – tactfully – to get them to masturbate near the end of the hour, how to hold a whip, and what to do when they say they want one thing but really want something else. She said I was her best friend before making me her enemy.

She showed me pictures from her past. A chubby, spotty teenager with a bad perm playing the piano in a rather grand looking oak-panelled library – or was it a smoking room or the music lounge? There's a photo of her father standing beside a hazelnut vintage car, a collector's car. His smile was mischievous and handsome. She inherited his eyes. She tells me he's a brilliant lawyer, has a passion for cars. There's one of her mother twenty years ago, slender in bikini and big sunglasses, reclining beside a swimming pool. 'She was a nurse then. And she's always been a bitch, impossible to please, moody, downright frightening. The entire house lived in dread of my mother's bad moods. She was cruel to my father and hideous to me, but my brother was her angel. She used to tell me I was ugly. She sent me to ballet classes, riding lessons, piano lessons, the dermatologist and the beautician just to try and make me a lady.'

When I met Angel she was teetotal, slipping off to AA meetings, visiting the dentist a lot, and dead serious about rock climbing. She used to practise at a climbing wall in Manor House. She taught me rope-tying tricks, which I applied to bondage. She went off to Wales and Scotland on a few climbing expeditions before an old knee injury flared up and she had to quit. Next it was meetings at the Jewish community centre, kabala classes, talks with the rabbi, and reconnecting with her

Jewish identity. When it was warmer outside and the knee had rested, she took up t'ai chi and attended a few ballet classes with me. Through a family connection she swung lessons from a professional opera singer. The sound of her practising travelled through the garden, that is, until her teacher went on tour. And then it was computer hacking, computer games, you name it, she dabbled in it. There were always detailed plans to make fetish videos, plans to renovate the house and the cottage, plans to run a second dungeon from her house, plans, plans, and more plans.

I met her father once. He was even more handsome in the flesh, very charismatic and jocular, but sad and beaten around the eyes. He was down from Yorkshire on a last-minute thing and he thought he'd pay his daughter a visit. It was summer. It was a Saturday. I'd already seen Bernie and Michael, and I felt like calling it a day, but Angel was keen for me to meet her father. 'He'll like you. He'll think you're great. He'll find our friendship reassuring.'

The dungeon was nothing new to him. She introduced us, we had our visit, and then somehow it happened: either Angel wasn't feeling well or maybe something had gone on between father and daughter that I'd missed but, in any case, I found myself having lunch alone with him at a nearby pub. The idea of eating in her filthy house did not appeal to him, apparently.

'The child doesn't eat,' he said, shaking his head. 'Poppy doesn't eat, you know. She puts up a good act. That's for sure. Always has done. You didn't know she was called Poppy? Well, there you go. She's so secretive. She has many disguises. We've been through so much with her, between the drugs, the alcohol, the rehab, the hospitals, the eating disorders. Even as a child she was always sick, often in hospital. Terrible thing, but I started suspecting that she did it to get back at her mother, or to get away, or get some attention. She doesn't get along with her mother. They were at each other's throats since she was nine. Lynda was hard on her, no question, but nothing's changed and I'm worn out from worry. The child's lost. What a waste. And those piercings, the pink dreadlocks, that cyber gothic look, the fads, the false starts . . . and to think I worked hard to send her to good schools. I can't stand it. My heart's dry. But enough of all that. Please excuse me. I haven't said those things in a while, perhaps never. Well then, it's a darn good thing you're Poppy's friend. She needs a friend. Shall we order some lunch?' For a second I thought he might cry but then he looked up and smiled, having quickly recovered his charm.

I felt a fool for not having guessed that Angel had an eating disorder. In retrospect it seemed obvious enough: the hiding in the house, the lies, the deceit, the shame she must feel, the visits to the dentist, dizzy spells, endless cups of soup and tea, all her addictions and demons . . . I changed the topic over a pint of beer and a plate of fish and chips. I told him about a June day in Canada, just over a year before.

I was in Toronto visiting my parents. I'd just quit the restaurant in London and I hadn't yet taken the job at the mansion. It was Father's Day, and I was on holiday, having a lie-in. That evening my siblings, their partners, my nieces and nephews, and my ninety-two-year-old grandmother would be coming over for a barbecue in the backyard. It was nearly eleven when I awoke and, still in my pyjamas, went drowsily downstairs where my mother was waiting for me. She had something she wanted to tell me, and would I please go outside with her and sit down on the porch.

'Why? Just tell me now. I just woke up, what's going on?'

'Please, Susan, please just come sit down outside.'

And so, mildly annoyed at this early urgency, I followed her outside and sat down.

'Well,' she said, containing her calm, 'some of the staff at the school (she worked at a small primary school) have been putting money into a lottery syndicate these last few years, and this morning I got a call from one of the teachers to say that we've won. Now don't stand up just yet because I want to say that I want everyone to share in it. Nobody knows yet. Dad's at the club this morning.'

'I'm so happy for you,' I said standing up and embracing her. 'Nonsense, it's your money, you keep it. I'm so happy for you. How much did you win?'

'I told you to sit down because you're not going to believe it.' I sat down. 'We won the big one, ten million dollars.'

'Mother! You've known that you won ten million dollars for over an hour and you didn't want to wake me up?!' And I got up and embraced her again.

'It's ten million but it's divided among the syndicate.'

'Still!'

'Now listen. Dad's going to be coming home soon. It's Father's Day and I got him a shirt. Don't say a thing when he comes through the door. I'm giving him the shirt that I've bought him and I've written a cheque for the amount we've won which I've stuck in the card.'

And so I told Angel's father how my father came home around lunchtime, and as he walked in the door I ran to wish him a Happy Father's Day. 'Dad,' I couldn't resist saying, 'this is going to be your best Father's Day ever.'

'Oh, I don't know, it's been good so far, what more could I want?'

And when he opened my mother's gift without first reading the card, he said, 'Well you're right, now I have everything. I love it, thank you.' And he gave my mother a kiss on the cheek.

'But the card,' I said. My mother just sat there smiling quietly. And he opened the card, read the sentiment, and looked indifferently at the cheque.

'What's this? Another one of your jokes? This cheque is going to bounce if I try to cash it.'

And then my mother said, 'It'll bounce today, that's true, but it won't bounce on Monday.'

It took a good forty minutes to convince my father (an accountant, born during the Depression, and very cautious with money) that my mother had really, truly won the lottery. And then she sent us away, told us to go shopping and buy anything we wanted while she made some phone calls. In a bleary, giddy daze we wandered through a big shopping mall – and bought not a single thing, even though we could have had it all.

After telling Angel's father about that fantastic day, there was nothing more to say. And I never said anything to Angel, nor she to me until she collapsed a few months later and was taken to hospital. And then it all came out.

We had maybe one good year before things began to separate

and sour. She became less and less reliable. She neglected her duties, hid in her house, stopped visiting me. And she got careless with the phones – when she could be bothered to answer them at all. She made some bad judgement calls and let 'unsuitable' clients pass through the filter. Men who wanted sex; men who had no intention of showing up for their appointment. Thoughtlessly, or greedily, she double booked, overbooked, overlapped, or booked my sessions back to back. I had to turn clients away, which was extremely uncomfortable. These were men that had come from far away, had taken time out of their day to visit, and she didn't care. When I tried to discuss my growing frustration and concern, she told me to go somewhere else if I was so miserable. 'See if things aren't worse somewhere else. You'll realise how good you've had it here. There are lots of nasty dungeons out there, believe me.'

It was a bluff – sort of. She'd be lost without me. Who else was going to put in the time and dedication, and run the place so efficiently? But another part of me feared there was truth to her threat. She knew I'd never worked at another dungeon, and that I was reluctant to begin anew. It was probably true that the city was full of unequipped, unsanitary dungeons where you worked late into the night and gave more than half your money to a mean Madam, paid off a maid to answer the phones and receive the clients, and competed with bitchy, critical women in less sanitised settings. There'd be no garden, no time alone to read, or freedom to make my own hours and set my own pace. There'd be no locking up and getting a falafel when I felt like it. I'd probably have to build up a new clientele since I'd certainly lose most in the shuffle. What if my clients didn't like the new space or location? Where else would I find the quirky charm, independence, and discretion of the cottage? No, I preferred to stay where I was, rather than take my chances somewhere else.

But the truth of the matter was that after a couple of years I felt I was squandering my creative and loving energy. What was I making and what was I taking? I'd prepare sweet and savoury soufflés when most of my clients would have gone away just as happy with a pickled egg. Although he adored me for an hour, I never saw him again. He goes back to his life and his wife and I go home alone. In the dungeon, as with sex, there are no resolutions or conclusions, only pressure, build up and release. Even the most elegant lancing of boils, the finest psychosexual feast, could leave me feeling empty and unfulfilled at the end of the day.

I started hinting to my clients that I was going away and that I didn't know when or if I'd be back. More than anything, I wanted to step back, move forward, and relieve my mind of certain scenarios.

The last thing Adam said to me before closing the door to my flat on our twenty-hour date was, 'Don't be a stranger.' And then he wouldn't allow it. He called me from his car the following day, just to say hello. He had nothing else to say. And the same a couple of days later. Then he dropped by the cottage on his way home from work for a social visit. It was like no other time he'd been in that space. And it was a challenge to us both. We embraced right away and I found myself ensconced in lavender-scented laundry detergent and spicy aftershave. I felt safe and protected in the shade of such towering manliness. You could say I was losing my power, shedding my role. It was distressing and disorientating, for I didn't know how to be. He held me at arm's length, studied my face, and to his happy discovery he saw that I was shy.

'What? Why do you smile like that?'

'I like you being shy. It's beautiful. It's honest.'

And so it registered with me, with relief and suspicion, that he was just as pleased to see me vulnerable. I let him see his file. I wonder what he thought when he saw himself labelled Adam the Masochist. Did he see himself that way? He flipped through the paper trail – years worth of sessions, four different Mistresses . . . but he must have been disappointed to find nothing more psychologically telling than: nice, polite, not submissive, takes medium amount of pain . . .

We went into the dungeon, where I bent over the whipping bench that had already been wiped clean twice that day of someone's nervous sweat, and hugged it in a playful sort of way. I liked his strength behind me. I felt his enormous hand touch the back of my thigh, the inside of my thigh, the heat of my groin. Slowly I felt my skirt rising and then my knickers being lowered to my knees . . . It wasn't just the excitement of being half naked and half dressed, it was his control, his confidence, something supremely expert in his touch. I felt his lips kissing my bare bottom, and his sagely fingers stroking the backs of my knees and the top of my spine. He spanked me, caressed me, was very gentle with me. I could feel the silk and the bulge of his trousers against my hot flesh . . . before he made me climax. And then, phantom-like, he vanished, went home to his wife, his son, his home-cooked dinner and the rest of his life.

I met him on his lunch break in the City. We sat on a park bench in Finsbury Circus surrounded by a circle of suits. I touched his nipple over his pink shirt, and it gave him an erection. It was a strange tableau: the green lace of trees, the affair, the married businessman, the masochist, the Mistress in trainers with a book and ballet tights in her knapsack.

He met me after my ballet class on a Sunday afternoon. I noticed the way his eyes lit up when he saw my healthy glow and perceived my grace and self-discipline. We went shoe shopping at Selfridges because his pointy, polished leather ones looked ragged and old. To please me he bought a pair of patent-leather square-toed shoes, but I learned later that he hid them in his car so as not to arouse his wife's suspicion.

Of his wife, he said practically nothing. He called me from his bathtub after they'd had an 'enormous row'.

'What was the fight about?'

'Nothing. Never is. Actually, to be fair, we don't normally fight. We don't normally talk. I take out the garbage, she cooks dinner. We operate on automatic.'

'Is she a good cook?'

'No, not really.'

'How can you share the same bed and not talk?'

'We sleep in separate bedrooms and we haven't had sex in three years.'

'How can you live like that?'

'People do it all the time.'

Do they? How awful.

He called me from Hawaii where he was competing with free-divers from around the world. I was at the cottage reading *Madame Bovary* between clients. He was on a beach at sunset. I was using the gynaecological chair as a chaise-longue, my legs resting in the stirrups. He'd just broken his record for the fifth year in a row. I was going to a ballet class in Farringdon if this six-thirty bondage and CBT guy didn't confirm. I wanted to be on a beach in Hawaii. He wanted to be in a North London suburb with me.

A few times he left his house at five in the morning, drove south to Brixton, missing the traffic and breakfast with his son, so he could crawl into bed with me for an hour or two before going to work. That arrangement couldn't last but such was the urgent state of our passion, hunger and excitement. That was September, October, November.

Things literally came to blows one morning with Angel and me. Judging by the violence of the knock on the cottage door and then the sight of her flushed, windswept face, she had stormed across the garden with a mission. She wanted to tell me that she didn't like my tone of voice. She was sick to death – that's what she said, sick to death – of trying to please me. 'You're an unforgiving perfectionist. You're arrogant. You're cold and critical. I live in fear of your sneers, of listening to your teeth suck if I've done something wrong. Sick of thinking: have I made a mistake? Is Anna going to criticise and humiliate me today? Did I screw up the schedule, should I take the telephone into the toilet with me? Fuck it, I'm not perfect and I'm sick of you bullying me like I'm one of your bloody slaves.' Her lip was quivering, and her eyes were wild and livid. She seemed on the verge of foaming or exploding when, instead, she sucker-punched me, crazy thing, and ran back home through the garden.

When I try to understand how it came to such a violent end my right eye and temple begin to throb with pain. Where had all that hatred come from, and how was I to blame? Violent fantasies assailed me at that moment, but I left it at that, feeling victimised, traumatised and sorely shaken. I walked to the high street pub, where I drank whisky before lunch and wrote Angel an interminable letter, in which I unleashed all my bitter, poisoned feelings, and let them run rampant across the page. But by page sixteen I was working through regret and shame for having given so much grief to such a fragile child. I don't know, by then it was nearly two, and I was drunk.

I threw away the letter, journeyed back to Brixton, and spent the next two weeks wrapping things up at the cottage informing my regulars that I was leaving, and seeing as many regulars as I could. She stayed out of my way. I made two thousand, six hundred pounds, gave her a very reduced cut, stole a Wagner CD, and dropped the keys through the letter slot in her door. I've heard rumours but I haven't seen or spoken to her since.

I'd been wanting to get out of London and take a break from domination for so long; and now the time had come. I went to Istanbul to stay with my friend, the young English diplomat with whom I'd lived in the Brixton Massive. He'd been living in

Turkey nearly a year and had played the generous host to many of his friends. He said I could stay as long as I liked. Two months was my plan, and Adam drove me to the airport.

He called me every morning in Istanbul. It was nothing that he said because, as I've stressed, he wasn't a talker, but he made himself a daily presence in my life. Intimacy evolved with every phone call. I began to suspect that the physical distance and those five minute talks were the new constraint, and that our relationship would only thrive in the presence of constraints.

I had been in Istanbul for six weeks when he called one evening to say he'd taken off his wedding band. I couldn't breathe when I hung up the phone. And then all I could do was breathe in a whirlwind of comprehension, apprehension, fear, possibility, and the absence of constraints. He was leaving his home, his wife, he would stay with me. He's so extreme. Did I want this? What was this? I remember his eagerness, his clean-shavenness when he greeted me at the airport and the silence of driving back to Brixton, where, together, we'd live without constraints.

CHAPTER 13

Steps

7:21 p.m.: *Forty-one minutes without moving from this pose is one of the craziest things I've done. I've overcome myself, having passed through mental, physical, and emotional barriers. And what have I gained? I'm afraid to move – petrified, in fact. My joints are locked into place. My blood and bones have fallen asleep and I'm afraid to wake them up. It's him who needs to wake up. And yet the whole meaning and significance of the gesture would be lost if I were to stop. He needs to find me and release me; suffering makes no sense without him. But then I cheat by quietly whispering his name. He doesn't hear me. I called him again, this time louder, and pleadingly . . . and damn it, still nothing! The light has faded and I'm hungry. It's finally insufferable. And yet I'm almost relieved when he doesn't awake to my call. I don't want to spoil such a heroic effort by cheating. And so I bribe myself, tell myself just a little longer, five more minutes, and then I'll give up.*

*

We slept in the same bed that first night living together, but I couldn't bear to have him touch me. His infatuated gaze frightened me. The change in our circumstances had been too sudden, too extreme. We'd probably spent a total of eighty-six hours, or four days, together, spread over a period of years, and now we were to spend every unstructured, unconstrained night and day together. It was radical. What if we'd made a mistake? We didn't even know each other.

He'd just walked out on an eighteen-year relationship, breakfast and bedtime with his son five days of the week, the handsome home he'd worked so hard to buy, his chiropractic rubber mattress, Jacuzzi bathtub, staid routine and solitude, just to live with me, in Brixton, until he bought a new flat. Yes, it was rash, but on the other hand, as my friend Louise said, 'Why waste time? Why *not* see if it works?' I told myself, and he confirmed, that I was the catalyst to his walking out but not the cause of his marriage's collapse. But when he ducked his head as he passed through the door and entered my bedroom for the first time, I caught him at an angle or in a light I'd not seen before: who's that tall man standing in my room? Was he awkward, ugly, callous and cruel? Was he crazy, empty, lazy? Did I even like him?

But in the morning I woke up in a perfect coil, my ankle resting on the soft arch of his foot, my arm in the fold of his, my hand wrapped around his thick wrist, the small of my back cupped in the basin of his firm, soft belly, my bottom in the hammock of his silk-haired groin. I awoke to him kissing my shoulder, which he insisted was his favourite thing. And that night we discovered new ways of kissing and touching. I sucked his chin. He sucked my tongue until I got scared; it's such a vulnerable thing. I kissed fourteen of his teeth. He pressed all of my buttons.

I woke up extra early to cook him breakfast while he slept. I steamed greens, toasted and buttered rye bread, fried two eggs with the whites completely cooked and crispy at the rim and the yolk thick and runny. I made a cucumber carrot tomato salad with some mint and feta and sunflower seeds, and lemon juice and flax-seed oil and brewed the coffee. I watched him dress for work, put on the pinstripe suit trousers, the cufflinks, knot the tie, and disguise his amazing nudity in order to become City Man.

In the evening we made our first trip to the supermarket and tittered over the oddity and novelty of sharing everyday activities like choosing tea, discovering that he liked rice milk, showing him how to pick a ripe melon, buying toilet paper, him buying razor blades and shaving cream. He hung my clothes up to dry, I stirred the sauce; he stripped the onion, layer by layer. I kissed his sweet coffee breath and we held hands in the park. The first week was extraordinary in a very ordinary way.

Our crash course in cohabitation called for some creative means of catching up and getting acquainted, so I invented a game that took three days for us to play. The object was for each of us to write down three lies about our past, our aspirations, our fears, things we had done, etc. without telling the other, seal them in envelopes, and spend the next three days trying to convince the other of our lies, while listening for theirs.

On the third day we sat down across from each other at the dining-room table with the envelopes in front of us and took turns guessing each other's lies. I had convinced him of nothing and he'd convinced me of everything. And I thought I was a fabulous liar. Maybe that was my problem; the lies I chose were too ambitious, too extravagant. His lies were much more subtle and prosaic. Still, coming at the truth from the back door, so to speak, felt exciting and subversive. It seemed to be our way.

He came up with the game on the stairs a few days later. The idea was simple to begin with, but it evolved into an enduring and intricate dialogue, an art form. We took turns waiting on the landing at the top of the stairs, naked on all fours and completely still. He chose that position because of its submissiveness, its exposure, and for its beauty and elegance. It was a statement of readiness and willingness; it was an offering of openness. Whoever was home first the following evening would text the other to say so. They in turn had to say when they'd be back and text again when they were exactly ten minutes away, at which point the other would get into position.

It was me who arrived home first on the following day. When I received the ten minutes text, I removed my bathrobe and folded it under my knees to protect them from the hardwood floor when I got down on all fours. I dropped my head, hung my ankles over the top step, and waited. And discovered the challenge of staying perfectly still for even one minute. Try it and you'll know what I mean. I felt the strain in my lower back and a stretch in my wrists. Imperceptibly, I adjusted my weight for better support, although nobody but me would know if I suddenly decided to move.

My body caught a draught, my nipples were erect, and my mind would not relax. I kept thinking about what he'd see and how he'd react when he walked in the door and looked up the stairs and saw me there: the soles of my feet, the backs of my thighs and my slightly raised ass and tensed back. It was still light outside; the light was penetrating the flat. He was going to see me as he'd never seen me, as I'd never seen myself. The hair between my legs, the slit between my ass, my callused heels, my bunions, scars and blemishes. Would he see my imperfections or would he see only beauty and willingness? Will he find what he sees erotic? In the dungeon I hid behind my costume, the hazy light, and an invulnerable role. Here I felt exposed, self-conscious, and foolish.

My mind wandered through negative terrain and trampled through doubts, but I also felt brave, beautiful and excited. I had the sense that I was hallowing myself, and it felt sanctified. And embarrassing. I wondered if in doing what I was doing I'd lose my embarrassment and self-consciousness, and therein temper my vanity. Do I want that? Is that ideal? Is that freedom? Isn't there such a thing as getting too familiar with nudity? What about mystery? What about the partial view, the fleeting glimpse, the suggestion, the taste, the tease, the appetiser? What about the tension between wanting to hide and wanting to be exposed?

Who else would do this for him? Nobody. Nobody else does this. Will it be my vulnerability that pleases and excites him? Or the opposite – my boldness, my strength, my dedicated effort. What's he going to *do* when he sees me? He has permission to do as he pleases with me. Does he know what pleases him? Can he separate his own pleasure from wanting to please me? Can they ever be separate? Will I submit? I am already submitting. How will he receive my effort?

My knees were hurting and so was my back and I was getting bored by the time I heard the key turn in the lock and then it was my heart thrown open. Interesting how his presence changed everything. I forgot my physical discomfort, I'd stopped waiting, and my self-consciousness became intense, acute. He slipped off his shoes as quietly as a thief, and then I heard his trousers rub and the stairs creak as he climbed closer, closer, out of step with the wild drumbeat of my heart, the flow of thought in my head. What does he see? What does he think? What's he going to do? Is he pleased? I did not move.

Say something, do something, acknowledge me, I thought in my stillness and silence. I felt the air spinning off his clothes, saw the cuffs of his trousers, felt good, felt happy he was there. And then he was going, going away! I couldn't believe it. He walked right past me and disappeared into the adjacent room. I collapsed inside. I didn't move an inch but I collapsed all the same. 'Coward,' I thought. And cruel. I'd waited ten minutes, naked, cold, uncomfortable and embarrassed for nothing. Was it not enough? Did he think I should wait longer? Endure more?

But then I realised he was stalling, not to be cruel, not to shock, not to prolong my discomfort, but because he didn't know what else to do. *What would you do?* His reaction was honest; it's difficult to be given so much freedom. I will remain still and silent for as long as it takes.

I did not wait long, for the response was in the ear. When I realised that the sound of tumbling silk and falling cotton was the sound of him undressing, then the sound of his nudity, I was brought to life with desire.

A couple of days later the vision I saw on the top of the stairs was his firm bottom, his broad back dipping, and his intense stillness.

He was so severely silent, and the vision so startling, so powerful, that it's branded in my mind. He turned himself into a gift that evening, a statue, an entrée, a feast for my eyes. I saw my lover supplicating and offering himself to me – and that was enough. I didn't want to *do* anything, I really didn't, but he was waiting, and I knew what that was like.

I climbed the stairs and then I saw he was biting the handle of a whip and two clothes pegs were clamped on his nipples and there was a strawberry on his back. My lover was an artist. My lover made this effort just for me. It was beautiful and I thought: people should see this vision of a lover's sheer effort.

But he was waiting. I could do whatever I wanted to do to him, but he'd suggested the whip. So he wanted to be whipped by me, or for me, because he thought it would please me? Does he want pain or does he want to show me that he'll hurt for me? It was too confusing. He wants me to be myself but he wants that self to be a Mistress, to be strong, sexual and persuasive; a vixen, a vision, the one who can fix him.

I'd never whipped him before because the whip left marks. I bit the berry and took the whip from his mouth and gave him a fruity kiss. I teased him and prepared him with the suede tails of the whip before I swivelled and got ready to strike him with full force. I saw his effort not to move. I was still wearing my coat and the neighbours were downstairs. I snapped my wrist like a lion trainer and landed one heavy lash across his bare ass. The adrenaline, not knowing how he'd react, the sound of the smack, my expert aim were but brief rewards before the tidal wave of his roar. He sounded so angry and resentful, and that in turn made me angry and resentful; I was not his foe and he'd turned on me again. He gives me power and then he yanks it away. Who put the whip there in the first place? I was upset, but I leaned over his body and kissed his moist neck, and at the exact same time we whispered, 'Thank you.' And it was over for the night.

The next time, I bought three bunches of roses, three different shades of pink, and plucked off the petals of all but three flowers. I made a trail of the petals leading to me, and then beyond and into the bedroom where I sprinkled the white duvet and the pillowcases with powder-pink petals. When I got into position, I put the last three thorny rose stems between my teeth – that prickly mouthful was a trial. And I'd placed the whip on the floor in front of me and thought about nothing but the unknown pain that awaited me.

Having whipped so many others, I thought the time had come for me to surrender. I was investing him with so much trust and power, I was curious to see how he'd use it. Meanwhile, it made me feel brave and emboldened to submit to a painful unknown. I wanted him to be impressed and surprised. Instead, he took me by surprise.

Carefully, he took the flowers from my mouth and lay them under the tent of my body and said, 'Turn over and lie on your back.' Was he testing me? I'd prepared to be whipped but I hadn't offered this. Was he bluffing? Did he really want me to lie down on a bed of thorns when there were petals and pillows in the bedroom? To test myself, to shock him, and because it was such a romantic image, I lay down on the floor, on the thorns, and faced my handsome lover with a sly smile on my face. And actually, it didn't hurt; it wasn't so bad.

It was worth it, worth the response: his gratitude, his musty excitement, his salient eyes, my name being chanted over and over again in that underwater voice of his. Then he turned me over and kissed my scratches, licked my wounds and cradled me from behind. Then he penetrated me from behind, holding my frame and kissing the nape of my neck. After we showered and dressed, he dropped to his knees and kissed my feet most devotionally. And then we went out for dinner.

Next time I sent Adam a text to say I was about twenty minutes away, he replied that he was going to begin. So he wanted to extend the time he waited motionless in position. I came back twenty-six minutes later by no fault of my own, and there were tea lights, dozens, guiding me to him. When I found him, he was on all fours with a full cup of water balanced on his back, and the handle of the whip was inserted in his backside. He looked like a donkey or a pony, and it was startling. All the possibilities of our art opened up to me, gave me hope, and inspired me. I was in love with him. In love with the idea of us. In love with our way of loving. I tipped the cup of water and let it trickle down his lower back and watched him struggle not to move. 'You are an incredible man,' I said, as I slowly extracted the whip.

And so it evolved. I balanced piping hot tea; he burned me. I whipped his hands; he held his pose for thirty minutes. I slapped his face. He squeezed my nipples and spanked me with a wooden spoon. I balanced weights; he posed in a ring of fire.

I prepared for him a stunning feast. I steamed opal rice until it was cooked and cloudy and the grains held their shape. I fanned the rice to cool it quickly in one hand and folded it gently with a spatula and the other hand. I did everything as I had seen and done it at a Japanese restaurant where I worked in Montreal. I seasoned the sushi rice with syrup made of sweet mirin and rice vinegar, drizzling a couple of tablespoons over the rice and gently folding simultaneously so that the syrup evenly glazed the grains. And then I moistened a muslin cloth with warm water and placed it over the cooked rice. I made miso soup. I sharpened my knife on a clay stone. I sliced the pink belly of deep-red tuna into quarter-inch strips. I peeled and sliced a ripe avocado, which is such a satisfying thing, and shaved raw beetroot and carrot into paper-thin slices and then used my knife skills to shave the orange and purple strips into the finest angel hair. I mixed wasabi powder and water into a thick paste. I washed my hands. I followed a rhythm, I was precise and efficient, and I thought of him throughout. I fingered the rice onto a sheet of nori seaweed in such a way as to spread it without crushing it. And then I placed the ingredients in the centre and rolled as I've practised doing. Finally, I prepared a seaweed salad and a dessert serum, and sliced a honeydew melon, squirted it with lime juice and sprinkled it with finely chopped spearmint.

About twenty minutes before he was due to arrive, I took a bath. After drying myself, I rubbed a thin layer of sesame oil into the flesh of my back, shoulders and bottom. And the dessert serum – maple syrup thinned with ginger tea – I massaged into my belly and my breasts and on the inside of my thighs. I rinsed the bath and ran it scalding hot so it would be just right for him when he arrived. I placed a cup of sake on the side of the tub. It would lose its heat and be tepid to his lips, but that would have to do. I lit the candles and left a clean bathrobe and slippers by the side.

I cleared a space in the living room, where I rolled out a blue batik tablecloth and placed the bowl of melon, a cup, and a pot of green tea. In the kitchen, I sliced the maki rolls and transported all the food on a tray to the living room. And then came the very awkward, painstaking bit. I got down on the cloth, on my hands and knees, and transformed myself into a table onto which I slowly, carefully, placed the food. Slices of maki one at a time, the seaweed salad on a square of banana leaf, the juice running down my sides, a mound of pickled ginger, a mound of wasabi and, finally, most delicately, the small cup of miso soup, not quite full but warm to the touch, I balanced on the flat of my coccyx. And then I put a pair of chopsticks in my mouth and waited.

A couple of minutes later, no longer, I heard the key in the lock, and then a silence which I interpreted as him reading my note which instructed him to bathe and then come to the living room with his appetite, where I'd be waiting. He talked about his desire for my body in terms of food all the time. I heard the splash in the tub, the quiet of his footsteps, and finally the sweet sound of his amazement. He took the chopsticks from my mouth and ate in silence. Afterwards, as suggested in my note, he turned me over to eat the melon off my maple-glazed chest.

He would wash my hair, dab my fingers dry, anoint me with almond oil or olive oil, powder me, brush my hair. I sponged his back, lathered him with spicy soaps, kissed his long wet eyelashes and the caps of his knees. He loved the water. He looked most himself, most unearthly in the water. How many times had I photographed him in the water, or just sat at the edge of the tub, reading out loud to him. So many times I kneeled and kissed his large, soft, sturdy feet and shapely ankles with the concentration of a supplicant, the fervour of a worshipper. I felt I'd become myself, and yet transcended myself while I worshipped his beauty. I felt so present, and such abandon. I was nourished by the act, fuelled by his response.

We covered our bodies in costume paint one colourful, fantastical night. We drew words on each other's body, words that we wore under our clothes throughout the day. I wrote letters and notes to him by the dozen, by the hundreds. I sketched him. I prepared spectacular meals for him. He tied me up, wrapped me in breathtaking compliments, and ravished me whole, wholly, and in minuscule mouthfuls that took hours to savour and digest. Once we tied ourselves together and slept that way all night. Once I rewarded him with five minutes of naked ballet.

Our relationship became a series of rituals and intensifying demonstrations. We took the time that was required, and made the concerted effort to transform everything ordinary into something extraordinary. It was the point of our union, the purpose of our chemistry. We were both drawn to the extremes of expression.

7:48 p.m.: *I've been getting through every second by clinging to the hope that in the next he'll wake up and rescue me. It's gone on like that for sixty-eight minutes, and so I get up. My bones feel ancient and brittle, like shards of glass, like snapping twigs, and as I feared, exactly as I feared, the resuming flow of blood, the waking of my muscles and creaking of my bones is more painful than the sixty-eight minutes of bondage. I can't remember having ever felt more defeated and saddened. And lonely, unbearably lonely. I get partially dressed and go downstairs to wake him up.*

He's lying on his side, his arms folded, and I shake his shoulder and call his name until he opens one eye. I ask him to come upstairs. I ask persuasively. He nods and makes an affirmative sound, so I go upstairs and get into bed.

Should I tell him what I'd done while he was sleeping? How can I keep such a thing from him? But if he knew that I suffered while he slept, that would surely upset him. It would be more difficult but less hurtful not to mention it. That's my conclusion. All I really want is his presence, his attention, his acknowledgement; that's all I've been craving for the last hour. And now where is he? I refuse to call him again. It's ridiculous, and I can't bear to go through the waiting all over again. Tears of abysmal frustration began to blur my vision, and then the silhouette of him was hovering in the doorway.

At last he had come to me. Thank God he'd come to me. Then he turned me over on my belly without saying a word. I don't think he knew I was crying. I don't think he knew anything. But what did it matter? I was suddenly so happy that at long last he had come to me. All that agony had vanished as he raised my top to my shoulders and lowered my trousers and knickers to my knees. He could do what he pleased. Then I felt the caress of a thick felt marker tracing designs on my back, down my spine, along my sides, across my bottom, and down the backs of both legs. The last traces of loneliness were erased, replaced by scribbles on my back.

'Don't you want to know what I've written all over your body? Should I read it to you?'

I nodded, but it didn't really matter because he'd said so much already.

'Grace, beauty, elegance, intelligence, dignity, strength, bravery, foxy and fiery, strange Mistress Susan . . .'

My nose was running and I was shivering, I felt more lamb than fox, but I was very happy.

CHAPTER 14

Distortion

In April, when I'd been living with Adam for over a month, I heard about a dungeon in central London that had vacancies. A few thousand sessions had taught me a lot, but I recognised there were limits to how much I could learn in the dungeon, especially since my journey had taken a deeper, more intimate turn. But the plain fact was I needed money. It had been nearly four months since I'd worked. I remember thinking that domination had finally become a job, a great job in many respects, but a job nonetheless. I was an experienced, skilled, sensitive dominatrix. I could work three days a week and still fund other interests and activities. So I arranged to meet this new Mistress at her dungeon in the basement of her flat off the Tottenham Court Road.

There were two entrances – one leading directly to the basement, and the other, at street level, led me into her living room. It was a bright, airy, magnolia-painted room with varnished hardwood floors, a white plush rug, a fireplace with an enormous gilded mirror over it, a framed Georgia O'Keefe print on the adjacent wall, tall lilies in pretty vases, and a red velvet settee by the muslin draped windows. I remember the natural light, the sounds coming in from the street, the open windows and the muslin blowing in the breeze. It felt sort of ticklish and thrilling to be privy to this new scene.

The tall, slender woman with the amazing cheekbones, stringy blonde hair, wide blue eyes and an endearing dimple on her left cheek introduced herself as Mistress Ariel. She was forty-seven years old but looked at least ten years younger. She swore by wheat-grass juice and facial exercises every morning. She was born and raised in Ireland, educated at 'good Catholic schools', earned a bachelor's degree in Irish literature, and had worked in the social welfare department until four years previously, when she met some people on the fetish scene. It started with the clubs, and then the smaller parties with the 'serious players', and it wasn't long before she befriended a couple of Mistresses. She found herself at the centre of a vibrant, cool new subculture where men treated her like a goddess. She was so dizzy and delighted with this lifestyle that she quit her office job and began working as a dominatrix.

Mistress Ariel was not an industrious, highly motivated woman, although she wouldn't have seen it that way. When it came to professional domination, she did one or two – maximum three – sessions a day, three days a week, charged two hundred pounds an hour, and complained about bad arches, sore wrists, draining sessions, whining men, and not being in the mood. She wanted to rent out the basement three days a week at a flat rate of two hundred pounds a day.

Angel and I had advertised in fetish magazines, even a car

retail magazine, and over the years I'd built up a regular clientele of over thirty. There came a time when I no longer relied on newcomers. The central chambers, on the other hand, operated off the tacky phone cards one used to find plastered in phone boxes all over central London. Police put an end to the practice, and there aren't enough phone boxes in use or existence anymore. The cards and the central location attracted a very different sort of client than I was accustomed to receiving at the cottage: men on their lunch break, tourists, horny and curious guys on a whim, men who wanted a simple tie-up-and-tease session – or sex. They didn't get the sex and, on the whole, it was a less inspired, seedier, more transient clientele.

In the four months that I was out of service, I'd lost most of my regulars. They'd either found someone else in the interim or, of the dozen or so men who stayed in touch, half found the central chambers too indiscreet a location, or else they didn't like the environment of the chambers themselves, which, aside from being larger, were admittedly shabby, dilapidated, and unimaginative. But instead of investing in new advertisements and committing to the job and the location long-term, I worked almost entirely off those phone cards.

At the central chambers a maid answered the telephone, booked the sessions, and charged fifty pounds a day plus ten per cent commission for every client she pulled in. Her name was Brittany and she was fifty, but like Ariel she looked ten years younger and she was beautiful. There were almost no wrinkles on her peaches and cream complexion. Her beauty secret was a combination of not smoking, not sitting in the sun, and never washing her face with soap or water. She always wore a wig, a blonde fringe, and carried a Versace bag or other expensive accessories. She had never done any work outside of the sex industry, never married, and was unable to have children. She'd been to the Heffner mansion as a Playboy bunny and had been a high-class escort to rich Arabs, business tycoons, rajahs, and princes. Later, she'd worked as a dominatrix, but for the last twelve years she said she was completely fulfilled in her work as a maid in dungeons and brothels.

She'd seen it all and done it all from every angle in the industry, yet she seemed completely ignorant, almost naïve, when it came to almost everything outside the sex industry. By three o'clock she was tipsy from the rosé that she uncorked at eleven in the morning. But until six in the evening, when she started repeating herself and slurring her words, she was full of fascinating stories.

Brittany must have been the best maid in the business, gifted as she was with the powers of persuasion. Each time the phone rang it was as if that genius voice of hers made itself a hand that reached through the telephone line and grabbed the caller by the collar, pulling him into the dungeon. An uncanny talent combined with a hustling, mercenary nature – and certainly my ability to keep up – made for some busy days. It wouldn't have been worth my clients' time to travel all the way to a North London suburb for a half-hour session, but in central London, Brittany could persuade anyone to come along for half an hour at a hundred pounds. The half hours added up and were most lucrative in the end, but they came at an expense: she would invite anyone to the dungeon, and I could do nine, ten sessions a day, almost back to back. Get them in and get them out, that was her thinking, whereas I was missing my regulars, and more involved, in-depth sessions.

My fondest memories of that place are of Brittany before six p.m. For the first time in my dungeon career I was never alone at work. She was aware of my every session. She kept me in the mood, bolstered my confidence, got me motivated. She used to make guest appearances in my sessions, depending on the client. I had her laughing at ballet boy doing his pliés, and even Trousers Dan got a visit from her – which he adored and still talks about. She was great fun, and it took immense restraint not to laugh when she came on the scene.

One day Mackintosh Gideon visited me at the central chambers.

He got himself undressed in the dungeon, and in the reception room I told Brittany all about him. She suggested I lock him in the closet in the hallway where the door was heavy and sticky, the lock finicky. She suggested that I pretend the lock got jammed so he'd think he was really trapped in the closet. So I did it. I was tipsy on rosé and although I suspected he wouldn't like it, I didn't really care.

I gagged him, hooded him, shackled him, attached weights to his balls, cuffs around his ankles, a collar around the neck, a ring around his cock. I teased his nipples, teased his mind, wore the mackintosh, and then locked him in the closet 'for a very, very, long time. Long enough to get a taste of the future. Time to meditate on your fate as my slave. You'll be here for ever.'

Back in the reception room Brittany poured us some wine and

we watched the cookery channel. After about twelve minutes, I went back to check up on Gideon.

'What's it like in there?' I spoke through the door. 'Feels like a long time, doesn't it? Feels like an eternity I bet, and it's only been seven minutes. And to think I have you for ever. When I come back, whenever that is, I'm going to bring my whip.'

Ten minutes later: I pretend to fiddle with doorknob and lock.

'The door appears to be stuck. Don't go anywhere while I get the maid.'

And then Brittany's shrill, 'Oh no, Mistress, I should have warned you about that door! That lock's sticky so we always keep it slightly ajar. This happened once before and we had to call the locksmith. He took three hours to get here. But we're not going through that again. Let me look for the spare key because I know there's one around here somewhere, we just didn't look hard enough last time.'

And then, after several moments, I flung open the door.

His penis was soft. I caressed his nipples but he didn't respond. I removed the gag and then the hood and he was really unimpressed. He was upset. He was scared. The real prospect of hours kept in a closet had no sexual appeal. And I'd known that, but I'd done it all the same. It took a lot of slow mackintosh seduction to make it up to him, and he finally ejaculated.

Another time a young tranny called up to ask if, since he was in the area, he could pick up his clothes that he had left there two years ago. It was a slow day and Brittany went to work on getting some money out of him.

'Well I don't know if they're here, but come along for a session while I take a look. You're extremely lucky today because Mistress Anna is here and she's absolutely gorgeous. She's young, she's Canadian, and between you and me, she's the best Mistress I've ever come across. You can afford such a privileged half hour while I look for your things – things, I might mention, that have had the benefit of free storage all this time. We actually charge for that sort of thing, but never mind, I remember you. I remember you had some lovely pieces . . . a silk blouse you say . . . stunning if I recall . . . and the shoes, what colour were they again? Ah, yes, I can certainly see why you'd want to get those things back.'

He rang the basement buzzer fifteen minutes later and Brittany led him into the dungeon. When I went in the room to greet him, it looked like he was there against his wishes.

'So what would you like to explore today?' I asked. He spoke lowly, slowly, weakly, said that when he felt like it he was into dressing-up and maybe an office scenario, but he didn't have his clothes with him for that.

'That's okay, we have plenty of outfits here. I'll find you the right thing. And what do you explore after you're dressed up?'

'I'm in the office. I'm a secretary and the boss is unhappy with me again, wants to humiliate me and embarrass me in front of my female colleagues, tell me I'm no good at the job, that I'm different from the other girls, etc.'

Back in reception, Brittany was waiting with a ruffled, powder-pink blouse, a grey pencil skirt and mauve high heels with the strap and button around the ankle – everything he'd left behind years ago. I looked at the clothes, and then at her, and she at me, and I could see we had the same idea.

I went back to the dungeon with a red spaghetti-strap dress, very slutty, fishnet stockings, a black and red suspender belt, shiny red stilettos, a black thong, and a long blonde wig. 'Put these on,' I said. 'When I come back in about four minutes, we'll begin.'

While he undressed in the dungeon, I undressed in the reception room. And then I put on the nicely fitting pencil skirt, the pink ruffled blouse, also very flattering, and the shoes – a size too large, but manageable.

Back in the dungeon he was standing, now dressed, in the middle of the room. 'Lower your head. Face the ground,' I said right away. 'Well, well, look at you. Look at you. So this is the kind of trash off the street they send us these days from the temp agency. I'll have to have a word with them, but as for the likes of you on this very busy day' – firmly eyeing him up and down – 'you look like you've been out all night on some boozy bender and you went home with a low-life man that ripped your clothes off, or rather you ripped them off, and then saw them as suitable attire to wear to the office on your first day. Is that how it went? Phew, you smell like sex, booze and stale ashtray.'

'Sorry, Madam, someone stole my clothes . . .'

'Nonsense! A liar, to boot. Not another word out of you all afternoon. And before I put you to work, take note of how I'm dressed. Head up! The way I'm dressed, that's exactly how I'd like to see you when you step foot in this office tomorrow morning. I'm told you're here with us all month. Lovely shoes, aren't they? And take note of my blouse, it's mauve and it's silk. I'm rather fond of both. Nobody's going to take you seriously unless you're dressed your best. Now get to work.'

*

At the end of an evening, having done anywhere between four and eleven sessions, I was invariably tipsy, tired and wired. I'd come home to Adam, who didn't much care for the post-work madam. He found my energy intense and aggressive, and my ego somewhat bloated. He was jealous of the high I got from playing with other men. He needed thorough reassurance that our sessions at the cottage, and especially the final breach, had never been repeated or could even compare to my sessions with other clients. It wasn't entirely true: I'd never had sex with another client, and the chemistry between me and Adam was on its own scale, but there's no denying that my best sessions were sensual, intense and extremely enjoyable. I never felt I was being disloyal to Adam; I was doing my job, and doing it well and enjoying it meant getting into it. But, as he put it, 'How would you feel if I was masturbating women all day long?'

I don't think it's a fair comparison.

In many ways, Adam's not artistic or creative. He has no interior design or fashion sense, and he neglects his palate. He doesn't dance, isn't a big film-goer, and the music he listens to hasn't changed since he was an angry teen. Yet when it comes to fulfilling his extreme sexual desires, he's poet, sculptor, director and creative inventor. Even his first masturbation episodes were of fixing himself into clever bondage traps, tying belts around his waist a notch or two too tight, and hurting his balls and nipples. His 'art' was an exploration of extremes and the championing of his body.

He wasn't a talker, never very eloquent or playful with his words, and could go hours without speaking . . . unless, that is, he was speaking through a submissive, sadomasochistic mouthpiece. Then he spoke so masterfully.

Adam has passionate explosions of expression, but otherwise he's unnaturally placid. Once we were driving past the Oval in South London. He was in the driver's seat and I was looking out my window when I heard a thump against his side of the car. I turned in time to see a cyclist crumpled by the side of the road. My first thought was that Adam was to blame. He's reckless. He attracts danger, and he has the power to destroy. I was paralysed by fear. I saw the fragility of things, how life could change irrevocably in a second.

I looked to Adam and could not comprehend his bloodless calm. Without a word, almost like a ghost, he opened the door and got out of the car. The cyclist was standing; he was all right. I wasn't able to hear what it was they were saying but the cyclist was gesturing – cordially? sheepishly? apologetically? – to Adam, which made no sense to me. I looked at Adam, but his expression was as unreadable as the face of a mountain. It gave me an eerie, awesome feeling. A few minutes later the cyclist, with a rip in his jeans extending from his back pocket to the knee, shook his head, made some hand gesture, and walked his damaged bicycle across the street.

When Adam got back in the car and started up the engine, it was as if nothing had happened. I had to ask, 'My God, what the hell happened?' Even after he explained that the cyclist had run a red light and ridden directly into his car, and was more stunned and sorry than hurt, I was still buzzing from the fright. It took some time for me to calm down, whereas I'm convinced that neither the rhythm of his heart nor the flow of his thoughts had been disrupted. That unnatural, heroic calm was mystifying to me.

I remember the first time his silence frightened me. I came home to him watching a DVD on his laptop. He didn't turn to look at me and he didn't respond to my greeting. Then it was chilling to see the absence of expression. I was looking at the hollow man. Without Adam, the atmosphere had become thick and compressed. No sound, no oxygen, like deep waters. Is this what it's like to freedive? Is this where he goes? His abundant, oceanic absence swallowed me up. For a second I was there with him at the bottom, seventy metres underwater, but I didn't know how to hold my breath . . . I felt so alone. Nobody sees me and nobody hears me, and I can't even open my mouth to scream. And then there is no more me.

When he was feeling submissive he would say, 'I'll do anything for you.' I began using, or manipulating these openings in order to get beyond his silence and learn about his life. I tied his hands behind his back, hung weights off his balls, blindfolded him, and said, 'For every question you answer I will remove one of the weights, and take off a layer of clothing.'

He agreed. He repeated that he wanted nothing but to serve me and please, and give me what I asked.

'So, tell me about your wife. I'm asking.'

I wanted to know something about the only other woman in his life. The mother of his child. The woman he has spent the last eighteen years with. How did they communicate without these games? What kept them together all those years? What did they talk about? What did they do together? I really craved to know. He couldn't appreciate my need to know, and the stubborn, silent man wouldn't budge. 'What's your son like? What's it like to be a father? Why did you wait fifteen years to conceive him? What was sex like? Does she know what you like? Does she know you?'

Only by taking advantage of his submission did I find out that she never called him handsome, and never complimented him. He was so beautiful; it was hard to believe. She collected crystal figurines. She wasn't artistic, she wasn't a 'babe', but she was attractive and a pretty good tennis player. She'd been anorexic in her twenties, and then she lost her brother to cancer. She studied holistic and alternative health therapies and nutrition. When she found out he'd been to see a dominatrix she said she was disgusted, and it was never mentioned again.

After tying him to the iron bed frame, having first removed the mattress, I lit a candle, held it over his body, and discovered that he had had an affair for three years with a co-worker. No amount of hot candle wax dripped on his cock and balls would make him tell me about their sex, only that she loved her bottom being licked and that he would do it for an hour at a time. She wanted him to leave his wife, and that's when he refused to kiss her ass, so she ended the affair. For all the wrong reasons, said Adam, she got engaged soon after their split. One night he'd worked himself into such a state, convinced she was making a mistake, that he sat up in bed and told his wife he was leaving, and the reason why. And then he got into his car at three a.m. and drove south.

In the early hours of the morning he pressed her buzzer. There was no answer. I don't know why he was sure she was there, and there alone, but never mind. He kept pressing the buzzer, then he called her landline and her mobile phone, banged on the door, knocked on the window and gave up trying. Apparently she was one of those extremely deep sleepers. He broke into her flat. Lucky she was there. Lucky she was alone. Lucky no curious neighbours caught him in the act. Never mind. Even when he was by her bedside she did not come to. He said it took twenty minutes to get her up. Whatever he said to her to try to make her change her mind, it didn't work. She kept repeating, coldly, sleepily, that it was too late. Too late. And it was very, very early.

When he returned home it was nearly noon. He found his wife sitting up in bed, dressed in her wedding gown, stockings, perfume, the mother-of-pearl shoes, her hair done up with a matching clip. She was fully made up, but tear-stained and mascara-streaked.

From my interrogations I deduced that when he sets his mind on something he wants, he goes to extreme lengths to get it. And if he lied to his wife for years, he'd probably lie to me. All his life his masochism had been his secret, the thing he did alone or with a stranger, but never as a kind of exposure. That was the difference with me: with me he could explore his masochism, indulge his taste for extremes, and attach a name and a cause to it. He could call it 'suffering for love'. I gave his need for pain a context, a purpose. I was his muse. I was the alternative to what he left behind. I was his escape, his outlet, and his freedom.

He gets down on the ground and flagellates himself – for me. He puts a dildo up his ass – for me. He yanks his nipples, puts two sets of clamps on each, and tells me in these wild tones how it's all for me. He will suffer anything – for me, do anything – for me. And yet, how is it 'for me', and what do I gain from a bag of ice tied around his cock and balls?

Adam is prepared to demonstrate his devotion to me through beautiful acts of submission and masochism, but if I want – if I ask – for a reply to my text message, to take a walk in the park with me (without one of us being naked under a long coat), to play Scrabble, to remember how I like my coffee, to buy me flowers just because, to feed me broth when I'm ill, to hold me when I'm sad or feel weak and needy, if I want stimulation or sympathy, I'm left wanting. He is either unable to offer me these things or else he refuses to do so.

I remember coming home one evening to find Adam in position at the top of the stairs. But he wasn't waiting for me. Instead of the usual silence he asked me for the time. When I told him, he boasted about how long he'd been in position. He wanted to be left alone for another twenty minutes, could I come back then? 'Why don't you take a walk around the block,' he suggested. And that was exactly what I did. I do believe that marked a change in the stairs game. He was playing with himself, playing by himself, it had gone from a dialogue to a soliloquy, and I felt sad and superfluous.

Another time, I remember kissing hungrily. A long dialogue of kisses on the bed. Moist, florid sentences written all over each other's face. I was so engrossed in this language of tongues, always taken by the possibilities of a kiss, that I bit his chin. I wouldn't have even noticed if he hadn't flown off the bed and roared, 'No!' before he'd even landed on the ground. It was our first session all over again, and the time he broke the leather straps in the rubber chamber, also the time I whipped him at home. It was that first session.

How many times had we deliberately hurt each other? How many times had he bled and welted and tortured himself? Damn it, how many times had he bitten my nose or my nipple or forcefully grabbed my ass because he just couldn't help himself? And I understood. I felt the same. Every time I looked at him, every time my body was anywhere near him, I felt the compulsion to grab hold of him, taste and consume him. I understood. So now I've bitten his chin – so what? Suddenly, as if from nowhere, so quickly, so violently, he becomes angry and accusatory. It terrified me to see the beautiful man that I loved instantly transformed into this monster. I couldn't stand his extremes. Didn't trust him, couldn't understand him.

When I was about five years old, I remember sitting with my twin brother in our eldest brother's bedroom. I remember the orange and brown carpet. I remember speaking into a tape recorder. Our brother, who would have been thirteen then, was interviewing us and playing back our answers. Unadulterated attention from the older sibling I adored, coupled with the strange, magical experience of hearing my own voice was pure delight. That is, until my brother's voice changed abruptly into a growl, and he said, 'That's it, game over, get out of here.'

My twin and I burst into a shock of tears. 'But why?' I wept. 'Why do we have to go?' The tape continued to record our sobs and protests, and my older brother, now laughing, now saying, 'Just kidding.' But I was unforgiving of that trick. He said it was an experiment to see how we'd react, but that sudden change in behaviour had a rancid flavour.

Adam's volatility tastes the same. It also makes me think of dogs. I've always had a good relationship with dogs. I grew up with a cairn terrier – he died on New Year's Eve twenty years ago and I still miss him. I think I fell in love with my landlady's half border collie, half Saint Bernard. I was living in Toronto that summer and I used to walk him to the beach every day because he was so fond of the water. It was the summer of the heat wave and that extraordinary dog used to lie on the tiled floor in the bathroom to get cool. That's not so extraordinary, but there was a terrycloth bath mat on the floor which the dog not only pawed aside to get to the cold tiles, but replaced when he left the bathroom – now that's extraordinary. The point is I've always had an untainted relationship with dogs.

Then, a couple of summers ago I was in Canada spending the weekend with my parents at their cabin in the Ontario wilderness. My parents have been going to 'the shack' every summer for thirty years, but I hadn't been back for six or seven. Things had changed, namely there was a new family in a cabin fifty yards away.

Just as I stepped out of the car, I was overwhelmed with the scent of cedar pine and maple, the rushing creek, and the clean air. I heard a woodpecker, crickets and cicadas. I heard the sound of speed, of something fast approaching. I heard ferocious barking. But as I turned to look, the big dog was literally upon me, attacking me. It tried to bite my face, which I was shielding with my hands. Three of them had to tear the bitch off me. I was so frightened that I burst into tears. I could smell fear's particular stench that had so quickly drenched my body, soaked my clothes, and was now evaporating off me. It was such a specific smell.

The neighbours said the dog was seven years old and had

never attacked anything before, not even chased a squirrel, a chipmunk, a porcupine, or a raccoon, and there were plenty of them around. They were flummoxed, and very, very apologetic. Thereafter, the dog was either tied up or locked in the cabin all weekend. But whenever she caught a whiff of me even fifty yards away, she went completely berserk. It was so disturbing and upsetting. I wish I could have asked her why she found me so offensive, so repellent and threatening. And what would she have said? I haven't been able to look a dog in the eye ever since.

CHAPTER 15

Domestic Violence

We lived together for four months before Adam bought his bachelor flat in North London, a few hundred yards from his wife and son. Four months felt like four years as we stretched the boundaries, experimented, pushed the limits, tested our bodies, played out ever-more bizarre dramas, tried to build an impenetrable fortress that would support a different way of existing together.

When I agonised over whether it was Susan that he loved or Anna, it occurred to me that that question and my agony resembled the questions all lovers ask themselves: does he love me, all of me, or an idea of me? It was just that *we* had dramatised, externalised and ritualised the tensions, demonstrations and tango of two.

And I asked myself as well; did I love Adam, or a man I had invented?

It was in those last six weeks that we started playing each other's slave for extended periods of time. A day, a weekend, the longest was a five-day stretch, for each of us. Every philosophical, metaphorical, and emotional implication of our non-stop play confounded and tormented me. But not him, I don't believe. Whatever drove him to extremes was more direct and came more naturally from him, whereas I was coming at it from the head, the heart, a place of art . . . and from somewhere else as well. But I had to push myself, override my instincts, and ultimately surpass myself. It was an enormous effort and, in the process, it was easy to lose touch with myself.

When he said, 'Take your pleasure, do with me as you will,' I did not know what it was that I willed. It tortured me, a question like that. Either it was a trick, a trap, or I should have known the answer. But I didn't. It was easier for me to please others, give them what they wanted, than it was for me to know my own desires and take my pleasure. Domination made it easy for me to avoid the question of my desires.

But here's my opportunity to explore my wildest fantasies. He's my occasion to discover myself and my desires. He wants that. I want that. But what do I will? *Is* this power that he gives me? It's certainly select and context-based, but is it real? What does it mean to take my pleasure and do as I will?

He would say, 'Please, Mistress.' He would use the word 'mistress'. 'Tell me what you want me to do to demonstrate my submission to you.'

He would get down on his knees and look up at me and implore me. 'Please, Mistress, what is it that you will from me?' And it would be nothing. Okay: wash the dishes, clean the stove, make me dinner, read to me, tell me your dreams, your favourite childhood stories, surprise me, stimulate me, ask nothing from me, and let me be. But that's not what he had in mind. He would like me to be constantly thinking up new and inventive ways to train him, push him, make him my slave.

The thought of ordering my lover to pleasure me was vulgar. I want him to pleasure me because he wants to, not because he has to, and not because it's the role he's playing. He wants me to have the will of a Mistress, not the will of Susan. Perhaps he thinks they're the same, but they're not the same. Playing Mistress was an effort, a performance, an act of precision and intense attention, a distillation of me, an improvisation, an unpredictable dance; I couldn't play the Mistress all the time. I can only do it when there is something to fall back on or step out of – contrast, boundaries, a nourishing base that can soak up the rich sauce, a beginning, middle and end.

When Adam was my slave I prepared a cold bath for him, filled it with bags of ice. It was one of the umpteen punishments or tests of submission I had concocted on behalf of an ever-consuming, demanding existence. I told him to get naked and get in the tub for three minutes. He wasted no time in getting naked. And then, without pause or hesitation he stepped into the bath.

'Okay,' I said after two minutes, 'okay, get out.' I was worried about his heart. But he begged me to stay in longer. 'No,' I said. 'You've more than proven your obedience. That's enough now.' And so he gets out of the bath with more resistance than when he got in.

I covered the bedroom floor with thumbtacks, dozens of them. I laid them down on their backs, points up, one at a time.

After he'd been denied any sexual contact for forty-eight hours, I lay naked on top of the bed, and told him he could have me if he could crawl over to me.

I whipped him in every room of the flat. I whipped the backs of his shoulders and the cheeks of his ass. I whipped his hands. I slapped his face so many times it was almost a reflex. I have to confess, I love slapping face. It's powerfully simple. It has a sound, requires aim, causes disproportionate humiliation and shame. But sometimes the look it produced in Adam when I said, 'Offer me your left cheek. I'm going to slap it as hard as I can' gave me a strange, unwholesome sensation. That look in his eyes was very specific – abject, hateful, fearful and sad; a look that perhaps lovers shouldn't show each other. He despised me. I despised him for pretending he was submissive when he wasn't, for giving me power and taking it away, for encouraging me to hurt him and then resenting me for it, for taxing and teasing my mind until I'd lost the point of it all.

I tied him to the metal bed frame and stuck pegs all over his body. And then I lay down on top of him. He wasn't allowed to ejaculate or masturbate without my permission. He wore humiliating words under his work clothes. He wore my underwear to work. I texted him and, no matter where he was, he had to masturbate. I had him wear the nipple clamps he bought for one hour, and then next night two hours and then two clamps on each nipple for two hours, and so on and on . . .

He bathed me. He washed my hair. He shaved my legs and dried my back. He made my dinner. He sat across from me at the table and I would drink wine but he would drink water. And yes, he fervently worshipped and excessively pleasured my body for hours at a time.

When I was his slave, I strived to be perfect. I would endeavour to understand all that's required to serve, and surrender. To know the feeling of submitting to anything. I did it for me. I did it for him. I thought about Bernie asking for anything.

I was a very good slave. I found grace in the strain. Serving was my passion's outlet; suffering was cleansing; worship proved wildly redeeming. I also took pleasure in excess, the extremes of the body, the challenge, the art, the romance of it. I prostrated myself, arched my back, and posed in seductive and painful ways. I stretched myself as I do in ballet, as I do when I run up the hill every morning, as I did in a kitchen twelve, fourteen, seventeen hours a day. I was humiliated, degraded, turned into a sex slave, a slut and an object. And I thought: if there is something to learn from humiliation, something to gain from facing one's shame, then I will know it. Sometimes I felt invincible. Look what I can do, look how much I can take, see what I will endure for you. I abandoned myself to a fever of servile devotion.

My submission excited him enormously. His response, so passionate, so generous, inspired me, and drove me to push on. I was not afraid. I was not afraid.

I was a terrible slave. I got very angry. Inwardly I criticised him. What did he know about being a master? Sometimes he was lazy. Sometimes, he was terribly insensitive, asked too much, pushed too far. I resented the harsh voice he put on as a matter of course. I don't respond well to being bossed around. He grew greedy with his power, selfish, gluttonous, and over-demanding.

He whipped me, clamped me, spanked me, tortured me, and made me call him 'Sir'. Sometimes it made my stomach ache and turn to see how aroused he became by my pain.

Four months all told. I don't know what would have happened had he not moved into his new flat and I not gone to Canada for the entire summer.

In Toronto, I rented a loft, bought a bicycle, signed up for yoga classes five days a week, took care of that genius border collie that belonged to my landlady, wrote all afternoon, and made handsome dinners for family and friends. It was scorching hot, and the sky was almost continuously a deep, cloudless blue. The flowers and gardens were in bloom, and the neighbourhoods were pastiches of tall, pretty houses and abundant trees. I had everything but Adam.

Distance, absence, limitations and constraints, these were the triggers of a new and bizarre twist in our relationship. He loved me most in my absence, in the abstract, when he could imagine me. Without my daily presence, he set about recasting me in a role of Mistress perfection. The woman that he missed was so much more powerful, omniscient and gifted than me.

He began calling me every day, like he'd done when I was in Istanbul. He began calling me Mistress. Then he asked permission to suffer for me on a Friday night. And then every Friday night. Friday nights rolled into Saturday nights, and then Wednesdays. He had some professional photographs of me in fetish wear, maybe a dozen that he pinned up, first on his wall, then in his closet, and finally on the walls of a bondage box he built for himself as a type of altar.

He would make elaborate preparations for these long nights, preparations that he would record in precise detail. He had barely written me so much as a note on the fridge, and no post-cards from Hawaii or Finland or Israel or Egypt; any of the places he went diving or vacationing. He had never composed a love letter, yet now he was sending me ten-page emails exploding with raw, descriptive detail of how he suffered and what he thought about while suffering. Having tapped into a well of pain, worship and sexuality, it poured forth in words.

He said he was suffering for me, even though I wasn't there. But by the force of his passion and this new-found, ten-fold adoration for me, I was drawn back in. I found myself applying myself as Mistress Susan all over again. He wasn't allowed to masturbate without my permission. He had to walk all day with a stone in his shoe. He had to hold his arms outstretched for five minutes while I was on the phone, then seven minutes, then eight, or beat his own cock so I could hear the slap through the telephone line. I posted him a pair of my panties, photographs of myself, a ring, a lock of my hair, a phial of my urine . . .

He would always call me up on his mobile to tell me when he was going to begin suffering, and what he was going to do. And then he would call me again, giving me the full description of what had happened and what he planned to do next, and will I stay on the phone and listen? And so it went. There were parents and siblings, nieces and nephews in the background, and he was panting on the other end of the phone, saying, 'I'm ripping off the clamps right now . . . they've been on for twenty minutes.' I can hear his agony, can almost smell his perspiration . . . and at my end the music's playing, the water is boiling, the onions are frying, a friend is laughing, a siren's screeching, a car is beeping, my laundry's drying. And then he says, 'Thank you.'

A typical Friday or Saturday, or sometimes Wednesday and Monday, goes like this: he gets into the bondage box he has built. He ties a shoestring tightly around the base of his penis; the shoestring is still attached to a heavy climbing boot. He has a small kettle, which he can plug in a socket near the box and still have the kettle inside the box. He is dressed in layers of rubber and PVC – outfits he has either purchased himself or things I have left behind. He wears a belt around his waist tight enough to act as a corset. He ties a plastic bag of ice around his balls, and attaches a couple of pairs of clamps on each nipple. Pictures of me are taped up on the walls inside the box, the kettle will be turned on. He hangs the boot attached to his cock outside the little window, sawn out of the wooden box. He calls me up before he's about to sit down on a rubber plug the girth of a rolling pin. I hear him as he makes wild sounds that are not quite a scream. When I'm not on the phone to hear him, he's chanting my name and looking at my photos for inspiration.

Somehow this is my doing; this is what I've inspired, encouraged, created. In marriage you make a contract to serve, to honour, to worship, and obey. Adam wants to give himself to me, full-time, as my slave.

I bought a ticket back to London. My flat was still on sublet but he said that what's his is mine, so, for the meantime, I would live with him. He met me at the airport. We had planned this: he would greet me as his Mistress and I would greet him as my slave. I would wear a skirt and high heels for the occasion (I almost never wear heels or skirts in public) and he would wear a collar around his neck. He would be waiting for me at Arrivals. He would approach me in front of two thousand strangers. In front of two thousand strangers he would walk up to me, and then stop. And I would slap his face. In front of all those people whose attention we now had, he would then drop to his knees and kiss my feet. It was a marriage ceremony, of sorts. The beginning of our contract. He wanted to say to the world, I submit to this woman. I worship this woman. He wanted the world to see that I owned him. Me, I was terrified, first of what the ceremony signified, what this contract meant, and second of making such a spectacle of myself.

It had been three months. He was tanned. He was chestnut. He was dark. He was blue. His beautiful presence was something untrue. I had missed that chemistry, that energy, the instant arousal, the charge that got stronger the closer we came to one another. I wanted to embrace him, I wanted to surrender into his powerful arms, and get lost in his scent. But I had to resist because it wasn't part of the plan.

As planned, I slapped his face. I saw that disturbing, contortionist's face he makes when he's slapped. I saw the battle in his face; him trying not to react, not to get angry, but to welcome it with courage. But then he dropped to the ground and he looked as if he was about to pray. It surprised me how dramatic, elegant and reverent it was. This is how you kiss the feet of your Mistress. And then for all to see, with such humility, he worshipped my ankles and kissed my feet.

'Get up,' I commanded, but it sounded wooden and false, and then I walked ahead. He followed behind with my luggage, and hundreds of eyes were on us, to be sure, but I didn't look. My heart was pounding so violently I thought I might faint. I just stared straight ahead, beyond murmurs of 'did you see that?' from the crowd, and passed through the sliding doors, into the haze and maze of London.

We arrived at his flat. There was no plan after that. Just that I was the Mistress and he was my slave. And I wanted to stop the game and make love. I wanted to devour him, kiss the crown of his head, feel his armpits, lick his kneecaps. I wanted no rules and no holds barred. I'm not a Mistress. I don't want to forfeit tenderness. I've also been denied.

And so, unlike Mistress and slave, we had sex. And in doing this, by simply making love, for the second time we broke the rules.

We went out to dinner. A heavy, oppressive air stifled the room – the feeling of failure, the feeling that something had ended, that these games were empty, or red herrings, or had outrun their purpose. We went to bed early that night and he went to work very early the following morning. When I got up, he was gone.

I took a good look around. One of the kitchen cupboard doors was off its hinges and fell to the ground when I merely touched it. Inside there were bottles of vitamins and homeopathic medicine, probably from his wife. It made me laugh to see health in pretty bottles but nothing else in the cupboards. I saw a stained coffee jug that I knew he must have used to give himself enemas before an evening of suffering. He believed that coffee enemas were purifying. There was a box of English breakfast tea, half a dozen tins of sardines, two cans of baked beans (organic), some dried pasta, a bag of potatoes with sprouting tentacles, a bag of onions (mouldy), a can of tomatoes, and a box of muesli. I was sure the floor had never been cleaned, never been swept in the three months he'd been living there. The fridge was bare except for a skin of Parmesan and some rice milk. The olive oil was rancid, the counters and cooker were sticky. There were a couple of dishes in the sink, a set of cutlery that I bought him before I left, and a few plates and glasses that his wife had probably given him. The bowl, the sauce spoon, the spatula, the dishtowel, the cutting board, the fish sauce and sesame oil and chef's knife were mine.

In his study there was a map on the wall. He'd marked all the places he'd been. He's travelled far for someone who had never strayed from the neighbourhood in which he grew up. The DVDs were all Hollywood blockbusters. He had a big screen TV. He had the entire thirty-three volume *Encyclopaedia Britannica* and the complete *Oxford English Dictionary*, and I don't know that he'd ever referred to them, but he said that he liked how they looked on the shelf.

Stuck between some freediving magazines, I found the only photos I'd ever seen that belonged to Adam: one of him and his wife, one of his parents, one of him as a toddler, a wedding photo, a photo of the son of Adam, a card written to Adam, and a note from his wife. The note was dated and composed at a time when I knew him only as a client. Written in a girlish hand with ballpoint pen, it thanked him for being so fun-loving, such a good husband and father, for being such a handsome man and great athlete, for fixing things around the house, for being such a good provider, and making her so happy. I did not know him as fun-loving, she *had* complimented him, and he had made her happy.

She was blonde and wrinkled and terribly expressive. She looked worn by emotions.

In the wedding photo he's looking down at his shoes and she's turning, twisting, careening to look up into his face. He's not smiling. In fact, I don't know what that expression reveals. I'm mesmerised by the photo of him, age four: the sepia skin, his features fully formed; the eyes look inwards, and outwards, glassy and remote. He looks serious. He looks like a man, not at all like a child. He looks spectral and beautiful, but also funereal, as if the photo was of someone who never existed – except within the photo and the frame. It was a child, but there never was such a child. I would have liked to have stolen the photo so I could study it, but I didn't risk it. He was a very private person and had he discovered I had violated his privacy, I can't think what he would have done. And that photo of his son. The child was a blond, curly-haired angel. He had Adam's eyes, spaced wide, extremely long-lashed and oceanic blue.

He hadn't bothered to buy furniture or decorate, or paint. There was a beanbag, a cardboard box standing in for a table, a tacky tie-dyed batik of a mushroom framed on the white stucco wall. In so many ways the place depressed me. It was barren, bland, and suburban. It was a fifteen-minute walk to the nearest shop and a twenty-five minute walk to the tube station. And this was meant to be my new home, my life for a while. And it didn't feel right. The honeymoon was over.

*

Before he came home that night I began cleaning, and I made three trips to the shop. I bought food, toilet paper, vinegar, sponges, cleaning products, salt and pepper, a dustpan, some flowers and a vase. I made him dinner. He didn't call to say when he'd be home. It was late, and if he noticed that the place was clean, he didn't mention it. In fact, he barely said a word. He came in with the post, kissed me on the forehead, and went upstairs to take a bath. Dinner had to wait, and then, I remember, we ate in suffocating silence before he simply went upstairs to bed without saying goodnight.

I couldn't believe it. And I couldn't bear it; the silence, the void. Such a contrast from his servitude, his passion. I needed to talk, needed him to listen, needed to feel welcomed. I couldn't stand his silence. I couldn't stand the suburbs, and his single mattress. I followed him upstairs yelling after him. I asked him what the fuck was going on. He whipped his head around and warned me with this violent expression. 'What more do you want from me?' he shouted. 'I've given you everything. I have no more to give and now I'm going to bed.'

And that was meant to be the end of the discussion. In other words: no discussion with Adam. But I wanted discussion. I wanted to talk, to shout, to mock. I just wanted anything but silence, anything but to be ignored.

'Shut up,' he roared with red murder in his voice.

'I don't want to shut up. Don't tell me to shut up. Why should I shut up? Who are you to tell me to shut up?' Like that I provoked; like that I pushed; like that it escalated. I remember a wild, insane look in his ocean-blue eyes.

'I will not shut up.'

Not until his enormous hands flew at me, landed around my neck, and threw me on the bed. His hands didn't leave my throat, or did they? Were they around my head, did he hold my head and shake me, did he squeeze my wrists or crush my collarbone? I remember one thing: the opposite of beauty, the heinous face of rage.

PART THREE

CHAPTER 16

Identity

There is this tiny village in the Scottish Highlands, population five hundred. The village sleeps in a crease on Lady H's ninety-eight-thousand-acre estate along with a castle; a long silver-birch path leads up to the castle and gardens, ultra-manicured but utterly fantastical. There are fruit orchards, old conifers, new forests, lochs and salmon-filled streams, fields of bracken and hills growing up into mountains. Larissa, an acquaintance from Toronto, actually the daughter of my parents' friends, had been one of the castle gardeners for eight or nine years, but after giving birth to her second child she switched to the upkeep of a relatively small vegetable/flower/herb garden located behind a formidable four-hundred-year-old house atop a hill.

Ever since I moved to London Larissa had been inviting me to visit them. Only weeks before, while I was in Canada, she'd sent me an email reiterating her invitation. She phrased it as a favour. 'I'm all alone here,' she wrote. 'There's almost no one my age that I can talk to and the girls would just love to have someone else around. Stay for nothing. It would be great if you could mind the girls sometimes, and bless us with some of your culinary magic – but no pressure. Just come. There's plenty of room and I think you'll find it's stunning here. You can write, do as you like, and stay as long as you want.'

I couldn't stay with Adam any longer. Pinned to the bed, his mighty hands gripping my neck, time expanded and contracted, thoughts and feelings overlapped. Perhaps it was only for a few seconds that I pierced the heart of the storm and saw Adam submerged underwater. There was no air . . . and then Bernie was coming up for air, as if waking from his drowning nightmare. I opened the door to those eyes, their sparkling blue matching the sea, but then they blinded me. I was always afraid of their intensity, but then I dared to stare directly into their dangerous glare, long enough to see an ugliness I could not bear. Mad merman, auroch, raging beast – layer upon layer. I felt shame and terror. I was the limp, lucid observer of a nightmare.

I wanted to be punished and purged by isolation. To leave behind my trauma and surround myself with mountains and heather and dominant weather, and see what followed me. I thought that being alone, out of the storm, would help me to see things more clearly. I needed – *needed* – to understand what really happened between Adam and me. Yes, there was failure, violence and exhaustion – that I wouldn't deny – but I was still left wondering how, what, what if, why . . .

We'd suffered for each other and because of each other. We'd made an extreme effort, taken time, applied our minds, and invented. We had both been searching for something. We share an intensity; we have this rare chemistry. Or was it an artistic, romantic inclination that compelled us to stretch ourselves until the fabric wore so thin that we lost ourselves?

I fled to the Highlands to solve conundrums. Not since the night I left Adam's had I had a proper sleep. I stayed with a friend for a couple of days and nights before getting on a train to Glasgow, and then another train to the small town where Larissa was waiting for me.

We embraced. She towered over me at six foot three, and then lowered her grand elegance to lift my suitcase, which she deposited in the boot of a robin's egg-blue vintage Mercedes that looked striking against the emerald-shaded foliage. In the back seat a three-year-old was silently sucking her fingers and clasping an egg carton.

For thirty minutes we drove along rising, falling, winding, wind-swept roads, through gnarled Caledonian forest, past expansive patchworks of ochre fields – a moss-green and rust-coloured tapestry. And then Larissa pointed out a standing stone. Everywhere I looked, whole tree trunks were uprooted and branches scattered like carnage – the aftermath of strong gales. I saw cows and communities of sheep, green dells, mountain goats, and a blanket of bluebells. We drove past hamlets of pretty houses in jagged, grey stone style, and at one point we had to stop and beep to encourage a bronze partridge to cross our path.

When at last we drove up a dirt road and parked on the pearly pebbled driveway, a large stone house stood in full view. Just before stepping out of the car, the little girl suddenly pulled her fingers from her mouth and opened the egg carton, which was eggless but colourful, and precociously squealed, 'Look, I used sparkle glue and indelible markers! It's lovely, isn't it?'

The immediate grounds were jewelled with red oaks and evergreens, as tall as I've ever seen, as well as pruned hedges and rhododendron bushes. There was a large eggplant-coloured barn behind the house, as well as two sheds, a nursery, and a greenhouse. And there, from on top of the hill, I looked down and saw the village and the church steeple, and beyond that a hem of regal-coloured mountains, their peaks crowned with dense, textured clouds.

The garden that Larissa tended was a lattice-work of sweet pea blossoms, French and runner beans, rows of baby lettuces, heads of savoy and Chinese cabbage, cauliflower, braids of garlic, and beetroot. She grew spring onions, shallots, rainbow-coloured chard, carrots, frothy fennel stalks, flowering thyme, bushes of purple basil, and velvet sage, as well as apple trees, artichoke plants and three types of potatoes.

When I arrived the wild strawberries were ripe enough to pick. I put one in my mouth and was shocked to discover that it tasted of – rather, it distinctly *suggested* – Roquefort cheese. A sloping stone wall and a tall wooden gate kept out the animals but welcomed the butterflies, the ravens, the crows, and the midges. The Highlands smelled floral and peaty, just like heather, burnt wood and fine whisky. The bench in the middle of the vegetable garden was where I sat alone at night, listening to the call of the wind and gazing at the firmament while thinking: I am under the shelter of celestial beauty and surrounded by the earth's nudity; it's everywhere I look, it's everything I feel, and yet, what am I to do with it?

In various ways Larissa made it known that she, her husband, and her daughters, three and five, were simple people living on very modest means. They paid a nominal rent for the old house on the hill, grew their vegetables, baked their own bread, and bought their clothes from a charity shop in the nearest town. Yet how rich and resplendent their lives appeared to me!

But the house was chaos and clutter, piles upon piles of paper, a litter of receipts, school notices, envelopes of garden seeds and pamphlets, a screwdriver, a sledgehammer, a couple of cameras and binoculars. A black cat was sleeping in a basket beside the telephone on a table near a window. There were photographs detached from their albums, children's art en masse, plastic farm animals, crayons, sheet music, records, cassettes and CDs tossed about. There was play dough on the shaggy rug in the corner, a thick plastic tablecloth on a large oval kitchen table and, underneath, a small red rubber boot, a pink slipper, jigsaw pieces and markers (indelible, no doubt) with and without their caps. Dishes were piled high and, in another corner of the room near the pantry, stacks of empty bottles, plastic containers, cans and newspapers to be recycled had spilled over into the piano area. The place was bursting with stuff, and my first thought was: I'm going to clean and organise and bring some order to this house.

From the kitchen we passed through a hallway, past a room where the door stayed shut, turned a corner, and entered an open corridor with desk and computer, more tools, toys, trinkets, and more trails of paper. On the warm yellow walls in the hall hung several framed paintings and against them leaned a dark wooden case, a sort of mantelpiece, an umbrella stand, and a podium. Then we climbed the winding stairs. The landing was avalanched with laundry, linen, boxes on top of boxes, bookshelves, tables, chairs and other furniture. Then came the girls' busy bedroom, the frenetic master bedroom, the bathroom and, finally, the room that would be mine.

I put down my suitcase and looked askance, amazed at its quiet, sparse elegance. It was unlike anywhere else in that busy house. The room was white and spacious, the ceiling very high. There were two walls of windows, draped with heavy velvet curtains that were half drawn. An enormous red oak tree dominated the belvedere, and half a dozen Persian carpets overlapped. Along one wall near the bed there was a low pine shelf like a shrine to Russian Orthodox church curios: miniature paintings of saints, a bronze incense burner, a slender prayer candle, a couple of spiritual books, and a little china vase filled with sweet pea blossoms which fragranced the room with their intoxicating perfume.

The bed was king-sized, or double king-sized, and covered in a powder-pink silk throw that had pieces of mirror and amber woven into the fabric. There was a small mahogany writing table in a windowed alcove, on which sat a green blotter. In the drawer I soon discovered a bottle of ink, a quill, fountain pens, sticks of gold, silver and red sealing wax, boxes of matches, lozenges of incense and bone-white stationery in stacks. There was a royal-blue tapestry hanging on a wall over a rattan rocking chair, and a couple of stout bookshelves stocked with antiquarian children's encyclopaedias, horticultural books, Russian fairytales, Scottish history and folklore. It was there, in that room, that I hoped to be purged and find peace.

Larissa briefed me on her husband's ancestry (they were doctors, war heroes, explorers, and archbishops), and his fascination with history and heritage – an introductory explanation of why the house was such an abundance of inherited *stuff* . . . and all that clutter and glitter was really gold. The glasses from which we drank the tasty Highland tap water had been blown in the seventeenth century. Some of the art on the walls had once hung in Scottish museums. The tapestries, carpets and antique furniture, the stamp collection, silver cutlery, swords and samovars, the ivory canes, crests and compasses, and even the old weather instruments, all had their stories yet to be told.

I slept on cotton sheets that had a thread count of a thousand, which meant nothing to me before, but which I now adore. There was jewellery and rubies and other precious stones here and there and everywhere. An emerald (no joke) sat in an empty plastic margarine tub, along with a bike key, a broken pencil and some elastic bands, for the duration of my stay.

And when I couldn't believe my eyes, couldn't believe the helter-skelter of extraordinary treasure, Larissa said, in a tone that was half jest, half honest exasperation, 'If you think this is a lot, let me show you the shed. There's more stuff than we know what to do with but he won't sell a single thing.'

Besides the firewood and coal, a wheelbarrow and the family's bicycles, there was indeed plenty more stuff in the shed. She encouraged me to look and to delve, and so I did. I saw equestrian gear – crops, harnesses, saddles – boxes of china, crates of crystal glass and mason jars. In one corner reams of stationery, fountain pens, spools of lustrous silk thread, tablecloths and napkins, lace doilies, old jigsaw puzzles made of wood, maps, ribbons, candlesticks and vases. There were copper pots and saucepans, and enough equipment to open a bakery. In the half year that I stayed there, I think I explored a twentieth of their treasure.

*

The striking contrast of their daily existence seemed personified in their children. The three-year-old was so earthbound, while the five-year-old had her head in the clouds. The younger was blonde with dark-blue, feline eyes, and was a bit plump. She was observant, mischievous, and fearless. The elder was worryingly thin, fey, and fairy-like. She had enormous brown eyes, delicate features, temper tantrums, and was often ill. The younger liked to get her hands dirty, to build in three dimensions, glue and stick things together, and she loved her food. The elder was dreamy, abstract and ethereal. She liked to draw butterflies, unicorns and other imaginary things, and write stories. She spoke to inanimate objects, got angry with the table if she accidentally banged into its corner, blamed a hedge for scratching her, but otherwise happily greeted the trees and the flowers. The younger was such a sneaky devil; she liked to hide things, test and try and lie, and play with words.

Now I'm in *their* life, following *their* rhythm and pace. It takes fifteen minutes to get the girls into their boots and hats, zip up their coats, and find their mittens. Mealtimes and bedtimes are full of complexity – cajolery and subtle bribes – and then downstairs and back upstairs with hot-water bottles stuffed into pink elephants and teddy bears. Two bedtime stories, sometimes three, and in so many ways the children challenged me. I wanted to be honest with them. I did not want to control or manipulate them. I never raised my voice to them. I tried to understand them. It required patience to play with and listen to them, to stimulate and inspire them. And in this way my affection for them blossomed.

I remember once the little one came into my room. She was

three, and she was interrupting me. I was in that beautiful room trying to write, but she wanted to be there beside me and she promised she wouldn't say a word. While I typed, she just stared at me, quietly sucking her two fingers. For five or six minutes all I could feel was her silent presence – and tenderness for her, because I well know how long even a minute of silence and stillness can be, and I am not three. Her young, clever self is abjured; she stands still and says not a word. It's I who breaks the silence with a laugh, a sloppy kiss, and a big hug and cuddle that the girls called a huggle.

Occasionally we drove to the castle a few kilometres away. Larissa knew the keepers from her years working at the garden. They were Joanne and Dean, a married couple in their fifties who were, coincidentally, Canadian. Joanne would answer the door in bare feet with cracked toenails and a thin red kimono, a cigarette hanging from her dry lips, and in a deep, hacking growl she welcomed us into their small, low-ceilinged hovel.

Besides a microwave, a coffee-maker, a small hob and a ripped linoleum kitchen that opened into a slightly larger bedroom/ living room, it was nothing but books. Hundreds of them, presumably because the days and months were lonely when the Lady was away. In any case, their very humble existence was a stark contrast to the extreme regal opulence to be found only a few doors and corridors away. On a couple of occasions, Dean led us to the oxblood walls and marble floors of the great grand castle foyer, adorned with gold-framed portraits twelve-foot high and the horns, coats, and heads of many dead animals.

Outside I stood on the highest tiers of grass and stone, and beheld a wonderland of passion and elegance, order and maze, and frivolous obsession: the castle gardens, something Alice dreamed up. I saw fruit orchards, herbaceous borders, hedges carved into corkscrews, arches and orbs, stripes and paisleys of flowers like the patterns of a playing card or tapestry. I saw ivy-covered archways and cupolas, leafy canopies, fountains, and white marble statues. There were peacocks and pheasants, and still my question roaming freely: what does one do with so much beauty?

The old stone house stands on a hill like a beacon, overlooking the hushed village which is all of one main street that trickles off into a few neighbourly roads. There's a general store and post office that sells newspapers, milk, postage stamps and other miscellaneous necessities, a petrol station, and a café that was never open. There was also an old church and cemetery dating from the fifteenth century, a primary school, a nursery school, two playgrounds, and a gymnasium that also served as a town hall, and two pubs.

The posh pub was also a B&B with a very good restaurant that offered an exciting menu, and at the workmen's pub, the ceilings were low, the carpet billiard green, and the white walls windowless. There was no ventilation, and the place stank of smoke, bathroom spray, and a sickly lemon product the barmaid used to polish the bar. The tables and chairs were so small they looked as if they'd been snatched from a nursery school. But it was there that I went to read and write, smoke and drink at night.

I had arrived early in September, a novice to the extreme and changeable Highland weather. There would be blustery rain, gales, mud, snow, hail, sunshine and bitter cold – sometimes all within the space of a day. So Larissa drove me to a charity shop in the nearest town where I equipped myself with all I needed for less than ten pounds. I bought a pair of black wellingtons for fifty pence, several pairs of wool socks, and a winter coat that cost me a pound. The canvas coat was the colour of overcooked peas, the inner lining was orange quilted nylon and down. It was hooded and was several sizes too big for me. It smelled of mildew, the bottom of an attic trunk, and the man who wore it last. Unattractive as I must have looked in it all those months, I was weirdly drawn to the new disguise. From rubber to canvas . . . I cast off one role and adopted another, wondering if one was more real than the other.

The girls were awake by six every morning, and because their room was next to mine I also woke up at that time. I lay in bed reading and listening to their excited play until, invariably, I heard their whispers outside my door. When they got the word of approval, they'd burst in like sunshine, and jump on my bed.

And when I volunteered to walk them to their schools in my sickly pea-green coat and wellies, holding their hands, they would ask over and over again, 'Are you a mother?'

'No.'

'Are you the cook and our babysitter?'

'No.' Not a wife, not a grandmother, and not a little girl. 'I am an adult. I was a chef. I write. I'm your friend and your parents' friend.'

And so I fell into the rhythm of their lives, kept my pain,

sadness and confusion in disguise, and quietly resented having to shake off so much of my near past. In that insular village, in that surrogate family, nobody knew me, and nobody asked. And had they asked, how should I have answered? I was not a babysitter, not a chef, not a dominatrix, not a lover, not a mother, not a tourist nor a settler . . .

There were no shortages of places to roam when I wanted to be alone. I could wander the village, walk in the fields, explore dense mossy forest, or travel further on towards the hills and mountains. But if I wanted shelter from the elements, a warm place to smoke and drink and write, then I went to the workmen's pub. There, I felt free to linger longer than at the plusher pub where they closed at odd hours and liked to reserve space for the diners. At first I went just once or twice a week, but by the time it was winter, I was a nightly fixture.

I would order a pint of Guinness from the barman, or barmaid, whom I called by their first names, and sit down at one of those elfin tables. Sometimes I wrote letters and postcards to family and friends, sometimes I read Russian fairy tales, but much of the time I spent writing volumes to Adam. Words I would never send. Words I knew he'd never read. By the end of those episodes, my fingers cramped from the tension of writing, my mind wrecked from inner fighting, I'd gather my things and snail back up the hill to the house.

What was he doing? What the hell had happened? How could he abandon me? Not contact me, no longer want to know me, not love me. For several months I woke up every night between three and four a.m., drenched with the sweat of tormented sleep.

This had never happened to me before. I would leap out of bed with a shiver, and a quiver in my throat, and this incessant quizzing in my mind. I'd want to scream or cry; instead, I crept downstairs, feeling my way through dark hallways and skirting the corners of ubiquitous clutter until I made it outside into the open night.

I'd stand in the middle of the fields or sit on the bench in the garden, playing out my turmoil to the indifferent, enormous Scottish night and thinking: who the fuck is Adam? With all his elusiveness and absence, did I invent him? Was he a man of immense beauty and possibility, a hero born in the wrong time, or a child trapped in a too-powerful body? Where should he put all that energy? I couldn't decide whether he was sick or cruel or lost. What had happened, and what was to become of Adam?

One night I bolted out of bed convinced of his death. He would dive too deep and not make it back to the surface in time. Perhaps he'd dive too deep deliberately. And what was he searching for? Deep silence, maybe. But it seems he doesn't know where to stop. Or maybe he dives thinking he's super-human, and then drowns in his own delusion.

I would text him during the night, just ask him if he was all right, but he wouldn't reply. Or couldn't reply. I didn't know which, or why. And every hour he wasn't there, or somewhere, his mythology would flare and I'd be driven deeper into despair.

I woke to the sound of a crash and I thought it was Adam driving too fast. Driving to his death. It seemed destined to be, and in that way it made sense to me; all those previous collisions, starting with the one in his mother's belly, and then his need for acceleration, and limit-breaking . . . but again, where does the driving, diving, searching end?

I called him in the morning but he didn't answer the phone. Maybe he died in that box he built for himself: burnt by steam, electrocuted by the kettle, passed out from heat, gone into shock when sitting on the huge rubber butt plug, or suffocated under a hood. And, depending on the day, it could be a while before his wife wondered why he hadn't picked up his son on Tuesday or Saturday. Found dead with belts around his waist, elastic bands around his balls, a collar around his neck, my photos scattered about, his nipples clamped – and I dare not imagine what else.

Weeks, sometimes a month would go by, and then I would get a call from him saying something paltry and insubstantial like hi, or how's it going? Once, after telling him I was hurting and lonely, that I missed him, that I'd been crying, that I didn't understand why, all he could find to say was 'Don't cry.'

Occasionally, I conjured images of him choosing life, finding himself at the scene of an accident, calm amid catastrophe, the survivor of a bombing or a crash. He'd be saving someone from drowning or rescuing a child from the flames; he'd be running in the streets with someone hanging over his sturdy shoulders, coming into his own, saving himself, finding his place and – at last – a use for his powers.

In vain I waited for him to stop hurting me and call, say he was sorry for hurting me, sorry that we weren't together, and sorry that it hadn't worked as planned. What was the plan? I waited for explanations, consolations, even confrontations. And I got nothing.

That was September, October, November, December.

*

The first week of the New Year, both pubs were shut. I was feeling abysmally lonely. I wanted a drink. I wanted to smoke. I wanted to sulk. So I went to the general store thinking I'd buy a couple of cans of beer and a bottle of whisky and sit in the shelter of the shed, the one that wasn't full of treasure, and exorcise my woes with the help of a pen and the light of a torch.

I took two cans of Guinness out of the fridge and placed them on the counter, to the shopkeeper's blatant surprise.

'Well,' she said in her thick Scottish accent, 'I would never have taken ye for a drinker . . . I mean you're so young and ye look so healthy and pure, m'dear. Tell you the truth, I couldn't believe ye were a smoker. But a *drinker* . . . don't know why, but ye don't look the type.'

True she usually saw me with the girls, buying candy and bubbles and what have you, or alone buying the newspaper and posting letters, but I wasn't prepared for her judgement and disappointment. I didn't bother to ask for the whisky that I wanted much more than the cold beer.

I walked away wondering: what *is* my type? It was sort of funny; and then again it wasn't. She sees me as some lovely person, as an innocent. I was half tempted to completely floor her, tell her that I'd beaten bankers, trodden on the toes of a judge, sewn a foreskin, inflated a scrotum with saline solution, shaved testicles, become a slave for my lover, branded myself and others with a red-hot poker, stuck needles in my nipples, made men cry, provoked the wrath of my ex-lover and ex-worker, raged in public, screamed at bus drivers, had had dozens of lovers, was now hung up on divers . . .

I don't seem the type.

*

It was February and it was dark by four p.m. It was windy and bitter and I ordered a whisky when I entered the pub. The regulars were gathered around the bar, six or seven men in their mid-thirties to late sixties. On numerous occasions they'd tried to engage me in conversation or invited me to join their card games, and although I preferred to sit alone and write, to be polite, we had the occasional exchange, even though I could barely make out their accents. One time I agreed to play cards with them. After they taught me the rules and we played two open-face rounds, the betting began. It was beginner's luck, but nonetheless I was pretty thrilled to clean up that night. I won a bottle of Scotch, and thirty-four pounds with which I bought them all a round.

But on the whole I kept very much to myself, which began to brew something more suspect and antagonistic than curiosity in the pub regulars. I wasn't a tourist and I wasn't a villager, and I wasn't there to socialise. I was, in their eyes, this unplaceable intruder.

In February it was dark by four p.m. One bitter cold night I had a prickly uneasiness, a sense of foreboding, before entering the pub. And as soon as I sat down, one bulky guy with whom I'd played cards and who had got a bit fresh and macho towards the end, was now approaching me, and was obviously drunk. He sat down on one of those small chairs, pulled right up beside me, far too close, and spoke in a derisive, Scottish slur.

'Aye, what you writing? Huh? Been doing a lot of that, haven't you?'

'It's a letter,' I said and closed my notebook.

'That's what you do the whole time? Write letters? You put us in your letters?'

'No,' I said.

'Well, why the hell not? You come in here all the time. Sit down by yourself, all proud and private, watching us. Maybe judging us. Scribbling it all down in your notebook, like you're hiding something. Huh? What is it? What are you hiding? You some kind of spy? Speak up. Tell us, is that what you are?'

'Now calm down, Terry,' admonished the barmaid.

'Aye,' said another, 'leave the lady alone. She ain't harming no one.'

'Well, why the hell doesn't she talk to us? Aren't we good enough? Eh? Seems she belongs at the other pub.'

'Pricey over there. Busy too. Bit stuck up, though. Which pub *do* you prefer?' asked the barmaid in earnest.

'Oh enough. Why're you interrogating the girl? She's friendly enough and she's entitled to sit by herself, not getting involved with you lot.'

'What I'm telling you,' slurred Terry, 'is she's stuck up. Hiding something. Judging us. Don't know. She doesn't belong here.'

I stood up, having gathered my belongings and taken a final swig of my drink. 'I prefer this pub –pardon me, I *preferred* this pub. Thought I made that obvious by coming here all the time. It's been a good place to have a drink, smoke a cigarette, and gather my thoughts. Never mind. I understand. I'm leaving.'

And then Terry made some kind of angry drunken pass at me and I had to back up and shove him off of me.

'Hit him,' someone shouted. 'Ay, hit him,' added another.

'Come on,' coaxed Terry, 'slap my face. You can do it. I know you can. I see it in your eyes.'

He was wrong; he saw nothing in my eyes. I wasn't angry. I

didn't want to slap him. But somehow he was in the right and I was in the wrong. I felt alienated, ashamed, even guilty. And he was right; I could have slapped him. I was capable of that. But I wasn't in a dungeon. There was a taunting chorus in the background, or was it my imagination that everyone, especially Terry, hoped that I would slap him? But why should I make such a spectacle, and give them something to gossip about for months to come. But it was strange, because for weeks I'd been anticipating a climax like this, getting that sense that what I was doing was wrong. I knew I didn't belong. It *was* odd for a single woman in her early thirties to have loitered for so long on the fringe. People can't place it, don't trust it, and I wasn't blaming them.

'I shouldn't be here. I'm not coming back.'

True to my word I never returned. But outside in the crisp Highland air, there I fell apart. How saddening, how mortifying to be chased out of that ugly green pub. And at the end of the earth, I felt nameless and homeless.

Larissa's husband drove me back to Glasgow. We were in the car by six-thirty a.m. I shall never forget that yellow sky as the sun rose over the mountains. I watched the scene unfold from the moving car and, like everything in that corner of the world, it was bold and powerful: changeable, wild, barren, yet bountiful and beautiful. I stared at the snow's lunar formations along the road, and the enormous sky, painted in thick strokes, of mustard, lemon, and muted gold.

From Scotland I went to Canada, where Toronto was experiencing its wickedest winter in memory. The temperature had dropped to minus twenty and stayed there for months. And if the wind chill was high, then the hairs inside your nose might freeze if you so much as dared to inhale the breeze without a mask, a scarf, or a balaclava. Oh, it was grey and grim. The snow was dirty, cars stalled from the cold, the bars and malls were packed, and there was no beauty.

I was jet-lagged, discombobulated, tongue-tied, disorientated, and deeply depressed. Whenever I was asked a seemingly straightforward question, such as how was I, or what my time in Scotland was like, a cloud of wax and cotton wool would clog my mind before the words could form. Speaking was no longer a simple, semi-automatic function. Imagine having to tell your eyes to blink every couple seconds because they'd forgotten how to do it automatically – it was that sort of breakdown. Something similar happened to me when I was eleven. The experience only lasted a few minutes, if that, but it was much more intense and harrowing. I was walking down the street and thinking about the mechanics of walking; walking and thinking, thinking about walking, until I'd somehow thought my way out of action. My body had temporarily *forgotten* how to walk . . . and I was paralysed.

It had been too much for me: the frictions and failures with Adam, the violent conclusion, escape to Scotland, identity crisis; the absence of Adam, and terrible isolation. Now I was back in the house where I grew up, staring at my old bedroom, still painted in what I once thought was an interesting concept, that didn't quite work. I'd chosen a periwinkle blue for the walls and terracotta for the ceiling: the ceiling was meant to be the earth and the sky was supposed to touch the ground and be all around, and I was supposed to feel upside down. But I got the tones wrong, or their chemistry, and it has always bothered me. My books were there. My box collection, my time capsules, magazine clippings, shelves of treasure like sea shells and driftwood, mason jars of broken pottery and beached glass, my stamp collection, and a tall cardboard box in the closet, stuffed with notes and letters from friends, posted from summer camps or just passed across our desks in class every day over a decade.

In the basement, where I am permitted to smoke, the windows haven't been opened in twenty years, and the ceiling's too low. I have my pick of a plastic lawn chair and a blue synthetic armchair. It's a place where nobody goes any more; a storage space for junk and disorder. There are empty shoeboxes, broken toys, board games, wires and extension cords. The light is dim and artificial, the air dry and stale, and amnesia coats all the memorabilia.

The ghosts of my childhood don't visit me down here where I sit huddled over an electric heater. The scenes in the dungeon, the thousands of brief connections, collisions, the breakthroughs, evolutions, magical improvisations – where do they go when I'm back in Toronto? My journey with Adam, the intense passion, the artistic vignettes, the failed experiments – where do they belong? What do I do with Scotland, the lunar landscape, the tormented nights, those children, that pub expulsion, those mountains . . . when I'm no longer inside them?

I remember looking in the mirror, desperately straining to see the face underneath my projections, alterations, expressions, distortions. Not a face I wished to be, not a face I imagined others would see, and it proved too difficult for me. The closest I came was to stare at the dark eyes of my father, and the chin and lower lip that belongs to my mother.

I wasn't able to talk to my parents about what I'd been doing since I quit the mansion. At first I said that a friend of a friend owned a small private theatre and needed a behind-the-scenes assistant. Well, the dungeon *is* a sort of theatre, so I wasn't really lying, but over the months, in subtle ways, these gaps, deletions, and aversions seemed to whittle away at our conversations and closeness.

One Toronto visit, my parents took me out to dinner after picking me up at the airport. We always went directly to the same Middle Eastern restaurant where they make this great lemon-marinated, griddled aubergine. My parents sat opposite me and, after we had ordered, one after the other, rapidly in stereo, asked me about the 'theatre'.

'How many people does this theatre seat?'

'What do you do there, exactly?'

'How much does a ticket cost?'

'How often do you put on performances?'

'What sort of plays do you put on?'

'Who comes to see them?'

I took a deep breath and thought quickly. I made up the price of the tickets (fifty pounds), the number of seats (twenty-six), told them it was an exclusive, independent theatre and that Angel was independently wealthy, had a big-shot lawyer for a father. She had hired me to help with the set design, the costumes, the scripts and directing the players' lines. And then, in order to excuse some of my awkward, stilted refrain, I told them that the theme of the theatre was a bit unusual. They looked at me, waited patiently.

'Well, have you ever heard of sadomasochism?'

I heard the long, scary, sibilant word coming from my mouth, and it sounded so – well, intimidating. The silence and blank stares that followed from my parents confirmed this. 'Do you know what that is?' I asked, almost angrily. My mother said nothing, and what could she be thinking? But my father replied. 'It's when two adults consent to hurt each other for sexual pleasure. Isn't that right?'

I swallowed. I stopped. I nodded. I was surprised by my father. 'Yes, that's right. And the English, they're very interested in that theme.'

They asked no more questions after that, but I wondered if what I'd told them was actually worse than the truth; wondered what was going through their heads. Actors hanging from the rafters? Cutting each other up with machetes and axes? I didn't want to disappoint them or worry them or shame them. I didn't want to lie to them. But I needed to protect them. When family and friends asked them what Susan was up to in London, I didn't want to put them in the awkward position of having to lie. That night they caught me off guard. Had I been prepared, I might have been able to explain my job to them in such a way that they'd understand . . . and come to see it as not such a bad thing. But time passed, and the opportunity to explain never came. And as time went on, I thought: soon I won't be doing this any more, and then maybe I'll tell them.

Three weeks in Toronto and I practically ran back to London, to the flat in Brixton. It was musty and cold, and it needed cleaning, reclaiming, the smell of cooking.

CHAPTER 17

Repast

11:43 a.m.: *I have seven hours to make an exquisite meal for seven, so it helps that I've been preparing for years. Experience, skill, and attention to detail – all shall be manifest while still giving the appearance of an almost effortless improvisation. I want to do something different, something daring, something that dazzles the senses. A symphony of dishes, a savoury tale inscribed in truffles and raspberry swirls.*

I could prepare a meal that explores the basic tastes, first in isolation, then in combination. For the first course, four simple starters: one sweet, one sour, one bitter, and one salty. The second course: the successful combination of two tastes, say something salty-sour, and something else that's bittersweet. And the main course would be a balancing act of all four. Or I could lay the stress on colour: a red dish, a green dish, a yellow dish; grilled rainbow trout, steamed rainbow chard. Or the opposite: blindfold my guests for a single course. I've seen it in the dungeon: when one sense is taken away the others will compensate. My guests will be feeling for their cutlery and the plate.

I imagine the smells grabbing them before the food, they know not what, first touches their mouths. No expectations, no eating with one's eyes, just pure taste and tactility. How enhanced is the texture, the temperature, the presence of others? Or I could blindfold them for half the course so they could then compare their blind taste with the colourful conclusion.

What about a feast of extremes that pushes the limits and challenges the palate? Spices that burn followed by a shot of frozen wine, stinging nettle soup, Stinking Bishop cheese, sea urchin. Or I could go for subtle elegance, like the four elements; a meal of air and water, earth and fire: a soufflé, some soup, a wild mushroom risotto, and chilli-pepper brownies or crêpes flambé. I wouldn't have to reveal my motif, but afterwards I could invite the guests to take a guess.

I was back in London less than one week, resuming my rituals and renewing my routine, when Adam called.

'How's it going? How's being back in Brixton?' he asked.

His tone was insultingly casual, and I could hear his lazy humour slithering around the back of his throat. I knew that encroaching laugh, knew that throat for that matter, and yet knew not why he found it perfectly natural to call me up after such an agonising hiatus (at least for me) and to speak like nothing had happened. In that mysterious (vacuous) mind of his, was he still on his knees flagellating himself for a kiss?

'Fine, I guess. Although for a long time I haven't been. Why are you calling?'

'I need to ask you a question. It's a question for a chef.' He wants to ask me how to make Pad Thai – what nerve. But no, that wasn't it. 'What happens when you eat a lot of raw chicken?'

'Is this a joke? What are you talking about?'

'No, it's not a joke.' But I heard the laughter slither upwards. 'I genuinely want to know what happens when you eat a lot of raw chicken.'

'A lot? What's a lot?'

'A whole chicken cutlet, minus a bite.'

'What? That's maybe a whole chicken breast, maybe two hundred grams of raw flesh. Who would do something like that?'

'Me, actually.'

'What are you talking about, Adam? You've done some crazy stuff, but that's just insane!'

'Susan, I didn't do it on purpose. It was an accident.'

'An accident!? Come *on*. Tell me how you *accidentally* eat a raw chicken cutlet?'

'Well, for starters, it was breaded. I bought it from the supermarket and I thought it was cooked. I even made a salad, the first one since I've lived in my flat. I was pretty chuffed. I made the vinaigrette just like you taught me. But when I got to the last bite of the cutlet, I tasted something strange so I looked at my fork. That's when I saw it was raw.' And then, at last, his laughter broke the surface.

'I can't believe it! Why are you laughing?'

'I don't know. Why not? You can't see the funny side?'

'No, I can't. It's not funny, it's, it's . . . so deranged! You're probably the only person on this planet who has ever eaten an entire raw cutlet, let alone the only, *only* one to eat it without noticing. Look, I've been through a lot, and, well . . . this is just too much. I mean, they're completely different in taste – I assume, and in texture – I know for certain. Where was your head? What were you thinking?'

'Susan, the cutlet was breaded, it wasn't that obvious – and I *did* notice something, which was why I looked. Just answer me. Do you think I'll be all right?'

'How should I know? You call me up after I don't know how long, no acknowledgement that our relationship suddenly ended, no apology for trying to strangle me, no –'

'I never tried to strangle you! You wouldn't stop pushing me, pressing my buttons. You really know how to press my butt –'

'Oh my God, and all those meals, all those perfect breakfasts and dinners I cooked for you! You rated them eleven out of ten every time.'

'I love your breakfasts. I love your cooking.'

'How can you possibly love my cooking when you've never tasted it? Ach, you have no palate, that's for sure. In fact there's nothing subtle about you. Can't even tell the difference between raw and cooked meat. It's barbaric, and you laugh, which is even crazier because it means you can't even appreciate your own extremism.'

After I hung up the phone I barely knew what to do with myself. What kind of man was this? Had he tasted anything I'd given him, made for him, done for him? Had we gone to such elaborate extremes because he was numb and incapable of savouring simplicity? What did it mean? I was spinning on myself, couldn't contain myself, I had to tell someone. I started writing an email to a friend of mine and as I typed the words 'raw chicken cutlet' it provoked a wave of disgust and I grunted in disbelief. But as I got absorbed in the telling I began to feel a giddy tickle crawling up my throat. And by the time I'd finished translating the conversation and my emotions into anecdote, I was laughing outright, laughing for all absurdity, and because who would have thought that a raw chicken cutlet could bring about an epiphany!

Being back in London, I needed an income. I didn't want to return to the central chambers, and I was done with working full-time as a dominatrix. I wanted to go in for the hour and then leave, three times a week. I was looking for chambers I could rent by the hour at some convenient location. With the rest of my time I could write, go to ballet, work on my treasure collection, my 'visual diary', cook, read, spend time with friends, start to date again. I would put up a very basic website and see the half a dozen clients or so that had kept in touch over the months and years.

I looked through some old fetish magazines for central dungeons and appealing ads. I'd seen most of their faces over the years and one had always intrigued me – Mistress K. So just like that I called her. When she answered the telephone, I could hear from her mellow voice that I'd made the right choice. We arranged to meet the following afternoon.

The chambers were in the penthouse of a handsome, Georgian-style apartment block in Marble Arch. An old-fashioned lift took me to the top floor and I entered a foyer that led off into six rooms: a toilet, a bathroom, two fully equipped dungeons, a kitchen, and a lounge for the Mistresses to hang out in and change into costume. And it could also be converted into a medical room.

The cupboards were stocked in bulk, orderly and thoughtfully, with all the essentials: latex gloves, toilet roll, kitchen roll, condoms, cleaning products, lubricant, bandages, adult nappies, bin liners, candles, disposable needles. A fridge in the foyer offered bottled water (still and sparkling), milk, juice, white wine and champagne. There was shampoo and conditioner, scented soap, a selection of combs, and a pile of plush towels in the bathroom. There was everything.

The two dungeon rooms were large, dark, atmospheric and fully equipped. Suspension racks, stretching racks, rubber, leather and canvas body bags, scores of ropes, whips, hoods, paddles, harnesses, gags, blindfolds. One of the dungeons had a rotating wheel: strapped in, you can be turned upside down or sideways or spun all around. Both rooms had whipping benches and a plenitude of dildos and electrics, canes, crops, and cock rings. Both had good sound systems with a vast selection of CDs. Most of the equipment, with slight variations, I'd seen before, either at the cottage or the central chambers, but never had I seen so much of it under one roof.

Half a dozen Mistresses were renting out the rooms by the hour. At any hour on any day two Mistresses could be working simultaneously, and if things were well organised (and because it was spacious enough), nobody ever needed to run into any of the others. The Mistresses rotated responsibility for the diary once a month. You called or texted the diary holder to see if the hour and day you wanted was available, and if it wasn't, then you could usually arrange something within the next couple of hours. Regardless of what the mistress was charging by the hour (a few of them charged a hundred and eighty pounds, one charged two hundred and fifty, but the standard was still a hundred and fifty), you paid your fifty to the house for every rented hour.

Mistress K was warmer, more attractive, and earthy, maternal in person. She was elegant, intelligent and snorted when she laughed. Aside from Mistressing, she was taking a course in couples counselling and another one in shiatsu massage. She said I could start right away but that it would best to meet the other Mistresses, who were all due for the monthly meeting and diary swap in a few days' time.

The meeting was called for ten-thirty so that it wouldn't interrupt the day's scheduling, and I was third to arrive. Mistress K was there, as well as a woman wearing a short plaid skirt, thick black tights and loafers. She was doubled over herself rolling a cigarette on her lap, and when she looked up she smiled sweetly and introduced herself as Sally.

'Well, well, look at you,' said the fourth as she entered the room. 'Look at those legs. I've never seen you wear a skirt outside of work. Sally in a skirt, ooh-we.' That was Karen speaking.

'I'm trying to be a lady. Thought it was about time.'

I could relate to that comment. In the dungeon I love to dress up, wear make-up and high heels, flaunt my figure, accentuate my feminine features. But in public I feel awkward in make-up and skirts. It feels like I'm pretending.

And then an earthy and curvaceous blonde, wearing wire-rimmed glasses, a long flowery skirt and Birkenstocks with socks burst in.

'Wow, Sally's wearing a skirt,' Laura giggled. Meanwhile, Sally was hunched over in a corner, puffing passionately on her cigarette.

'I'm trying, I'm trying.'

Laura began recounting some mishap she had had on her farm that week. She spoke so quickly I could hardly understand her, but then I caught on that she was making fun of her husband, then Sally, and next doing an impersonation of Mistress K. She spoke with speed and spirit, and a scathing sense of humour. I really liked her. She reminded me of Eve. The last to arrive was Jenny, carrying a tray of lattes and a box of croissants from the shop across the street. In an East End accent she introduced herself and apologised for being late. She was in her late forties, divorced, and the only one of the group who was a mother. The rest of us had only ourselves to support.

Karen was American, the baby at twenty-five, and recently married to a client. She has a Masters in Classics, attended an Ivy League college, teaches book-binding courses and only occasionally works as a Mistress, and as a submissive, when she needs the money. Her husband is English and a university lecturer.

Laura, it turned out, was also married to a client of hers, a man fifteen years her senior, and she was about thirty-eight.

'Am I the only one here that wants to get married and isn't?' asked Sally.

'Oh honey,' soothed Mistress K, who was bisexual. 'I didn't know you wanted to get married. That's so sweet. Well, why not? Doesn't your boyfriend want to get married?'

'I don't want to talk about it,' and Sally dropped her head.

'Of course not, I'm sorry.'

Sally was about thirty-three and Australian. Although she looked severe with her pale skin, dark-red lipstick, and jet-black bob, she seemed the most fragile of the bunch. And it was an extremely nice bunch.

Eventually we got around to the house meeting. Someone said they'd found an electrics box that wasn't clean, someone else said they should get some Styrofoam heads for the hoods. Sally felt that the equipment wasn't always put back in the same place, Jenny reminded everyone that if they're using amyl nitrate in a session to make sure the room gets aired out properly afterwards because it stinks. Everyone agreed. When the diary was reassigned, the meeting adjourned because Laura had someone arriving at noon, and I walked back to the tube station with Sally and Karen.

'Bet you know my boyfriend,' said Sally. 'He's seen every young, attractive dominatrix in London. He's German. Tall, really skinny, and he's got pretty wild grey hair. A bit arrogant, just turned fifty, name's Jan, and he loves being caned. A real legs man.'

'Yeah, I've seen him.' But sensing she was jealous, I added, 'It was a long time ago when I worked in North London. Actually, he was one of my first clients. In fact, I remember I wasn't so good with the cane and he kept stopping and correcting me. In a way, he was the one who taught me how to use the cane.'

'That's Jan all right. Doesn't think anyone knows how to cane properly, including me.'

'I saw him a few times, then he disappeared. I thought he was very handsome and charming. How long have you been together?'

'Two years. But we've broken up I don't know how many times. I have jealousy issues. I do. And you? Seeing anyone?'

'No, not really. Getting over someone. He was also a client of mine. Maybe you've seen him: tall, very fit, extremely handsome, dark hair, amazing blue eyes, late thirties. His name's Adam. He's a masochist.'

'No, don't think so. You remember the handsome ones, don't you? I'd definitely remember tall, dark, and handsome.'

I left there that morning feeling that the place had struck such a perfect balance: it was clean and organised but relaxed and supportive. Nobody took themselves too seriously but we were all professionals. I felt part of a community.

Before I booked any sessions I needed to retrieve some of my gear that I'd stored at Adam's. We arranged to meet close to his work near St Paul's Cathedral. I was nervous about seeing him. It was one thing to talk to him on the phone, but another to be face-to-face, our bodies within inches of each other. Therein lay the danger. I hoped I'd see him and feel nothing. See him and be free from his spell. Was it beauty that put a spell on me? If it was beauty I beheld, then I invariably wanted to own and possess it, *do* something with it. I would keep in mind his ugliness, how deranged he looked in anger, how I felt when I was pinned down to the bed, when he'd screamed 'No!', when he'd broken the straps in the chamber at the cottage, how he yelled when I accidentally bit his chin; how he looked when he was abject and weak, or absent and oblique. All those months he hadn't contacted me in Scotland.

I'd remind myself that he was the man who ate raw chicken without noticing. He was the man whose love for me was so mythic, and poetic, whose touch was electic, whose demonstrations and supplications were extravagant, but who would never answer for his actions. A man who wouldn't explain himself, probably didn't know himself, and wouldn't relieve me of a now long-standing confusion: about what had happened between us and why did he think it had failed, and what was fantasy and what was real. Did he miss me? Did he even think of me? It's not possible for two people to go through such a journey and ever be wholly free of each other. And yet, regardless of where we'd been and why, the relationship had nowhere else to go. There was nothing left for us to do.

And then I saw him across the street; he was waiting for the traffic light to change. How vividly I recall the suit – midnight blue, the shirt – baby blue, and the powder-pink tie. The azure eyes, even from across the street, looked like light striking a sheet of glass. As it had always been, my knees began to buckle, my body to perspire, and my heart to roller-coaster.

I couldn't tell whether I wanted to laugh or cry, freeze or bolt, but I smiled at him across the street, through the sunlight, with St Paul's Cathedral in the backdrop. That man in the dark suit in the City, I know him. I've seen him crawl, watched him lick my wounds, walk on thumbtacks, penetrate himself. I allowed that man to do the most intimate, erotic, unbelievable things to me. He has taken me somewhere I could never have imagined. He did these things . . . he is this . . . because of me. I know this man in the City. I know all these men in the City, their needs and desires lurking beneath their tailored suits; I know theirs better than I know my own.

Yet I don't know *this* man in the City. I've never known him. I keep reinventing and imagining him, but I don't know him. I know little more than I knew after that twenty-hour date. Maybe it's as he said: 'There's nothing else to know.' Could that be true? No. Impossible. What's the meaning of this chemistry? What *is* the purpose of chemistry? Was it, or wasn't it true that we'd done what we needed to do, our destiny: failed or fulfilled? It's my head, it's confused. I know nothing except what I feel right now: I'm embracing him, and his collar is rubbing against my burning cheek. I can smell him, he smells like dead lilies and tobacco, and this masculine strength envelops me.

He has to go back to the office in ten minutes, that's what he says. I followed him like a puppy dog into the deli.

'What do you want?' he asked.

'What are you getting?'

'A cappuccino.'

'Fine, make it two.'

He placed the order with surprising charm and familiarity. I'd never witnessed that in public; obviously he knew the server, was a regular, and she knew him too, in her way. What *did* she know? And he drinks cappuccino. I'd only ever seen him drink espresso. Apparently he did exist outside my imagination. Why is he so calm? He looks happy to see me.

And then he goes back to work. And I watch him walk away, until his midnight blue suit has become one in the City sea.

12:30 p.m.: *I've always wanted to do a full-fledged degustation. Fifteen, twenty courses, petite portions, like bite-sized sentences in a story. It could start with a single scallop drenched in a sauce of puréed raisins and capers. I'd approach the long sequence like a mathemati-*

cal challenge, and have to balance colour, square the texture, divide and multiply the flavours.

But if dinner's going to be so complicated, dessert must be simple. I definitely don't want to pull out scales and measuring spoons. I don't want to bake; I did so much of it in Montreal. For a year I ran my own bakery and catering business from the loft that I lived in. My dessert repertoire included jasmine tea cheesecake, flourless almond chocolate torte, an Italian chestnut cake, cranberry scones, the best oatmeal chocolate cookies, amaretto biscotti with the tips dipped in chocolate, espresso brownies, and maple syrup crème brulée. I made them each at least fifty times, and never lost my awe and wonder that in baking the same seven or eight basic ingredients make creations of infinite variation.

I've had porridge on my mind for a long time: wholesome, a serotonin booster, and delicious – but could I really make it for dessert? Nobody expects it. But I bet nobody knows how gourmet it can be, so why not? It's an ideal dessert, with a pinch of salt, spices, seeds, nuts, fruit, and milk or cream. I could make two different porridges then swirl them together or serve them in adjacent dishes. One of the porridges could have cloves, chopped almonds, sunflower, pumpkin, and cardamom seeds, a vanilla bean and nectarines. And I could sweeten it with moist brown sugar. The other porridge could be apple and cinnamon with currants, walnuts, blackberries to sharpen and turn the porridge mauve, fresh ginger and maple syrup. But if there's rhubarb at the supermarket then rhubarb instead of, or in addition to, the apples.

I'd finished saying my goodbye to Enema Larry and had just shut the door behind him when Sally and Jenny came out of the lounge. They'd been waiting until Larry left the premises to make their appearance, and then we all convened in the foyer. Both of them were expecting clients in twenty-five minutes. Sally was wearing a leather catsuit that laced up on either side from ankle to shoulder, and a pair of extremely intimidating leather boots that also laced up to her shins. Her lipstick was the colour of thin blood and she was wearing a leather cap and a basque. She looked pretty scary. Jenny on the other hand wasn't much softer in an SS military uniform, the full regalia from top to bottom. And since I'd just seen Enema Larry, I was wearing a cream-coloured rubber nurse's uniform, stilettos, black shiny hold-ups, and was in the process of taking off the long black rubber gloves.

'It's so warm for May, I love it,' I said.

'Tell me about it,' said Jenny. 'It's warm now, but just wait till summertime and you're melting underneath your rubber while trying to look so cool in front of the client.' Jenny was a bit of a whiner and a sigher.

'I like the heat,' I said. 'I like the slime and slither underneath the rubber. Makes me feel like a snail. I am a snail. I more or less carry my house on my back.'

'I like the heat, just can't stand the sunshine,' said Sally.

'How can you hate the sunshine, that's crazy,' I said.

'Ooh, it's yucky. I don't like it. I was a Goth for fifteen years, what do you expect? But I was outside all weekend soaking up the poisonous rays because Jan's two brats were staying with us and there was a festival in the park. Hey, and for dinner I made a roast chicken and put paprika on it so it would colour nicely, and stuffed it with rosemary and garlic, all like you told me, and it was delicious. The little angels ate it all and even asked for seconds – unheard of, so thanks.'

'You're welcome.'

At this point, Jenny, who'd been eating a bag of crisps interjected to offer us some.

It was then that I had an uncanny sense of double-vision, or was it the humorous juxtaposition? There I was on the inside, casually chit-chatting about recipes and the weather among colleagues, but also viewing it from the outside: the three of us were wearing the most unlikely combination of costume. I thought it redundant to point out my observation to my colleagues who were already, no doubt, well beyond the irony.

Jenny complained about her client who was due in a quarter of an hour for a water sports, anal play, and corporal punishment session . . . and we said nothing but we both nodded, which, in effect, said everything.

It was early in the morning and I was sitting at my desk by the window. The walls had been newly painted mossy green, and cherry for the ceiling. I was trying to write but I couldn't help staring out of the window at the neighbour's imprisoned cat. It was a black cat that lived on the top flat of a matching Victorian house.

The cat had probably never been outdoors beyond that ledge, which was only about six inches wide. From there it peeked over the edge onto the world: the birds, the trees, the people on the street four storeys below. It seemed so tragic that it could only watch, only look on and never participate. I imagined it was always contemplating the jump, about to do it, knowing it wouldn't. It was trapped, and it knew it. And then Adam called. The bell in his voice was uncertain and hesitant.

'Hi, how are you?'

'Fine.'

'I was wondering if I can book a session with you?'

I took some time to reply. What could we concentrate into an hour that we hadn't stretched, pulled and spread over days and months until we were buried in it? How could we go backwards? Back to a professional relationship? Back to being Mistress Anna and Adam the masochist? Does this mean that he chooses Anna over Susan? Or just Anna over other Mistresses?

'You still there?'

'I'm here. I'm thinking.'

At which point I thought: maybe this is how it ought to be, how it always should have remained, how it's always been; our rare chemistry, those games, the art contained within a gilded frame. But no, if that were how it had always remained, then what would I have really gained? We'd made a mistake, blurred the boundaries, dined on rich foods day and night, asked too much of fantasy, let it become our lives. I heard him breathing patiently on the other end. Think Susan, think. What do you want? I want clean, tidy closure. I want a place for me and Adam. I want to accept its limitations.

'You have to book a day in advance, that's how I work things now.'

'Fine, how about tomorrow at four?'

'That's okay, I guess. I'll give you the address.'

*

And then Adam was naked and erect, looking as sculpted and stunning as ever. I fell back on old routine. I put a hood on his head and it had the same effect: released me, let me perform, and made me feel free. We could focus on touch, heat, waves and vibrations. Suddenly all my confidence and powers had returned. I touched his chest, let my finger teasingly graze a nipple, hovered over him and let him feel the electricity between us. I stroked him so gently that I was really only stroking the air and hair just above his flesh. But there was so much activity between us. I stroked his penis because I could, because it was so present, so telling, and it was mine. My senses were heightened and I felt such fluid control. He was standing when I put my hands between his lithe legs, and parted them. I love those thighs, their smooth, gradual tapering into calves. There's nobody to compete with me – and he knows it. Only I know how to touch him, worship him, be worshipped by him, and bring him to his knees.

I tied his erect penis and his balls. I'd forgotten how the chemistry worked, how charged we became in each other's sphere. How could it be that this session surpassed the others? How was that possible? Because he wasn't really a client? Because he was a client? Because of our history? Because it had been so long? Because this is where we belong?

I ordered him to worship me, pleasure me. I'd never done that before, but in my mind it was our last session, the end of our story, and I could do whatever I wanted. Such freedom, if I only knew how to use it. Well, I took it, took my pleasure that I ordered from Adam. And it was bittersweet: having known such a lover as Adam, I was afraid I could never be free of him.

Towards the end of his suffering he had a powerful orgasm – and that's where it could have ended. But there was one thing that for years I'd been tempted to do, since those first sessions when he came prematurely so many times. I didn't have the confidence then, or the desire to make him carry on beyond the orgasm.

'Back on the whipping bench. There's something else.'

His look was uncertain, but he did as he was told. I strapped him down with the soles of his feet facing up, and chose a thin rattan cane. Weakened as he was from his climax, dissolved as he was of the erotic reward, it was meant to be painful, in isolation, and not exactly sexual. That's why I wanted to do it – see what happens when you separate the two. And yes, I was testing him this last time, to see if he'd endure pain for me without the sexual gain. Or maybe I exempted myself, and really I just wanted to punish him.

He wasn't gagged and he wasn't hooded. And he didn't scream. I felt ugly and cruel, and angry and powerful. And then empty, sad, and impotent. It wasn't what I wanted and I stopped. I undid his straps, and let him free.

I've been seduced by such beauty. Now I'm getting swept away by elaborate, indulgent ideas. All these savoury, salacious visions: orgies of food, outlandish contortions, vegetable perversions, exploding juices. Salty-sweet operettas have their place and time, and it's exciting to fantasise. I'm tantalised just by cooking in my imagination. But at the end of the day I don't want to dazzle, or be frazzled, or to go to such extremes. Tonight what I'm after is something fulfilling, modest and familiar, something I've made before. Preparing it with presence, employing all my senses, considering my guests, taking pleasure in the rhythm and precision of chopping, absorbed in the motions, the interactions, the minute effects, I aim to perfect something simple and rustic. Does it look auspicious? Does it taste delicious? Is it nutritious? Is it easy to clean up?

I've made a decision. I know what I'll do: the seven of us will share a peasant-style, Dupuy lentil stew. Sitting around the dinner table, I will dip the ladle in a cast-iron pot, and serve the hearty repast piping hot. We'll tear off pieces of bread from the same rustic loaf and soak up the burgundy juice that seeps from the mound of cooked lentils and settles around the ring of the plate. From a large wooden salad bowl, each guest will help themselves to fresh, foresty leaves tossed in a simple lemon juice and grape-seed oil vinaigrette.

It had been about a year since I'd seen Bernie, and that was at those seedy central chambers. When I gave him my new address over the phone, I sensed he wasn't paying attention so I insisted he write it down, which he found insulting, condescending. I dreaded the session. I tried not thinking about it because the dread was all in my head. But I couldn't help it; I knew exactly how it would go and those were two challenging, maniacally trying hours.

When he entered, I noted his indifference to the new surroundings. We chatted about what he'd been up to – same; how work was treating him – badly (so, same); and what he'd been reading – a Georges Perec novel I'd recommended, as it happened. It was nice to see him; he had that same infectious giddiness, the demeanour of a wagging dog. When he paid me, the cash didn't come in a clear sandwich bag like it had in the past.

When I returned to the room he was naked and I noticed that his chest and pubic area were shaved and covered in a rash and his nipples were tough and flaky; but more mysterious were those dark bruises like teacup rings around his nipples.

'What are the bruises?'

'Haven't you ever heard of cupping?' His nonchalance was probably a defence.

'So you've been seeing a Mistress that cups you? Whose idea was that?'

'Mine. No Mistress. I did it on my own.'

And that was as far as we got on that front. So I guess he *did* suffocate himself and he was obviously exploring new things. Maybe he didn't want the same session.

'Is there anything you want to tell me before we begin?'

Well, served me right; I got the same mistrusting, flummoxed look I'd seen a hundred times before . . . and the session was the same old scenario.

After Bernie left that afternoon I opened the dungeon door and in came Sally.

'Oh my God,' she said, waving her hand and pinching her nose. 'I know that smell, that's Coin Man.'

'You mean Bernie?'

'Of course, who else? Didn't know you saw him.'

'Didn't know *you* saw him,' I said. 'I've seen him since I first started domming in North London years ago. When did you start seeing him?'

'Nearly two years ago.' She took a drag of her cigarette while reaching for the room deodoriser. 'Pee-ew! I always spray Bernie with body deodorant at the beginning of a session.'

'You don't!'

'I certainly do,' she said. 'He smells. Why should I have to cope with that for two hours?'

'But you suffocate him, don't you?' I asked.

'Sure. And flip his nipples with coins.'

'And do you sit on his face the whole time?'

'God, no! I usually string his arms up to the suspension rack or tie him to the bondage bench and either tie a rope around his neck or us my hands.'

'But that's dangerous, Sally. How could you do that? So you flick his nipples with coins?'

'Yes, at some point in the session, but I also twist them with my fingers, electrocute them, rub them with sandpaper. And I use him as a human punching bag, kicking him with my knee or boot and punching him with my fist. I've even used a boxing glove. I just beat the shit out of him a week ago.'

'Do you hood him?'

'Never.'

'Do you enjoy the sessions?'

'Definitely not. So dull, but I really like Bernie. I think he's extremely clever, possibly a genius. We always go out for a drink after our session. I only do that with him and Apple Allan.'

'You're not tired of him after the two hours?'

'Not the same, is it? I mean I find Bernie fascinating to talk to. He's taught me a lot of things. And he's been going through a hard time, I feel sorry for him. Everything bad happens to Bernie, poor guy. Just the other night he called me to tell me he was mugged.'

'He calls you up to chat? And you don't mind?'

'No, not really. He's like a friend of mine.'

'When he came in today he didn't say anything about having been here before.'

'I don't know why they like to play those games. I don't mind that he sees other Mistresses, do you?'

'No, it's just the deceit that's unattractive.'

'Yah, I agree.'

When I think of lentils, I think of mighty and yet humble. I think ancient and enduring. Dark charcoal green, each is the size of a bird's eye, and they look like caviar. Lentils are somehow quiet, reticent, they require coaxing and time to break open and soften; more than an hour of boil and vigour to penetrate and tenderise the hard exterior. Once cooked, they glisten like pebbles licked by muddy waters. They taste like earth and they're mild, but they can support the most robust flavours, shapes and textures.

I'll cook them in red wine and stewed tomatoes spiced with cinnamon and cloves, a thumb of fresh ginger, sprigs of rosemary and a handful of peppercorns. And more, I'll roast spears of carrots and celery, cloves of garlic, layers of fennel, lots of shallots. When the mix is caramelised and golden, I'll add them to the pot.

In the eight or nine weeks following the session with Adam, first a text thanking me, then another one that said he loved me, followed by a third in the middle of the night saying he missed me. And then an early one to say, 'Good morning, Beautiful.' The sixth text was an official apology. The seventh said something astonishing: 'I need you.' The ninth one asked me out to dinner. The tenth was a genuine plea to see me.

We arranged to meet outside Marble Arch tube. I was twenty minutes late because my last session had gone over time and there was a lot to clean up. It was raining and chilly when I got outside. Rushing down the street I thought: he never carries an umbrella. His coat, it doesn't close properly, the zipper broke. He doesn't bother to fix that kind of thing. He doesn't take care of himself. He doesn't wash his sheets enough. Runs out of toilet paper, doesn't know how to cook, lives on pizza and Indian take-aways. He's just like so many men; he needs a woman to take care of him. He's never lived on his own. And if he's angry that I'm late? Well, then I'm free to leave. But he won't be angry, because he's the one who arranged to meet. He wants to see me. We're meeting in a public space and he'll have to talk. I have nothing more to say.

There he was, wrapped in his long brown coat with the broken zipper, wrapped in it and shivering. His hair was wet and both his posture and presence spoke of fragility and vulnerability. I felt sorry for him. I had this vision of him in ten years, bald, wrinkled, weathered, thick around the middle, bad teeth, and calcified loneliness. I saw him in London still in an unfurnished home . . . always alone, riding his fancy car, not diving any more, drinking, watching the same DVDs, reading the same five or six novels over and over again: *Anna Karenina*, *War and Peace*, Thomas Carlyle, *Lord of the Rings*, *Don Quixote*, *The Count of Monte Cristo.* There'd be another promotion, a few big bonuses, but the same job, and still in debt. Still masturbating with clamps on his nipples and rings around his cock . . . and why should he stop? Maybe he's happy that way. But me, I couldn't be happy with that. I want to travel. Maybe live on a farm, but move on – write a cookbook, own a home, have babies, maybe get married, embrace the next thing. We seem so out of sync. I felt deadlocked. I didn't want to let go but there was nowhere for us to go. So I collapsed inside and I felt dismally sad. And yet I wanted to warm him and to shelter him from the rain. Instead I barely looked at him and said, 'Come on, let's run.'

I knew a place nearby, a Lebanese restaurant on the Edgware Road, and we were just outside it when he halted in the downpour.

'Why are you stopping? It's right here. Come on, let's go inside.'

'Please, Susan, oh please kiss me.' His upper lip was wet, his lashes matted, his hair spiked and stuck to the trim of his face, and he looked so wanton, so wanting; it would have been cruel to deny him. I didn't want to deny him. I got swallowed up in a deluge of sympathy, and there in the pouring rain, briefly but passionately, we kissed. Would it ever end, if even the rain could not extinguish the flame? Could a flame keep burning for ever? I've heard of such a match, locked up in a vault, which can be struck indefinitely. I was wondering if we were that match when I then took his large hand and we went inside.

He was wearing the square-toed shoes we'd bought together. He wore them for me. He wouldn't stop staring at me.

'You're staring at me. It's making me uneasy.'

'I'm sorry, it's just that I've never seen you look so radiant.' That's because he sees that I'm free and because he's afraid he's lost me. My allure has increased with my intangibility. 'You look beautiful, healthy, confident, and happy. That's what it is. That's what I see.' I am healthier, I am happier, he's right to perceive that. 'Either I've never until this evening really seen you before or you've changed. Not that I didn't find you beautiful before, but you look like you've grown up; you look like a woman.'

A bit condescending, but nonetheless his charm is working. He lets me do the ordering, while he just sits there gazing and smiling. But his smile is sad. He put his giant hand on the table hoping that I'd hold it. I was hoping he'd talk, and thankfully, that's what he did. Not like he'd talked before, but openly, humbly, emotionally – and without the aid of a sadomasochistic mouthpiece. So, things can change, people can change, there has been some movement for both of us. The thought warmed me and filled me with hope. He's saying how sorry he is for the way he treated me. Like a flood, he says so many things, like how lonely he's been, how angry he's always been, how tired he is, how much he admires me, loves me, loves all of me, everything about me . . . and then the food came.

'Susan,' he said with a pickled turnip in his mouth, 'please don't hurt me any more.'

'Excuse me?' A stuffed vine leaf was thus interrupted on its way to my mouth. I looked at him quizzically. 'Me hurt you?' All I'd suffered, all the tears I'd shed, the isolation I'd endured, the confusion, the loneliness. 'Me hurt you! Tell me how I've hurt you?'

'Susan, how can you ask me that? You have beaten me, whipped me, caned my feet, and tortured my nipples until they bled, until it hurt for days afterwards just to put on my shirt. I never told you that. You slapped my face and slapped my cock.

You teased me and humiliated me. You made me bathe in a tub of ice water. I have never suffered more in anyone's presence, and absence, than I have suffered for you. Susan, I love you, but you have hurt me.'

It's not the same. You're a masochist. You wanted me to hurt you. It was in the contract of our union. My God, don't turn this around, it's not the same.'

'Don't get upset, my angel, although I love your passion . . . but don't get upset. Just acknowledge that it's not as simple and one-sided as you're pretending it is. How can it be all me? It was both of us. I need you to accept some responsibility for the things that we did, the pain that was inflicted, as well as the ecstasy. I've done a lot of thinking, and I've done some really extreme things in the past, and I don't want to hurt any more. I need healing. I need comfort and tenderness. I need your magic touch.'

It was so much more than he had ever said. He was partly right, wasn't he? I hadn't even thought of it that way, that he might have suffered more because he thought I wanted it . . . more than was good for him . . . because he thought it pleased me. Could that really be? True, he'd done so many things he had never done before he met me. Had he really suffered more because he thought it pleased me? Had I unleashed a beast? Maybe. He'd done things to please me and I'd done things to please him, and I doubted that lovers could ever distinguish between all these things.

'Would you be with me tonight? Just to lie beside each other, just to sleep together?'

*

I was relieved that his flat was tidy, until I realised that he must have planned everything. He just knew that I'd bend to his fragility. He knew I'd come back to his place. But maybe it wasn't like that. I hope it wasn't like that. No, he'd only *hoped* I'd come back with him, and just in case, he made sure the flat was clean. He knew I'd feel more comfortable in a clean flat – and I was, so he was right, and I appreciated it. He made us a pot of camomile tea and we sat on the floor by the gas fireplace. I wanted to prolong the moment, savour the taste of the herbal tea, and this new intimacy. I knew that it was only a matter of time before he would receive all the soothing and magic he yearned for. And he was patient; he would wait.

On his single bed he lay naked like a wounded god. I got in beside him. He was too scared to ask for the thing he most needed. And now it's time to heal him, to indulge him with tenderness. And what a joy to give him that! It suited me and I was happy to do it. If I had the opportunity, if right now he asked of me the same, I'd rhapsodically do it all again.

As I touched his shoulder and traced the length of his arm, I realised it was true; I don't know how, but it was true that I'd never been so soft with him before, never nursed him, never mothered him, never comforted him before. And I've always wanted to do that. He had never let me before. I had never introduced it before. Why not? The way he responded, every touch seemed to fix him. He had never felt safe being weak and wounded. So I made him feel safe. It's a big thing. The truth is, it's the very thing I want for myself.

It was night, just the purple white of a streetlight shining through a crack in the curtain. In that spectral light I saw that he was crying. Had I ever seen him cry? I didn't want to see him cry. Courage to look again, and thankfully he wasn't crying, not exactly. He was smiling.

'Susan, your touch is so healing, so delicate, so amazing; it's what I've always needed. This, just what you're doing to me now.' Then he sat up to look at me in the half dark, and kissed me. 'Why did we go to such extremes, why have *I* gone to such extremes, when it's this that I've needed all along? It seems so crazy to me right now: to go so far only to arrive at something so obvious. But what do you think?' A beautiful, happy ending, that's what I thought. He was laughing. In a second I'd be laughing too. He was swimming just a stroke ahead of me. He kissed me again but then he pulled back excitedly.

'I feel different. I feel light. Something's lifted and you've helped. I feel happy, and satisfied. You heal me. I love you.'

And then we made love. Of all the things we'd done, it was as if we'd never made love before, and it ripped open another layer of the universe. Such possibility, such a symphony, such epiphany, and then he whispered something in my ear. I wasn't sure I heard him correctly, but he whispered it again.

'I want to do things differently. Taste moderation. I don't feel I need to go to such extremes.'

It sounded hopeful. Sounded so trite. It made me think of something, and I started to laugh.

'Why are you laughing? Don't. Is that funny? Did I say something funny, my princess?'

'No, what you said was beautiful and I'm happy for you. But I was thinking about my session tonight.' He frowned. 'No, wait, let me tell you, it relates.'

'Go on, then.' And he kissed my bare shoulder.

'Well, I'm thinking about humiliation and shame. I'm thinking about everything you're saying: what we did, and how we behaved in order to come to this place . . . of tenderness.'

I told him that the reason I was laughing was because what he was saying and the session I'd had earlier that evening suddenly reminded me of my friend Helen. We moved to London around the same time. We used to walk around the city together taking photographs. It was her skirt I borrowed when I met Denise, the housemaid at Angel's. I used to tell her about my first domination sessions. I remember telling her about this humiliation client who'd come along. He didn't want role-play. He had a big nose – slightly crooked and at war with his weak chin – and a bad case of acne. He wanted me to insult his face and tell him how ugly he was, how grotesque and hideous he was – and I couldn't do it. I told Helen that of all the things, humiliation most perplexed and troubled me. Together we tried to get our heads around it.

'She asked an interesting question. I just thought of it again. What would happen, she wondered, if instead of humiliating him, telling him he was gruesome and ugly and pathetic and embarrassing to look at, I went right up to him, put my hands on his shoulders or hugged him and told him he was great. What do *you* think would happen?'

'I don't know, but it's a funny thought. Actually, I don't think he'd appreciate it. He'd probably never come back.'

'The client I had tonight was into humiliation. I was late to meet you because it took so long to clean up the mess. It was extravagant. And for what? I threw pies and chocolate éclairs in his face. I spat on them first. Told him he was fat and lazy. And the thing was, he wasn't fat, and I doubt he was lazy. And who cares if he was fat, lazy, and ugly as well? He wanted me to make him eat a chilli pepper and a stinging nettle! What would have happened if I did like Helen suggested? Because deep down, I'm sure he'd prefer tenderness and acceptance, to be loved, imperfections and all.' I want that, I was thinking. We all want that, I was thinking. But it doesn't happen until we're tender, loving, and accepting of ourselves – I was realising. 'It's so good to see you smiling,' I said.

I can never see you again, I thought.

We made love all night, spoiled each other with attention and tenderness. And when the daylight intruded, I got up and he watched me swan naked across the room to draw the curtains and return.

CHAPTER 18

Concertina

After the long tender night I didn't hear from Adam for almost a fortnight. But it was over . . . and I wanted that. In the meantime I kept thinking of the forest. I've always felt a distinct solitude in the forest. If I fall in love, I always thought, I'll know because I will no longer feel alone in the forest. Somehow, in some form, he'll be there with me. I'd never spoken to Adam about the forest, so it was strangely poignant when he called me and said, 'Let me take you away to the New Forest.'

But it was intolerable. We drove there without saying much. Then when we entered the forest, Adam walked ahead of me. A couple of hours, not saying anything, but the whole time he was smoking. We finally took a rest and I asked for the lighter. I tried lighting my cigarette but there was no more fluid, and just like that, in exasperation, I said, 'Give me a fucking break!'

Adam thought I was attacking him – which I wasn't, but then

he was shouting, 'Don't dare talk to me that way!' And he stormed off.

It enraged me that he should take my comment so personally, that he should do it again, suddenly turn on me . . . for what reason? And now he's walking away from me. For an hour I followed behind him, watching him get smaller and smaller until he disappeared completely. That was good, because I didn't want to see him. I was so full of hate for him.

I stopped for a while and sat underneath a tree. But up and walking again, I came to a fork in the road. It was getting late and I didn't have water, money, or my phone. Did he go left or right? The car was parked at one end or the other. Damn him, I thought. How could he just leave me all alone in the woods? I took a guess and went left. But after another twenty minutes and no one about, I started to fill with doubt. Should I turn back and go right? That might take another hour and by then it'll be dark. I started to walk back the way I came for another ten minutes, and then no, it didn't feel right, so I turned around and continued with my first guess, which was left. Maybe an hour later, I made it back to the car park. So it was left, and there was Adam's car, and there was Adam, sleeping in the reclined driver's seat. He woke up when I opened the door. 'Enjoy your walk?'

I looked at him with fury. 'I didn't know which way you went. Didn't know where the car was. It's getting dark and I could have been lost. I didn't know if I should go right or left.'

'It was obvious. I doubted it for a minute. Doubted that you'd get it. I even went back to the crossing to consider it . . . but you're Canadian. You've got good instincts . . . so then I figured you'd get it. And see, you did.'

That's all he said. We drove back to London in frigid, leaden, impossible silence. It would always be this way with us. We've been here before, at this cul-de-sac. We'll keep coming back. Unless . . . I finally, boldly, step out of this box, follow another track. The way it goes, the moment we get close, the trees disappear, the birds stop singing, there are no people, and huge chunks of the world get vacuumed up or crumble. But what remains is this intensity, this distinct, mysterious substance that flows between us. Now I see that the very same substance that rockets us into a euphoric frenzy of sensual possibility, scorches us and tortures us. Back and forth, up and down, expanding and then collapsing upon itself – that's its action. The substance needs to know its limits, needs to be contained, put in its box.

By two p.m. I'd fought my way through crowds and carcasses and cake stalls at Brixton and Borough Market. I bought all that I needed for dinner and dessert. I chose two walnut loaves, a creamy wedge of Roquefort cheese, and I found wild strawberries in season. I chose three beautifully ripe mangoes and a honeydew melon, and dark chocolate that reminded me of the kind we used to bake with at the mansion. It was painful walking through the common with all the groceries hanging from both hands and eight tall gladioli held under my arm. But I felt happy and enlivened.

My guests were Sally and Mistress K from Marble Arch, Sally's boyfriend, Jan, my friend Kathy, the radio producer who I'd lived with in the Brixton Massive, and her boyfriend, Terence, a video artist and stand-up comedian. I also invited Charles from down the road. He was Kathy's friend from college, and we'd met on several occasions. He'd recently moved to Brixton, and I ran into him the day before the party, so I invited him. That made us seven.

I chopped the vegetables, began boiling the stew, made the vinaigrette, tidied the flat, placed the flowers in the vase, washed and dried the lettuce and, with time to spare, most of my preparations were done. So I took the novel I was reading, a bottle of water, put on my sunglasses, and went to the park.

It was a bright, splendid day and I passed the red rhododendrons, the little pond, the weeping willow and the tall sunburnt grass, following a path until I came to a bench that looked onto the duck pond. There were people around and I was a bit disgruntled at the fact that there was nowhere outside where I could really be alone. But I was reading a great book by my favourite author, Heinrich Böll, and I had my sunglasses to shield me, and so there I sat on the bench, reading.

After some time I heard people approaching. I looked up over my sunglasses and saw two men in their early forties – maybe much younger, it was hard to tell – unwashed, dishevelled and derelict. Maybe they lived in a halfway house or a shelter nearby. They were thin and ashen, their clothes grey and very worn, but they were walking and talking cheerfully, and carrying ice-cream cones. I returned to my book and thought: that's nice . . . they obviously don't have much but they have friendship . . . and that's a lot, and on top of it, they've treated themselves to ice cream on this hot summer's day. It touched me, and then I carried on reading.

When I looked up again I saw that they'd stopped at the pond just in front of me, and now they were feeding the ducks. Well, that's really something I thought: they are down and out and yet they really have so much; they have friendship and ice cream and time and bread to feed the ducks. At that I returned to my book. It really was a wonderful book. So when I heard them laugh just a few minutes later, I did not look up but just carried on reading and thought, that's really great . . . they are joshing, sharing a joke, and laughing like people laugh maybe once a year. It was deep, bellowing, almost fitful laughter that went on and on, but I was reading my book, enjoying it, so I didn't look up.

But a minute or two later, when I heard them walking away, I looked up from the page and over my sunglasses. I watched them as they walked away, saw them from the side and then the back, and, bizarrely, they were wearing their ice-cream cones upside down on their heads. Just like that they walked away, almost dignified, and no longer laughing.

I didn't know what to do with it. But nothing, there's nothing to do with it. And with that I turned once more to my book. But I looked up again just seconds later because now a father and his toddler in a pushchair were strolling by. I looked up when I heard him thinking out loud, saying to his oblivious, thumb-sucking daughter: 'Poppet, did you see that?' She clearly hadn't. 'Those two men were wearing their ice-cream cones on their heads! Isn't that silly?' So he also had to say it in order to do something with it.

Just before the guests arrived I was conscious that the temperature in the room was just right. I smelled the spicy incense of dinner and the sweet aroma of fresh flowers. The windows were open and the evening breeze was mild. I felt giddy on hearth and home, and the anticipation of good company and ripe festivity. When I first enrolled in cooking school people asked me why, and flippantly I'd say it was because I wanted to have extravagant dinner parties. I was envisioning a long wooden table in a gothic-style room, candlelight, theatrical music, fascinating guests engaged in lively conversation, and feasting upon abundant, delicious offerings.

For a while the music was Pat Metheney and Charlie Haden's *Beyond the Missouri Sky*. It never failed to evoke the wild-wind-in-hair sensation, the tall grass of lonely plains in swaying motions, and the exact feeling that is travelling into a blazing, setting sky. Charles was telling adventure stories, making flapping gestures with his hands. Then he was talking politics with Jan. He seemed to know so much, conversed so eloquently, and was hugely entertaining. Yet he could listen, asked interesting questions, and inspired trust with his hazel eyes. In fact his presence served as a balancing factor, the congealing, special-sized ingredient that brought the entire meal together. How differently things would have been had I not by chance met him in Brixton, and invited him along.

I served them all two ladles of steaming stew, textured as it was with large treasures of roasted root vegetables, melting potatoes, and a tattered cloth of slow-cooked tomatoes. But before they raised their forks, for the sake of creamy depths, fresh contrast, sharpness and spike, the stew needed its garnishes. So each bowl was finished with paper-thin slivers of Parmesan, caper berries, chopped parsley, and splashes of sherry vinegar. The humble lentil dish had become something elegant and complex. Bach was playing. Mistress K was probing Charles about his first love, and in turn I caught snatches of her ongoing romantic obsession. Sally told Charles about a client of hers whose fetish was to hear his name spoken over and over again. And his name was also Charles. I noticed Jan growing quieter in the corner. He was a man that liked to be the centre of attention, and with Charles's animation, the quirks and loquaciousness of the others, the soothing music, the scent of white and pale pink flowers, and the handsome, well-balanced dinner, I thought I saw him stepping back, gazing outside of himself, and taking in this new pleasure in others.

Kathy had been travelling in South America and she brought along a strange and bitter drink called maté that was brewed in a gourd. After dinner was done and the table cleared, we passed it around according to ritual, and sipped it from a metal straw. Sally refused to have a try. Terence liked it more and more, Charles had tried it before, and I enjoyed the difficult taste, and the attention that was placed on ceremony.

Dessert rewarded our palates after the trial of the maté. Cream crackers served with a spread of crumbled Roquefort smeared in the blood of freshly wounded wild strawberries. And there was more, there was a wooden chopping board and on it, twenty slices of honeydew melon flecked with spearmint, and sprinkled with lime juice. In a black lacquered bowl there were cubes of ripe mango spiced with crushed peppercorns. And, at last, a milky coloured plate, on top of which sat a jagged, exquisitely dark chocolate mountain. And there were still two carafes of red wine.

I told them about the two men in the park who wore their ice-cream cones on their heads. And as I told them, these things occurred to me. I realised how reassured I was by the absurdity of that episode, placed as it was in that everyday setting. I'd been thinking about the theatre of the dungeon: the influx of people, their nudity, their beauty, their absurdities, the brief and intimate collisions, the surplus of stories. Men are taking time out to play. They're all wearing cones on their heads. But I was wondering about life outside the dungeon. Would I find as many stories? Where would I look for them? Seeing those men in the park reminded me that if I poised myself just right, those weird and tender moments were to be found everywhere.

Having been absorbed in the sheer pleasure of telling my story, dishing it out slowly, feeding off my listeners as they devoured every morsel, I realised that being present for the surprising experience was only part of it. My great delight was in the telling, the reporting of my findings, and serving them to others.

The evening seemed to vibrate with its own harmony and fullness. As a portrait, it was not divided along double lives, the boundaries were less shaded, and there were many lives intertwining and overlapping. It was colourful and comforting with its warm crimsons, berry reds, rosy wines and flushed faces. And there was no Adam. And that was okay. I liked it that way.